Guilt: Man and Society

ROGER W. SMITH teaches political theory at the College of William and Mary. He was born in Alabama in 1936 and was educated at Harvard and the University of California at Berkeley.

Guilt: Man and Society

EDITED BY
ROGER W. SMITH

ANCHOR BOOKS
DOUBLEDAY & COMPANY, INC.
GARDEN CITY, NEW YORK
1971

125518

The Anchor Books edition is the first publication of GUILT:
MAN AND SOCIETY

Anchor Books edition: 1971

Library of Congress Catalog Card Number 70–131114
Copyright © 1971 by Roger W. Smith
All Rights Reserved
Printed in the United States of America

For Matie

Man is the being who is capable of becoming guilty and is capable of illuminating his guilt.

Martin Buber

Preface

For several years now I have been trying to understand what is involved in the idea of "guilt" and, in particular, what the relationships between man, guilt, and society might be. I have come to see that guilt is a basic category, like power, identity, death, or love, without which it is difficult to explore seriously the human condition. But it has also seemed to me that guilt has generally been ignored, taken for granted, or used for purposes of exploitation. What guilt is, how we are related to it, and how it can illuminate much of our experience of society and of ourselves are problems that have not received the attention they call for. There are, however, a few excellent essays that speak to these problems; yet they are not as widely known as they should be. Excellent as these essays are individually, they gain additional force when brought together with other important essays on guilt. What I have done, therefore, is to attempt to get the best essays possible and bring them together in a single volume.

My hope is that this book will initiate a dialogue on guilt—the "most important problem in the evolution of culture," according to Freud—and that this dialogue will help us to understand better the rich and painful reality of guilt. But if there is to be a dialogue, it seems important to me that everyman, and not just the specialist, enter into the conversation. For guilt, like death, is a *human* problem, and thus no respecter of persons.

R.W.S.

Contents

Preface   11

  I. Introduction   17

 II. The Origin of Guilt   27
FRIEDRICH NIETZSCHE
"Guilt," "Bad Conscience," and Related Matters

III. The Compulsions of Guilt   63
SIGMUND FREUD
Dostoevsky and Parricide

IV. Existential Guilt   85
MARTIN BUBER
Guilt and Guilt Feelings

 V. Guilt, Ritual, and Culture   117
MARGARET MEAD
Some Anthropological Considerations Concerning Guilt

VI. Social Guilt and Preventive Innocence   135
GRESHAM M. SYKES and
DAVID MATZA
Techniques of Neutralization: A Theory of Delinquency

VII. Guilt as Social Drama   149
KENNETH BURKE
On Human Behavior Considered "Dramatistically"

VIII. Guilt and Awareness   171
      ROLLO MAY
      The Meaning of the Oedipus Myth

  IX. Politics, Guilt, and Theory   185
      A. Purification and Change
      ROGER W. SMITH
      *The Political Meaning of Unconscious
      Guilt*
      B. The Mark of Cain
      DONALD CLARK HODGES
      Fratricide and Fraternity

   X. Radical Evil   217
      HANNAH ARENDT
      Total Domination

  XI. Collective Guilt   255
      HANNAH ARENDT
      *Organized Guilt and Universal
      Responsibility*

 XII. The Stains of War   269
      J. GLENN GRAY
      The Ache of Guilt

Bibliography   309

Guilt: Man and Society

I

Introduction

Guilt is one of the earliest inventions of man, yet it is still one of those least understood. Guilt broods over twentieth-century existence, yet the more its presence is felt, the less we seem able to come to grips with it. What is "guilt"? What is its origin? Are there different modes of guilt? Does the idea of "collective guilt" make any sense? Has guilt changed over the centuries or has it remained basically the same? How do culture and social organization affect the problem of guilt? Why do men in certain periods of history experience guilt much more intensely than those living in other periods? What is the relation between guilt and creativity, and between guilt and art? What are the functions of guilt? Under what conditions is reconciliation possible? Can man ever lead a guilt-free existence? These are some of the important questions raised by the essays in this volume. That the conclusions are not final, perhaps goes without saying: no comprehensive and settled theory of guilt, in fact, is possible at this time. But considered as reflections on guilt rather than as finalities, the essays included here are always suggestive, always illuminating. They are, I believe, the necessary starting point for any future discussion of guilt. Moreover, as reflections on guilt, they are inevitably reflections on man and society as well. To take the essays in this volume seriously would, in fact, be to change much of our understanding of man and society, and would lead necessarily to a change in our social theory. We would, for example, no longer view man as the utilitarian and instrumental creature he is ordinarily assumed to be. Rather, we would come to understand him as the being who seeks meaning, and who, therefore, does not live by consequences

alone. But to follow out the implications of this shift in
perspective would in itself lead to a transformed understanding of ourselves as persons and to demands for a
critical re-examination of the social and psychological
sciences. A revolution in our thought would be under-
way.

Guilt is the province of man; it is he who is "capable of
becoming guilty"; it is he who is "capable of illuminating
his guilt."[1] But it is true also that the word "guilt" can
easily lead us astray. When we notice the psychoanalyst
talking about guilt *feelings,* the judge about overt *acts,*
and the existentialist about the human *situation,* and each
claiming to speak of guilt, we can only ask: Is "guilt" so
protean a word that its shape and meaning change with
each speaker? If so, communication ceases; our thoughts
are no longer sharable. If, on the other hand, we restrict
"guilt" to one specific meaning, such as that of guilt feelings, we rob the term of what is most fruitful about it—
its richness of association—and we force ourselves to
ignore much of what we presently think of as guilt. In
short, by narrowing the word, we make it less useful; in
making it more spare, we make it arbitrary. Is there, then,
any way in which we can escape the temptations of both
relativism and restrictionism in our understanding of
guilt? I suggest that there is, and that it consists of recognizing that "guilt" is a concept of a peculiar sort, a concept
with "blurred edges."

When Wittgenstein introduced the idea of a concept
with blurred edges,[2] what he was concerned with was not
guilt, but "the proceedings we call 'games.'" He wanted
to know why we call different kinds of games by the same

[1] Martin Buber, "Guilt and Guilt Feelings," in *The Knowledge
of Man,* ed. Maurice Friedman (New York: Harper & Row,
1965), p. 146.
[2] Ludwig Wittgenstein, *Philosophical Investigations,* 2d. ed.,
trans. G. E. M. Anscombe (Oxford: Blackwell, 1958), sections 65–84.

generic name. Could it be that "board-games, card-games, ball-games, Olympic games, and so on" have one thing in common by virtue of which we call them "games"? Wittgenstein concludes that this is not the case, that games do not, in fact, have any one thing in common, but that they are related, nevertheless, in other ways. For games involve a "complicated network of similarities overlapping and criss-crossing: sometimes over-all similarities, sometimes similarities of detail." These similarities Wittgenstein calls "family resemblances," for, in his view, "the various resemblances between members of a family: build, features, colour of eyes, gait, temperament, etc. etc. overlap and criss-cross in the same way." Wittgenstein comes to the conclusion that the various things we call "games" thus form a "family," an intellectual cluster that holds together despite the lack of a common center. The concept "game" is not rigidly bounded; there is nothing within it to "stop up all the cracks"; it is capable of extension. He concludes, then, that "the concept 'game' is a concept with blurred edges." But is a concept with blurred edges a concept at all, one might ask? Wittgenstein's reply is in the form of another question: "Isn't the indistinct one often exactly what we need"?

The concept "guilt" involves, with one exception, all that Wittgenstein found characteristic of the concept with blurred edges. The reason for this discrepancy, moreover, has nothing to do with guilt as such, but rather with an error in Wittgenstein's own analysis. For he implies (on the basis of his analysis of the concept "game") that the absence of a conceptual center is what produces the blurring of conceptual edges. The idea of guilt, however, and one could find other examples, does not lack a center. The basic idea involved in guilt—the center of the concept, as it were—is that of the boundary, or limit, which is *trans-gressed*, that is, literally, the boundary which is "overstepped." Yet the boundaries of guilt are nevertheless soft, indistinct, muted: the ideas of crime, debt, and the unclean can all find accommodation there. The con-

cept of guilt, moreover, refers not to the trespass alone: it
refers also to the boundary and the attempts to restore the
boundary. The focus of guilt, in other words, is on the
creation, maintenance, and repair of boundaries, within
society and within ourselves.[3] The concept of guilt is thus
broader than is generally assumed, but it is still not a free-
floating concept: its anchor is deep within the human
condition, tied always to the boundary and the overstepping of the boundary, with the consequent reactions.

If guilt, then, is a concept with blurred edges, we can
say that the cluster of ideas associated with it—sin, punishment, repentance, purification, and the like—form a
family. And within this conceptual family (the family of
guilt) those basic similarities, or "family resemblances," of
which Wittgenstein spoke, can be found: the similarity,
for example, between Freud's notion of unconscious guilt
and the Greek notion of purification; the similarity between
the moral indignation that we turn toward ourselves
(guilt feelings) and that which we turn toward others
(nemesis); the similarities involved in separating the
transgressor from society through exile, imprisonment, or
death.

But there are other types of relationship present as well,
relationships that Wittgenstein failed to see, due to the
limited applicability of his example, the game. The various
concepts within the family of guilt move beyond the similarities of which Wittgenstein spoke, to structural and
functional relationships. There are, for example, certain
structural pairs within the concept of guilt, among them
judge and thief, crime and punishment, pollution and
purification, repentance and forgiveness. More important,
though, is the basic structure of guilt itself, which revolves
around the notion of boundary, the overstepping of the
boundary, and the return to a boundary. To express it
in linear dimensions, one can speak of the structural se-

[3] The only work I know that includes all six elements of guilt
is the *Oresteia* of Aeschylus. Could it be that guilt requires the
art of the poet for its fullest expression?

quence of guilt: a *boundary* is *transgressed,* the offender
is *separated* from the rest of society (sometimes physically, sometimes through withdrawal of solidarity), various
attempts are made (nemesis, guilt feelings, punishment,
etc.) to *reassert the boundary,* and finally the boundary
is either restored or a new one takes its place (*reconciliation*), and society finds itself at one with the offender
(*atonement*). Moreover, many of the concepts within the
family of guilt can be considered as structures that perform certain functions. The concepts of debt, uncleanness,
and crime are all structures that indicate modes of transgression; nemesis and punishment are structures that
perform a cleansing function in society, i.e., the re-
establishment of solidarity. As these examples indicate, di-
verse structures can, at times, perform similar functions.
Similar structures, on the other hand, can perform vastly
different functions: the function of the modern scapegoat, for example, is to avoid guilt by transferring responsibility to another; the function of the scapegoat in
ancient Israel was to force men to accept collective responsibility for the community.[4]

Guilt is, then, a richer concept than we had previously
thought. But it is more: a basic category, like power,
identity, death, or love, without which it is difficult to
understand either the human condition or the day-to-day
life of man. For the creation, maintenance, and reparation
of boundaries—precisely what we have seen is involved in
the concept of guilt—is an inherent and pervasive aspect
of human life. Men, even in their rebellion, live by and
through boundaries,[5] so much so that it is almost impossible for us even to conceive of human life apart from
boundaries or limits. Thomas Hobbes, to be sure, "feigns
the annihilation of the world" and thus is able to sketch a

[4] Lev. 16:21. See also T. H. Gaster, "Sacrifices and Offerings,
OT.," *The Interpreter's Dictionary of the Bible* (New York:
Abingdon Press, 1962), Vol. 4, p. 153.
[5] Cf. Albert Camus, *The Rebel,* trans. Anthony Bower (New
York: Vintage Books, 1956).

state of nature that knows no boundaries, except that of death. But this is, I suspect, a terrible ordeal for Hobbes,[6] and he undertakes it only in order to create the conditions for a civil order that will be both tightly structured and immortal. And if Nietzsche gazes into the abyss, what he, too, sees is the need for limits, for not even the philosopher—who is both beast and god—can live without them.

An anarchic tendency is inherent in a book of essays. And this is as it should be, for much of the flavor, as well as the marrow, of the work derives from the parts rather than from the whole. Nevertheless, where a theme is involved, it is important to impart some kind of structure so that we may gain perspective on the problem under consideration. I have, therefore, arranged the essays on guilt in a sequence that, though not immutable, has at least a kind of rhythm to it. Those who read the essays closely, moreover, will be able to detect the harmony, counterpoint, and, admittedly, the touches of dissonance that are present.

The book begins with Nietzsche's reflections on the origin and evolution of guilt; the historic coupling of guilt, debt, and pain; and the possibility of man's overcoming "bad conscience" through creativity. Freud, in his essay on Dostoevsky, continues to probe the origins of guilt, adding the element of parricide. But he also describes the compulsions of neurotic guilt, and inquires further into the relationship between guilt and art. Martin Buber then addresses the psychotherapist, and suggests that unless the "doctors of the soul" are aware of *existential guilt*, they are not likely to be able to help men achieve a true wholeness. But the relevance of this mode of guilt, Buber would be the first to say, is not confined to psychotherapy—existential guilt is, in fact, human

[6] On what the philosopher *does not* tell us and why, see Nietzsche's *Beyond Good and Evil*, trans. Walter Kaufman (New York: Vintage Books, 1966), sections 289–90.

guilt in the fullest sense, non-neurotic, universal, and inescapable.[7] Next, Margaret Mead outlines the contributions that anthropological research, resting heavily on psychoanalytic perspectives, has made to theories of guilt. In particular, she clarifies the relationship between ritual and guilt, and shows the wide variation of cultural patterns with regard to guilt. Sykes and Matza also focus on society, but do so in terms of what might be called "preventive innocence." That is, they are concerned with the fact that the juvenile delinquent, rather than being a member of a deviant sub-culture, learns techniques from society that allow him to neutralize the social norms that he *believes in.* One need only add that there is a striking resemblance between the delinquent of Sykes and Matza and the "family man" of Hannah Arendt. Even the most respectable among us may contain more of the delinquent than he would care to be aware of or acknowledge.

The next two selections focus on the dramatic aspects of guilt. In the eyes of Kenneth Burke, the *drama* of human relations is primordial, unchanging, and enduring. Societies are always the same: they always rely on the same "collective motives," namely, on Guilt, Redemption, Hierarchy, and Victimage. Yet the age-old pattern could be broken, Burke believes, if we could only become aware of the symbols by which we live and what they do to us. In this connection, Rollo May's study of the Oedipus myth is revealing. May would agree with Burke that men live by symbols and that their life is highly dramatic. The meaning of the Oedipus myth, he shows us, is universal, but, at the same time, it is not a drama of aggression or sexuality. Rather, it is a drama of self-awareness and gradual maturity, of a man coming to know himself.

In the next section of the book, Smith and Hodges turn their attention to the problems of guilt and politics, both doing so by examining Freud's theory of guilt. Smith

[7] Cf. Rollo May, in Rollo May and others, ed., *Existence: A New Dimension in Psychiatry and Psychology* (New York: Basic Books, 1958), pp. 50–55.

argues that "unconscious guilt" is a metaphor rather than an explanation, a weapon of war in the struggle to shape political society. But it is a weapon, he believes, that is also destructive of the plurality of politics. Hodges, on the other hand, sees two ethics in Freud, one growing out of parricide and the other out of fratricide. Fratricide, he suggests, is the more serious problem, and has given rise to the ethic of brotherly love. To strengthen this ethic and make it effective in the community is the task before us.

Hannah Arendt continues the theme of political guilt in her essays on the concentration camps and on "German guilt." The first, "Total Domination," raises the question of a radical evil, different from the ordinary crimes of men, which can be neither punished, forgiven, nor wholly understood. Though we can see the results and feel its presence, radical evil goes beyond the limits of the human imagination: it is *in-human* guilt. The second, "Organized Guilt and Universal Responsibility," considers the problem of collective responsibility for the administrative mass murders of the Nazi period. In this connection, Arendt makes it clear that the privatization of life in the modern period is an important source of collective guilt, particularly in its most virulent form, radical evil. But she also introduces the idea of "metaphysical guilt" (though she does not use the term), a type of guilt that involves identity more than causality, but requires each of us to assume responsibility for all the evil done in the world.[8]

The final essay, Glenn Gray's "The Ache of Guilt," is a study of the soldier's relationship to guilt. But in Gray's hands it becomes much more: a summation of all that has gone before. We come back to the origins of guilt, the role of conscience, the problem of existential and metaphysical guilt, the functions of guilt. But Gray does something even more important: he awakens us to what it

[8] See also Karl Jaspers, *The Question of German Guilt,* trans. E. B. Ashton (New York: Capricorn Books, 1961).

means to be *awakened*. "If guilt is not experienced deeply enough to cut into us," Gray argues, "our future may well be lost." But Gray concludes his essay on a note which moves beyond good and evil. For he knows that if we are to survive as men, we must learn to love more. "There is," as he puts it, "no other way."

In closing, I simply want to thank the authors for allowing me to reprint their work. Without their generous cooperation, and that of the various publishers, this book, of course, would not have been possible.

II

The Origin of Guilt

FRIEDRICH NIETZSCHE

"Guilt," "Bad Conscience," and
Related Matters

To breed an animal with the right to make promises—
is not this the paradoxical problem nature has set itself
with regard to man? and is it not man's true problem?
That the problem has in fact been solved to a remarkable
degree will seem all the more surprising if we do full justice to the strong opposing force, the faculty of oblivion.
Oblivion is not merely a *vis inertiae,* as is often claimed,
but an active screening device, responsible for the fact
that what we experience and digest psychologically does
not, in the stage of digestion, emerge into consciousness
any more than what we ingest physically does. The role
of this active oblivion is that of a concierge: to shut temporarily the doors and windows of consciousness; to protect us from the noise and agitation with which our lower
organs work for or against one another; to introduce a
little quiet into our consciousness so as to make room for
the nobler functions and functionaries of our organism

which do the governing and planning. This concierge maintains order and etiquette in the household of the psyche; which immediately suggests that there can be no happiness, no serenity, no hope, no pride, no *present*, without oblivion. A man in whom this screen is damaged and inoperative is like a dyspeptic (and not merely *like* one): he can't be done with anything. . . . Now this naturally forgetful animal, for whom oblivion represents a power, a form of strong health, has created for itself an opposite power, that of remembering, by whose aid, in certain cases, oblivion may be suspended—specifically in cases where it is a question of promises. By this I do not mean a purely passive succumbing to past impressions, the indigestion of being unable to be done with a pledge once made, but rather an active not wishing to be done with it, a continuing to will what has once been willed, a veritable "memory of the will"; so that, between the original determination and the actual performance of the thing willed, a whole world of new things, conditions, even volitional acts, can be interposed without snapping the long chain of the will. But how much all this presupposes! A man who wishes to dispose of his future in this manner must first have learned to separate necessary from accidental acts; to think causally; to see distant things as though they were near at hand; to distinguish means from ends. In short, he must have become not only calculating but himself calculable, regular even to his own perception, if he is to stand pledge for his own future as a guarantor does.

This brings us to the long story of the origin or genesis of responsibility. The task of breeding an animal entitled to make promises involves, as we have already seen, the preparatory task of rendering man up to a certain point regular, uniform, equal among equals, calculable. The tremendous achievement which I have referred to in *Daybreak* as "the custom character of morals," that labor man accomplished upon himself over a vast period of time, receives its meaning and justification here—even despite the brutality, tyranny, and stupidity associated with the process. With the help of custom and the social straitjacket, man was, in fact, made calculable. However, if we place ourselves at the terminal point of this great process, where society and custom finally reveal their true aim, we shall find the ripest fruit of that tree to be the sovereign individual, equal only to himself, all moral custom left far behind. This autonomous, more than moral individual (the terms *autonomous* and *moral* are mutually exclusive) has developed his own, independent, long-range will, which dares to make promises; he has a proud and vigorous consciousness of what he has achieved, a sense of power and freedom, of absolute accomplishment. This fully emancipated man, master of his will, who dares make promises—how should he not be aware of his superiority over those who are unable to stand security for themselves? Think how much trust, fear, reverence he inspires (all three fully *deserved*), and how, having that sovereign rule over himself, he has mastery too over all weaker-willed and less reliable creatures! Being truly free and possessor of a long-range, pertinacious will, he also possesses a scale of values. Viewing others from the center of his own being, he either honors or disdains them. It is natural to him to honor his strong and reliable peers, all those who promise like sovereigns: rarely and reluctantly; who are chary of their trust; whose trust is a mark of distinction; whose promises are binding because they know that they will make them good in spite of all accidents, in spite of destiny itself. Yet he will inevitably reserve a kick for those paltry windbags who promise irresponsibly and a rod for those liars who break their word even in uttering it. His proud awareness of the extraordinary privilege responsibility confers has penetrated deeply and become a dominant instinct. What shall he call that dominant instinct, provided he ever feels impelled to give it a name? Surely he will call it his *conscience*.

His conscience? It seems a foregone conclusion that this conscience, which we encounter here in its highest form, has behind it a long history of transformations. The right proudly to stand security for oneself, to approve oneself, is a ripe but also a late fruit; how long did that fruit have to hang green and tart on the tree! Over an even longer period there was not the slightest sign of such a fruit; no one had a right to predict it, although the tree was ready for it, organized in every part to the end of bringing it forth. "How does one create a memory for the human animal? How does one go about to impress anything on that partly dull, partly flighty human intelligence—that incarnation of forgetfulness—so as to make it stick?" As we might well imagine, the means used in solving this age-old problem have been far from delicate: in fact, there is perhaps nothing more terrible in man's earliest history than his mnemotechnics. "A thing is branded on the memory to make it stay there; only what goes on hurting will stick"—this is one of the oldest and, unfortunately, one of the most enduring psychological axioms. In fact, one might say that wherever on earth one still finds solemnity, gravity, secrecy, somber hues in the life of an individual or a nation, one also senses a residuum of that terror with which men must formerly have promised, pledged, vouched. It is the past—the longest, deepest, hardest of pasts—that seems to surge up whenever we turn serious. Whenever man has thought it necessary to create a memory for himself, his effort has been attended with torture, blood, sacrifice. The ghastliest sacrifices and pledges, including the sacrifice of the firstborn; the most repulsive mutilations, such as castration; the cruelest rituals in every religious cult (and all religions are at bottom systems of cruelty)—all these have their origin in that instinct which divined pain to be the strongest aid to mnemonics. (All asceticism is really part of the same development: here too the object is to make a few ideas omnipresent, unforgettable, "fixed," to the end of hypnotizing the entire nervous and intellectual system; the ascetic procedures help to effect the dissociation of those ideas from all others.) The poorer the memory of mankind has been, the more terrible have been its customs. The severity of all primitive penal codes gives us some idea how difficult it must have been for man to overcome his forgetfulness and to drum into these slaves of momentary whims and desires a few basic requirements of communal living. Nobody can say that we Germans consider ourselves an especially cruel and brutal nation, much less a frivolous and thriftless one; but it needs only a glance at our ancient penal codes to impress on us what labor it takes to create a nation of thinkers. (I would even say that we are the one European nation among whom is still to be found a maximum of trust, seriousness, insipidity, and matter-of-factness, which should entitle us to breed a mandarin caste for all of Europe.) Germans have resorted to ghastly means in order to triumph over their plebeian instincts and brutal coarseness. We need only recount some of our ancient forms of punishment: stoning (even in earliest legend millstones are dropped on the heads of culprits); breaking on the wheel (Germany's own contribution to the techniques of punishment); piercing with stakes, drawing and quartering, trampling to death with horses, boiling in oil or wine (these were still in use in the fourteenth and fifteenth centuries), the popular flaying alive, cutting out of flesh from the chest, smearing the victim with honey and leaving him in the sun, a prey to flies. By such methods the individual was finally taught to remember five or six "I won'ts" which entitled him to participate in the benefits of society; and indeed, with the aid of this sort of memory, people eventually "came to their senses." What an enormous price man had to pay for reason, seriousness, control over his emotions —those grand human prerogatives and cultural showpieces! How much blood and horror lies behind all "good things"!

But how about the origin of that other somber phenomenon, the consciousness of guilt, "bad conscience"?
Would you turn to our genealogists of morals for illumination? Let me say once again, they are worthless. Completely absorbed in "modern" experience, with no real
knowledge of the past, no desire even to understand it,
no historical instinct whatever, they presume, all the
same, to write the history of ethics! Such an undertaking
must produce results which bear not the slightest relation
to truth. Have these historians shown any awareness of
the fact that the basic moral term *Schuld* (guilt) has its
origin in the very material term *Schulden* (to be indebted)?
Of the fact that punishment, being a *compensation,* has
developed quite independently of any ideas about freedom of the will—indeed, that a very high level of humani-
zation was necessary before even the much more primitive
distinctions, "with intent," "through negligence," "by accident," *compos mentis,* and their opposites could be made
and allowed to weigh in the judgments of cases? The pat
and seemingly natural notion (so natural that it has often
been used to account for the origin of the notion of justice
itself) that the criminal deserves to be punished *because*
he could have acted otherwise, is in fact a very late and
refined form of human reasoning; whoever thinks it can
be found in archaic law grossly misconstrues the psychology of uncivilized man. For an unconscionably long time
culprits were not punished because they were felt to be
responsible for their actions; not, that is, on the assumption
that only the guilty were to be punished; rather, they were
punished the way parents still punish their children, out
of rage at some damage suffered, which the doer must pay
for. Yet this rage was both moderated and modified by
the notion that for every damage there could somehow be
found an equivalent, by which that damage might be com-
pensated—if necessary in the pain of the doer. To the
question how did that ancient, deep-rooted, still firmly
established notion of an equivalency between damage and
pain arise, the answer is, briefly: it arose in the contractual

relation between creditor and debtor, which is as old as the notion of "legal subjects" itself and which in its turn points back to the basic practices of purchase, sale, barter, and trade.

As we contemplate these contractual relationships we may readily feel both suspicion and repugnance toward the older civilizations which either created or permitted them. Since it was here that promises were made, since it was here that a memory had to be fashioned for the promiser, we must not be surprised to encounter every evidence of brutality, cruelty, pain. In order to inspire the creditor with confidence in his promise to repay, to give a guarantee for the stringency of his promise, but also to enjoin on his own conscience the duty of repayment, the debtor pledged by contract that in case of nonpayment he would offer another of his possessions, such as his body, or his wife, or his freedom, or even his life (or, in certain theologically oriented cultures, even his salvation or the sanctity of his tomb; as in Egypt, where the debtor's corpse was not immune from his creditor even in the grave). The creditor, moreover, had the right to inflict all manner of indignity and pain on the body of the debtor. For example, he could cut out an amount of flesh proportionate to the amount of the debt, and we find, very early, quite detailed legal assessments of the value of individual parts of the body. I consider it already a progress, proof of a freer, more generous, more *Roman* conception of law, when the Twelve Tables decreed that it made no difference how much or little, in such a case, the creditor cut out—*si plus minusve secuerunt, ne fraude esto.* Let us try to understand the logic of this entire method of compensations; it is strange enough. An equivalence is provided by the creditor's receiving, in place of material compensation such as money, land, or other possessions, a kind of *pleasure.* That pleasure is induced by his being able to exercise his power freely upon one who is powerless, by the pleasure of *faire le mal pour le plaisir de le faire,* the pleasure of rape. That pleasure will be increased in proportion to the lowliness of the creditor's own station; it will appear to him as a delicious morsel, a foretaste of a higher rank. In "punishing" the debtor, the creditor shares a seignorial right. For once he is given a chance to bask in the glorious feeling of treating another human being as lower than himself—or, in case the actual punitive power has passed on to a legal "authority," of seeing him despised and mistreated. Thus compensation consists in a legal warrant entitling one man to exercise his cruelty on another.

It is in the sphere of contracts and legal obligations that the moral universe of guilt, conscience, and duty, ("sacred" duty) took its inception. Those beginnings were liberally sprinkled with blood, as are the beginnings of everything great on earth. (And may we not say that ethics has never lost its reek of blood and torture—not even in Kant, whose categorical imperative smacks of cruelty?) It was then that the sinister knitting together of the two ideas *guilt* and *pain* first occurred, which by now have become quite inextricable. Let us ask once more: in what sense could pain constitute repayment of a debt? In the sense that to make someone suffer was a supreme pleasure. In exchange for the damage he had incurred, including his displeasure, the creditor received an extraordinary amount of pleasure; something which he prized the more highly the more it disaccorded with his social rank. I am merely throwing this out as a suggestion, for it is difficult, and embarrassing as well, to get to the bottom of such underground developments. To introduce crudely the concept of vengeance at this point would obscure matters rather than clarify them, since the idea of vengeance leads us straight back to our original problem: how can the infliction of pain provide satisfaction? The delicacy —even more, the *tartufferie*—of domestic animals like ourselves shrinks from imagining clearly to what extent cruelty constituted the collective delight of older mankind, how much it was an ingredient of all their joys, or how naïvely they manifested their cruelty, how they considered disinterested malevolence (Spinoza's *sympathia malevolens*) a normal trait, something to which one's conscience could assent heartily. Close observation will spot numerous survivals of this oldest and most thorough human delight in our own culture. In both *Daybreak* and *Beyond Good and Evil* I have pointed to that progressive sublimation and apotheosis of cruelty which not only characterizes the whole history of higher culture, but in a sense constitutes it. Not so very long ago, a royal wedding or great public celebration would have been incomplete without executions, tortures, or *autos da fé;* a noble household without some person whose office it was to serve as a butt for everyone's malice and cruel teasing. (Perhaps the reader will recall Don Quixote's sojourn at the court of the Duchess. *Don Quixote* leaves a bitter taste in our mouths today; we almost quail in reading it. This would have seemed very strange to Cervantes and to his contemporaries, who read the work with the clearest conscience in the world, thought it the funniest of books, and almost died laughing over it.) To behold suffering gives pleasure, but to cause another to suffer affords an even greater pleasure. This severe statement expresses an old, powerful, human, all too human sentiment—though the monkeys too might endorse it, for it is reported that they heralded and preluded man in the devising of bizarre cruelties. There is no feast without cruelty, as man's entire history attests. Punishment, too, has its festive features.

These ideas, by the way, are not intended to add grist to the pessimist's mill of *taedium vitae*. On the contrary, it should be clearly understood that in the days when people were unashamed of their cruelty life was a great deal more enjoyable than it is now in the heyday of pessimism. The sky overhead has always grown darker in proportion as man has grown ashamed of his fellows. The tired, pessimistic look, discouragement in face of life's riddle, the icy *no* of the man who loathes life are none of them characteristic of mankind's evilest eras. These phenomena are like marsh plants; they presuppose a bog—the bog of morbid finickiness and moralistic drivel which has alienated man from his natural instincts. On his way to becoming an "angel" man has acquired that chronic indigestion and coated tongue which makes not only the naïve joy and innocence of the animal distasteful to him, but even life itself; so that at times he stops his nose against himself and recites with Pope Innocent III the catalogue of his unsavorinesses ("impure conception, loathsome feeding in the mother's womb, wretchedness of physical substance, vile stench, discharge of spittle, urine, and faeces"). Nowadays, when suffering is invariably quoted as the chief argument against existence, it might be well to recall the days when matters were judged from the opposite point of view; when people would not have missed for anything the pleasure of inflicting suffering, in which they saw a powerful agent, the principal inducement to living. By way of comfort to the milksops, I would also venture the suggestion that in those days pain did not hurt as much as it does today; at all events, such is the opinion of a doctor who has treated Negroes for complicated internal inflammations which would have driven the most stoical European to distraction—the assumption here being that the Negro represents an earlier phase of human development. (It appears, in fact, that the curve of human susceptibility to pain drops abruptly the moment we go below the top layer of culture comprising ten thousand or ten million individuals. For my part, I am convinced that, compared with one night's pain endured by a hysterical bluestocking, all the suffering of all the animals that have been used to date for scientific experiments is as nothing.) Perhaps it is even legitimate to allow the possibility that pleasure in cruelty is not really extinct today; only, given our greater delicacy, that pleasure has had to undergo a certain sublimation and subtilization, to be translated into imaginative and psychological terms in order to pass muster before even the tenderest hypocritical conscience. ("Tragic empathy" is one such term; another is *les nostalgies de la croix*.) What makes people rebel against suffering is not really suffering itself but the senselessness of suffering; and yet neither the Christian, who projected a whole secret machinery of salvation into suffering, nor the naïve primitive, who interpreted all suffering from the standpoint of the spectator or the dispenser of suffering, would have conceived of it as senseless. In order to negate and dispose of the possibility of any secret, unwitnessed suffering, early man had to invent gods and a whole apparatus of intermediate spirits, invisible beings who could also see in the dark, and who would not readily let pass unseen any interesting spectacle of suffering. Such were the inventions with which life, in those days, performed its perennial trick of justifying itself, its "evil"; nowadays a different set of inventions would be needed, e.g., life as a riddle or an epistemological problem. According to the primitive logic of feeling (but is our own so very different?) any evil was justified whose spectacle proved edifying to the gods. We need only study Calvin and Luther to realize how far the ancient conception of the gods as frequenters of cruel spectacles has penetrated into our European humanism. But one thing is certain: the Greeks could offer their gods no more pleasant condiment than the joys of cruelty. With what eyes did Homer's gods regard the destinies of men? What, in the last analysis, was the meaning of the Trojan War and similar tragic atrocities? There can be no doubt that they were intended as festivals for the gods, and, insofar as poets in this respect are more "divine" than other men, as festivals for the poets. In much the same manner the moral philosophers of Greece, at a later date, let the eyes of God dwell on the moral struggles, the heroism, and the self-mortification of the virtuous man. The "Heracles" of stern virtue was on stage and was fully aware of it; to that nation of actors, unwitnessed virtue

was inconceivable. Might not the audacious invention,
by philosophers of that era, of man's free will, his absolute
spontaneity in the doing of good or ill, have been made
for the express purpose of insuring that the interest of the
gods in the spectacle of human virtue could never be exhausted? This earthly stage must never be bare of truly
novel, truly unprecedented suspense, complications, ca-
tastrophes. A truly deterministic world, whose movements
the gods might readily foresee, must soon pall on them:
reason enough why those friends of the gods, the philosophers, would not foist such a world on them. Ancient
humanity, an essentially public and visual world, unable
to conceive of happiness without spectacles and feasts, was
full of tender regard for the "spectator." And, as we have
said before, punishment too has its festive features.

We have observed that the feeling of guilt and personal
obligation had its inception in the oldest and most primitive relationship between human beings, that of buyer
and seller, creditor and debtor. Here, for the first time,
individual stood and measured himself against individual.
No phase of civilization, no matter how primitive, has
been discovered in which that relation did not to some
extent exist. The mind of early man was preoccupied to
such an extent with price making, assessment of values,
the devising and exchange of equivalents, that, in a certain sense, this may be said to have constituted his thinking. Here we find the oldest variety of human acuteness,
as well as the first indication of human pride, of a superiority over other animals. Perhaps our word *man* (*manas*)
still expresses something of that pride: man saw himself
as the being that measures values, the "assaying" animal.
Purchase and sale, together with their psychological trap-
pings, antedate even the rudiments of social organization
and covenants. From its rudimentary manifestation in interpersonal law, the incipient sense of barter, contract,
guilt, right, obligation, compensation was projected into
the crudest communal complexes (and their relations to

other such complexes) together with the habit of measuring power against power. The eye had been entirely conditioned to that mode of vision; and with the awkward consistency of primitive thought, which moves with difficulty but, when it does move, moves inexorably in one direction, early mankind soon reached the grand generalization that everything has its price, everything can be paid for. Here we have the oldest and naïvest moral canon of justice, of all "fair play," "good will," and "objectivity." Justice, at this level, is good will operating among men of roughly equal power, their readiness to come to terms with one another, to strike a compromise —or, in the case of others less powerful, to *force* them to accept such a compromise.

Keeping within the primeval frame of reference (which, after all, is not so very different from our own) we may say that the commonwealth stood to its members in the relation of creditor to debtor. People lived in a commonwealth, enjoying its privileges (which we are, perhaps, inclined to underestimate). They lived sheltered, protected, in peace and confidence, immune from injuries and hostilities to which the man "outside" was continually exposed, since they had pledged themselves to the community in respect of such injury and hostility. But supposing that pledge is violated? The disappointed creditor —the community—will get his money back as best he can, you may be sure. It is not so much a question of the actual damage done; primarily, the offender has broken his contract, his pledge to the group, thus forfeiting all the benefits and amenities of the community which he has hitherto enjoyed. The criminal is a debtor who not only refuses to repay the advantages and advances he has received but who even dares lay hands on his creditor. Hence he is not only stripped of his advantages, as is only just, but drastically reminded what these advantages were worth. The rage of the defrauded creditor, the community, returns him to the wild and outlawed con-

dition from which heretofore he had been protected. It
rejects him, and henceforth every kind of hostility may
vent itself on him. Punishment, at this level of morality,
simply mimics the normal attitude toward a hated enemy
who has been conquered and disarmed, who forfeits not
only every right and protection but all mercy as well. The
offender is treated according to the laws of war and victory celebrations, brutally, without consideration; which
may explain why war, including the martial custom of
ritual sacrifice, has provided all the modes under which
punishment appears in history.

As the commonwealth grew stronger, it no longer took
the infractions of the individual quite so seriously. The
individual no longer represented so grave a danger to the
group as a whole. The offender was no longer outlawed
and exposed to general fury. Rather, he was carefully
shielded by the community against popular indignation,
and especially against the indignation of the one he had
injured. The attempt to moderate the rage of the offended
party; to obviate a general disturbance by localizing the
case; to find equivalents, "arrange things," (the Roman
compositio); but most of all the attempt, ever more determined, to fix a price for every offense, and thus to disso-
ciate, up to a certain point, the offender from his offense
—these are the traits which characterize with increasing
clarity the development of penal law. Whenever a community gains in power and pride, its penal code becomes
more lenient, while the moment it is weakened or endan-
gered the harsher methods of the past are revived. The
humanity of creditors has always increased with their
wealth; until finally the degree to which a creditor can
tolerate impairment becomes the measure of his wealth.
It is possible to imagine a society flushed with such a
sense of power that it could afford to let its offenders go
unpunished. What greater luxury is there for a society to
indulge in? "Why should I bother about these parasites
of mine?" such a society might ask. "Let them take all they

want. I have plenty." Justice, which began by setting a
price on everything and making everyone strictly accountable, ends by blinking at the defaulter and letting him go
scot free. Like every good thing on earth, justice ends by
suspending itself. The fine name this self-canceling justice
has given itself is *mercy*. But mercy remains, as goes without saying, the prerogative of the strongest, his province
beyond the law.

A word should be said here against certain recent
attempts to trace the notion of justice to a different source,
namely rancor. But first of all, let me whisper something in
the ear of psychologists, on the chance that they might
want to study rancor at close range: that flower now
blooms most profusely among anarchists and anti-Semites—
unseen, like the violet, though with a different odor. And
as the like spirit begets the like result, we must not be
surprised if we see these recent attempts hark back to
certain shady efforts, discussed earlier, to dignify vengeance by the name of justice (as though justice were simply
an outgrowth of the sense of injury) and to honor the whole
gamut of *reactive* emotions. I am the last person to object
to the latter notion: in view of the long neglected relationship between our biological needs and our emotional reactions, it is a consideration of the utmost importance. Yet
I want to draw attention to the fact that precisely out of
the spirit of rancor has this new nuance of scientific
"equity" sprung to the service of hatred, envy, malevolence, and distrust. For "scientific equity" ceases immediately, giving way to accents of mortal enmity and the
crassest bias, the moment another group of emotions comes
into play whose biological value seems to me even greater
and for that reason even more deserving of scientific ap-
praisal and esteem. I am speaking of the truly *active* emotions, such as thirst for power, avarice, and the like (*vide*
E. Dühring, *The Value of Existence, A Course in Philosophy*, and elsewhere). So much for the general tendency.
Against Dühring's specific proposition that the native soil

of justice is in the reactive emotions, it must be urged that
the exact opposite is the case: the soil of the reactive emotions is the very last to be conquered by the spirit of
justice. Should it actually come to pass that the just man
remains just even toward his despoiler (and not simply
cool, moderate, distant, indifferent: to be just is a positive
attitude), and that even under the stress of hurt, con-
tumely, denigration the noble, penetrating yet mild objectivity of the just (the *judging*) eye does not become
clouded, then we have before us an instance of the rarest
accomplishment, something that, if we are wise, we will
neither expect nor be too easily convinced of. It is generally
true of even the most decent people that a small dose of
insult, malice, insinuation is enough to send the blood to
their eyes and equity out the window. The active man, the
attacker and overreacher, is still a hundred steps closer to
justice than the reactive one, and the reason is that he has
no need to appraise his object falsely and prejudicially as
the other must. It is an historical fact that the aggressive
man, being stronger, bolder, and nobler, has at all times had
the better view, the clearer conscience on his side. Conversely, one can readily guess who has the invention of
"bad conscience" on his conscience: the vindictive man.
Simply glance through history: in what sphere, thus far,
has all legislation and, indeed, all true desire for laws, developed? In the sphere of "reactive" man? Not at all.
Exclusively in the sphere of the active, strong, spontaneous,
and aggressive. Historically speaking, all law—be it said to
the dismay of that agitator (Dühring) who once confessed:
"The doctrine of vengeance is the red thread that runs
through my entire investigation of justice"—is a battle waged
against the reactive emotions by the active and aggressive,
who have employed part of their strength to curb the excesses of reactive pathos and bring about a compromise.
Wherever justice is practiced and maintained, we see a
stronger power intent on finding means to regulate the
senseless raging of rancor among its weaker subordinates.

This is accomplished by wresting the object of rancor from vengeful hands, or by substituting for vengeance the struggle against the enemies of peace and order, or by devising, proposing, and if necessary *enforcing* compromises, or by setting up a normative scale of equivalents for damages to which all future complaints may be referred. But above all, by the establishment of a code of laws which the superior power imposes upon the forces of hostility and resentment whenever it is strong enough to do so; by a categorical declaration of what it considers to be legitimate and right, or else forbidden and wrong. Once such a body of law has been established, all acts of highhandedness on the part of individuals or groups are seen as infractions of the law, as rebellion against the supreme power. Thus the rulers deflect the attention of their subjects from the particular injury and, in the long run, achieve the opposite end from that sought by vengeance, which tries to make the viewpoint of the injured person prevail exclusively. Henceforth the eye is trained to view the deed ever more impersonally—even the eye of the offended person, though this, as we have said, is the last to be affected. It follows that only after a corpus of laws has been established can there be any talk of "right" and "wrong" (and not, as Dühring maintains, after the act of injury). To speak of right and wrong *per se* makes no sense at all. No act of violence, rape, exploitation, destruction, is intrinsically "unjust," since life itself is violent, rapacious, exploitative, and destructive and cannot be conceived otherwise. Even more disturbingly, we have to admit that from the biological point of view legal conditions are necessarily exceptional conditions, since they limit the radical life-will bent on power and must finally subserve, as means, life's collective purpose, which is to create greater power constellations. To accept any legal system as sovereign and universal—to accept it, not merely as an instrument in the struggle of power complexes, but as a *weapon against struggle* (in the sense of Dühring's communist cliché that every will must regard every other will as its equal)—is an anti-vital principle which can only bring about man's utter demoralization and, indirectly, a reign of nothingness.

One word should be added here about the *origin* and the *purpose* of punishment, two considerations radically distinct and yet too frequently confounded. How have our genealogists of morals treated these questions? Naïvely, as always. They would discover some kind of "purpose" in punishment, such as to avenge, or to deter, and would then naïvely place this purpose at the origin of punishment as its *causa fiendi*. And this is all. Yet the criterion of purpose is the last that should ever be applied to a study of legal evolution. There is no set of maxims more important for an historian than this: that the actual causes of a thing's origin and its eventual uses, the manner of its incorporation into a system of purposes, are worlds apart; that everything that exists, no matter what its origin, is periodically reinterpreted by those in power in terms of fresh intentions; that all processes in the organic world are processes of outstripping and overcoming, and that, in turn, all outstripping and overcoming means reinterpretation, rearrangement, in the course of which the earlier meaning and purpose are necessarily either obscured or lost. No matter how well we understand the utility of a certain physiological organ (or of a legal institution, a custom, a political convention, an artistic genre, a cultic trait) we do not thereby understand anything of its origin. I realize that this truth must distress the traditionalist, for, from time immemorial, the demonstrable purpose of a thing has been considered its *causa fiendi*—the eye is made for seeing, the hand for grasping. So likewise, punishment has been viewed as an invention for the purpose of punishing. But all pragmatic purposes are simply symbols of the fact that a will to power has implanted its own sense of function in those less powerful. Thus the whole history of a thing, an organ, a custom, becomes a continuous *chain* of reinterpretations and rearrangements, which need not be causally connected among themselves, which may simply follow one another. The "evolution" of a thing, a custom, an organ is not its *progressus* towards a goal, let alone the most logical and shortest *progressus*, requiring the least energy and expenditure. Rather, it is a sequence of more or less profound, more or less independent processes of appropriation, including the resistances used in each instance, the attempted transformations for purposes of defense or reaction, as well as the results of successful counterattacks. While forms are fluid, their "meaning" is even more so. The same process takes place in every individual organism. As the whole organism develops in essential ways, the meaning of the individual organs too is altered. In some cases their partial atrophy or numerical diminution spells the increased strength and perfection of the whole. This amounts to saying that partial desuetude, atrophy and degeneration, the loss of meaning and purpose—in short, death—must be numbered among the conditions of any true *progressus*, which latter appears always in the form of the will and means to greater power and is achieved at the expense of numerous lesser powers. The scope of any "progress" is measured by all that must be sacrificed for its sake. To sacrifice humanity as mass to the welfare of a single stronger human species would indeed constitute progress. . . .

I have emphasized this point of historical method all the more strongly because it runs counter to our current instincts and fashions, which would rather come to terms with the absolute haphazardness or the mechanistic meaninglessness of event than with the theory of a will to power mirrored in all process. The democratic bias against anything that dominates or wishes to dominate, our modern *misarchism* (to coin a bad word for a bad thing) has gradually so sublimated and disguised itself that nowadays it can invade the strictest, most objective sciences without anyone's raising a word of protest. In fact it seems to me that this prejudice now dominates all of physiology and the other life sciences, to their detriment, naturally, since it has conjured away one of their most fundamental concepts, that of *activity*, and put in its place the concept of *adaptation*—a kind of second-rate activity, mere reactivity. Quite in keeping with that bias, Herbert Spencer has defined life itself as an ever more purposeful inner adaptation to external circumstances. But such a view misjudges the very essence of life; it overlooks the intrinsic superiority of the spontaneous, aggressive, overreaching, reinterpreting and re-establishing forces, on whose action adaptation gradually supervenes. It denies, even in the organism itself, the dominant role of the higher functions in which the vital will appears active and shaping. The reader will recall that Huxley strongly objected to Spencer's "administrative nihilism." But here it is a question of much more than simply "administration."

To return to the issue of punishment, we must distinguish in it two separate aspects: first its relatively permanent features: custom, the act, the *drama*, a certain strict sequence of procedures; and second, all that is fluid in it: its meaning, its purpose, the expectations attending on the execution of such procedures. In keeping with the views I have stated earlier, I presuppose here that the procedure itself antedates its use for purposes of punishment and that the latter has only been projected into the procedure, which had existed all along, though in a different framework. In short, I absolutely part company with the naïve view which would see the procedure as having been invented for punitive purposes, as earlier the hand for prehensile purposes. Concerning that other, fluid, "meaning" aspect of punishment, I would say that in a very late culture such as our present-day European culture the notion "punishment" has not one but a great many meanings. The whole history of punishment and of its adaptation to the most various uses has finally crystallized into a kind of complex which it is difficult to break down and quite impossible to define. (It is impossible to say with certainty today *why* people are punished. All terms which semiotically condense a whole process elude definition; only that which has no history can be defined.) However, at an earlier stage that synthesis of "meanings" must have been more easily soluble, its components more easily disassociated. We can still see how, from one situation to the next, the elements of the synthesis changed their valence and reorganized themselves in such a way that now this element, now that predominated at the expense of the others. It might even happen that in certain situations a single element (the purpose of *deterring*, for example) absorbed the rest. To give the reader some idea how uncertain, secondary, and accidental the "meaning" of punishment really is, and how one and the same procedure may be used for totally different ends, I shall furnish him with a schema abstracted from the relatively small and random body of material at my disposal.

1. Punishment administered with the view of rendering the offender harmless and preventing his doing further damage.

2. Punishment consisting of the payment of damages to the injured party, including affect compensation.

3. Punishment as the isolation of a disequilibrating agent, in order to keep the disturbance from spreading further.

4. Punishment as a means of inspiring fear of those who determine and execute it.

5. Punishment as cancellation of the advantages the culprit has hitherto enjoyed (as when he is put to work in the mines).

6. Punishment as the elimination of a degenerate element (or, as in Chinese law, a whole stock; a means of keeping the race pure, or of maintaining a social type).

7. Punishment as a "triumph," the violating and deriding of an enemy finally subdued.

8. Punishment as a means of creating memory, either for the one who suffers it—so-called "improvement"—or for the witnesses.

9. Punishment as the payment of a fee, exacted by the authority which protects the evil-doer from the excesses of vengeance.

10. Punishment as a compromise with the tradition of vendetta, to the extent that this is still maintained and invoked as a privilege by powerful clans.

11. Punishment as a declaration of war, a warlike measure, against an enemy of peace, order and authority.

However incomplete, this list will serve to show that punishment is rife with utilitarian purposes of every kind. All the more reason why we should delete from it a fictitious usefulness which looms very large in popular thought these days, and which reckless writers are using freely to buttress our tottering belief in punishment. Punishment, these men claim, is valuable because it awakens a sense of guilt in the culprit; we should therefore view it as the true instrument of the psychological reaction called "remorse," "pangs of conscience." But this is a blunder, even as far as modern man and his psychology are concerned; applied to early man the notion becomes wholly absurd. True remorse is rarest among criminals and convicts: prisons and penitentiaries are not the breeding places of this gnawer. All conscientious observers are agreed here, though the fact may disappoint their innermost hopes and wishes. By and large, punishment hardens and freezes; it concentrates; it sharpens the sense of alienation; it strengthens resistance. If it should happen that now and again it breaks the will and brings about a miserable prostration and self-abasement, we find that psychological effect even less gratifying than the one which is most common, i.e., a dry, self-absorbed gloom. But if we stop to consider the millennia of prehistory, we may say with some assurance that it is precisely punishment that has most effectively retarded the development of guilt feeling, at any rate in the hearts of the victims of punitive authority. For we must not underestimate the extent to which the criminal is prevented, by the very witnessing of the legal process, from regarding his deed as intrinsically evil. He sees the very same actions performed in the service of justice with perfectly clear conscience and general approbation: spying, setting traps, outsmarting, bribing, the whole tricky, cunning system which chiefs of police, prosecutors, and informers have developed among themselves; not to mention the cold-blooded legal practices of despoiling, insulting, torturing, murdering the victim. Obviously none of these practices is rejected and condemned *per se* by his judges, but only under certain conditions. "Bad conscience," that most uncanny and interesting plant of our vegetation, has definitely not sprung from this soil, indeed for a very long time the notion that he was punishing a "culprit" never entered a judge's mind. He thought he had to do with a mischief-maker, an unaccountable piece of misfortune. And in his turn the man whose lot it was to be punished considered his punishment a misfortune. He no more felt a moral pang than if some terrible unforeseen disaster had occurred, if a rock had fallen and crushed him.

Spinoza once, with some embarrassment, perceived this fact (to the annoyance of some of his commentators, like Kuno Fischer, who have gone out of their way to misconstrue his meaning). Teased one afternoon by heaven knows what memory, he was pondering the question of what really remained to him of that famous *morsus conscientiae*. Had he not relegated both good and evil to the realm of figments and grimly defended the honor of his "free" God against those blasphemers who would have God invariably act *sub ratione boni* ("But this would mean subordinating God to fate, and result in the worst absurdity")? The world for Spinoza had returned to that state of innocence which it had known before the invention of bad conscience—but what, in the process, had become of the sting of conscience? "It is the opposite of joy," he says finally, "a sadness attended by the memory of some past event which disappointed our expectations,"

(*Ethics* III, Propos. 18, Schol. 1. 2.). In much the same way for thousands of years, all evil-doers overtaken by punishment would think, "Something has unexpectedly gone wrong here," and not, "I should never have done that." They would undergo punishment as one undergoes sickness or misfortune or death, with that stout, unrebellious fatalism which still gives the Russians an advantage over us Westerners in the management of their lives. If actions were "judged" at all in those days, it was solely from the prudential point of view. There can be no doubt that we must look for the real effect of punishment in a sharpening of man's wits, an extension of his memory, a determination to proceed henceforth more prudently, suspiciously, secretly, a realization that the individual is simply too weak to accomplish certain things; in brief, an increase of self-knowledge. What punishment is able to achieve, both for man and beast, is increase of fear, circumspection, control over the instincts. Thus man is *tamed* by punishment, but by no means *improved;* rather the opposite. (It is said that misfortune sharpens our wits, but to the extent that it sharpens our wits it makes us worse; fortunately it often simply dulls them.)

I can no longer postpone giving tentative expression to my own hypothesis concerning the origin of "bad conscience." It is one that may fall rather strangely on our ears and that requires close meditation. I take bad conscience to be a deep-seated malady to which man succumbed under the pressure of the most profound transformation he ever underwent—the one that made him once and for all a sociable and pacific creature. Just as happened in the case of those sea creatures who were forced to become land animals in order to survive, these semi-animals, happily adapted to the wilderness, to war, free roaming, and adventure, were forced to change their nature. Of a sudden they found all their instincts devalued, unhinged. They must walk on legs and carry themselves, where before the water had carried them: a terrible heaviness weighed upon them. They felt inapt for the simplest manipulations, for in this new, unknown world they could no longer count on the guidance of their unconscious drives. They were forced to think, deduce, calculate, weigh cause and effect—unhappy people, reduced to their weakest, most fallible organ, their consciousness! I doubt that there has ever been on earth such a feeling of misery, such a leaden discomfort. It was not that those old instincts had abruptly ceased making their demands; but now their satisfaction was rare and difficult. For the most part they had to depend on new, covert satisfactions. All instincts that are not allowed free play turn inward. This is what I call man's interiorization; it alone provides the soil for the growth of what is later called man's *soul*. Man's interior world, originally meager and tenuous, was expanding in every dimension, in proportion as the outward discharge of his feelings was curtailed. The formidable bulwarks by means of which the polity protected itself against the ancient instincts of freedom (punishment was one of the strongest of these bulwarks) caused those wild, extravagant instincts to turn in upon man. Hostility, cruelty, the delight in persecution, raids, excitement, destruction all turned against their begetter. Lacking external enemies and resistances, and confined within an oppressive narrowness and regularity, man began rending, persecuting, terrifying himself, like a wild beast hurling itself against the bars of its cage. This languisher, devoured by nostalgia for the desert, who had to turn *himself* into an adventure, a torture chamber, an insecure and dangerous wilderness—this fool, this pining and desperate prisoner, became the inventor of "bad conscience." Also the generator of the greatest and most disastrous of maladies, of which humanity has not to this day been cured: his sickness of himself, brought on by the violent severance from his animal past, by his sudden leap and fall into new layers and conditions of existence, by his declaration of war against the old instincts that had hitherto been the foundation of his power, his joy, and his awesomeness. Let me hasten to add that the phenomenon of an animal soul turning in upon itself, taking arms against itself, was so novel, profound, mysterious, contradictory, and pregnant with possibility, that the whole complexion of the universe was changed thereby. This spectacle (and the end of it is not yet in sight) required a divine audience to do it justice. It was a spectacle too sublime and paradoxical to pass unnoticed on some trivial planet. Henceforth man was to figure among the most unexpected and breathtaking throws in the game of dice played by Heracleitus' great "child," be he called Zeus or Chance. Man now aroused an interest, a suspense, a hope, almost a conviction—as though in him something were heralded, as though he were not a goal but a way, an interlude, a bridge, a great promise. . . .

My hypothesis concerning the origin of bad conscience presupposes that this change was neither gradual nor voluntary, that it was not an organic growing into new conditions but rather an abrupt break, a leap, a thing compelled, an ineluctable disaster, which could neither be struggled against nor even resented. It further presupposes that the fitting of a hitherto unrestrained and shapeless populace into a tight mold, as it had begun with an act of violence, had to be brought to conclusion by a series of violent acts; that the earliest commonwealth constituted a terrible despotism, a ruthless, oppressive machinery for not only kneading and suppling a brutish populace but actually shaping it. I have used the word "commonwealth," but it should be clearly understood what I mean: a pack of savages, a race of conquerors, themselves organized for war and able to organize others, fiercely dominating a population perhaps vastly superior in numbers yet amorphous and nomadic. Such was the beginning of the human polity; I take it we have got over that sentimentalism that would have it begin with a contract. What do men who can command, who are born rulers, who evince power in act and deportment, have to do with contracts? Such beings are unaccountable; they come like destiny, without rhyme or reason, ruthlessly, bare of pretext. Suddenly they are here, like a stroke of lightning, too terrible, convincing, and "different" for hatred even. Their work is an instinctive imposing of forms. They are the most spontaneous, most unconscious artists that exist. They appear, and presently something entirely new has arisen, a live dominion whose parts and functions are delimited and interrelated, in which there is room for nothing that has not previously received its meaning from the whole. Being natural organizers, these men know nothing of guilt, responsibility, consideration. They are actuated by the terrible egotism of the artist, which is justified by the work he must do, as the mother by the child she will bear. Bad conscience certainly did not originate with these men, yet, on the other hand, that unseemly growth could not have developed *without* them, without their hammer blows, their artist's violence, which drove a great quantity of freedom out of sight and made it latent. In its earliest phase bad conscience is nothing other than the instinct of freedom forced to become latent, driven underground, and forced to vent its energy upon itself.

We should guard against taking too dim a view of this phenomenon simply because it is both ugly and painful. After all, the same will to power which in those violent artists and organizers created polities, in the "labyrinth of the heart"—more pettily, to be sure, and in inverse direction—created negative ideals and humanity's bad conscience. Except that now the material upon which this great natural force was employed was man himself, his old animal self—and not, as in that grander and more spectacular phenomenon—his fellow man. This secret violation of the self, this artist's cruelty, this urge to impose on recalcitrant matter a form, a will, a distinction, a feeling of contradiction and contempt, this sinister task of a soul divided against itself, which makes itself suffer for the pleasure of suffering, this most energetic "bad conscience"—has it not given birth to a wealth of strange beauty and affirmation?

Has it not given birth to beauty itself? Would beauty exist if ugliness had not first taken cognizance of itself, not said to itself, "I am ugly"? This hint will serve, at any rate, to solve the riddle of why contradictory terms such as *selflessness, self-denial, self-sacrifice* may intimate an ideal, a beauty. Nor will the reader doubt henceforth that the *joy* felt by the self-denying, self-sacrificing, selfless person was from the very start a *cruel* joy.—So much for the origin of altruism as a moral value. Bad conscience, the desire for self-mortification, is the wellspring of all altruistic values.

There can be no doubt that bad conscience is a sickness, but so, in a sense, is pregnancy. We shall presently describe the conditions which carried that "sickness" to its highest and most terrible peak. But first let us return for a moment to an earlier consideration. The civil-law relationship of debtor to creditor has been projected into yet another context, which we find it even more difficult to understand today, namely into the relationship between living men and their forebears. Among primitive tribes, each new generation feels toward the preceding ones, and especially toward the original founders of the tribe, a *juridical* obligation (rather than an *emotional* obligation, which seems to be of relatively recent origin). Early societies were convinced that their continuance was guaranteed solely by the sacrifices and achievements of their ancestors and that these sacrifices and achievements required to be paid back. Thus a debt was acknowledged which continued to increase, since the ancestors, surviving as powerful spirits, did not cease to provide the tribe with new benefits out of their store. Gratuitously? But nothing was gratuitous in those crude and "insensitive" times. Then how could they be repaid? By burnt offerings (to provide them with food), by rituals, shrines, customs, but above all, by obedience—for all rites, having been established by the forebears, were also permanently enjoined by them. But could they ever be *fully* repaid? An anxious doubt remained and grew steadily, and every so often there occurred some major act of "redemption," some gigantic repayment of the creditor (the famous sacrifice of the first-born, for example; in any case blood, human blood). Given this primitive logic, the fear of the ancestor and his power and the consciousness of indebtedness increase in direct proportion as the power of the tribe itself increases, as it becomes more successful in battle, independent, respected and feared. Never the other way round. Every step leading to the degeneration of the tribe, every setback, every sign of imminent dissolution, tends to diminish the fear of the ancestral spirits, to make them seem of less account, less wise, less provident, less powerful. Following this kind of logic to its natural term, we arrive at a situation in which the ancestors of the most powerful tribes have become so fearful to the imagination that they have receded at last into a numinous shadow: the ancestor becomes a god. Perhaps this is the way all gods have arisen, out of *fear*. . . . And if anyone should find it necessary to add, "But also out of piety," his claim would scarcely be justified for the longest and earliest period of the human race. But it would certainly hold true for that intermediate period during which the noble clans emerged, of whom it may justly be said that they paid back their ancestors (heroes or gods) with interest all those noble properties which had since come to reside abundantly in themselves. We shall have an opportunity later on of dealing with this "ennoblement" of the ancestral spirits (which is not the same thing as their "consecration"), but first, let us bring to a conclusion the story of man's consciousness of guilt.

Man's firm belief that he was indebted to the gods did not cease with the decline of tribal organization. Just as man has inherited from the blood aristocracies the concepts *good* and *bad*, together with the psychological penchant for hierarchies, so he has inherited from the tribes, together with the tribal gods, a burden of outstanding debt and the desire to make final restitution. (The bridge is provided by those large populations of slaves and serfs, who, either perforce or through servile mimicry, had adopted the cults of their overlords. The heritage spreads out from them in all directions.) The sense of indebtedness to the gods continued to grow through the centuries, keeping pace with the evolution of man's concept of the deity. (The endless tale of ethnic struggle, triumph, reconciliation, and fusion, in short, whatever precedes the final hierarchy of racial strains in some great synthesis, is mirrored in the welter of divine genealogies and legends dealing with divine battles, victories, and reconciliations. Every progress toward universal empire has also been a progress toward a universal pantheon. Despotism, by overcoming the independent nobles, always prepares the way for some form of monotheism.) The advent of the Christian god, the "highest potency" god yet conceived by man, has been accompanied by the widest dissemination of the sense of indebtedness, guilt. If we are right in assuming that we have now entered upon the inverse development, it stands to reason that the steady decline of belief in a Christian god should entail a commensurate decline in man's guilt consciousness. It also stands to reason—doesn't it?—that a complete and definitive victory of atheism might deliver mankind altogether from its feeling of being indebted to its beginnings, its *causa prima*. Atheism and a kind of "second innocence" go together.

So much, for the moment, about the connection of "guilt" and "duty" with religious presuppositions. I have deliberately left on one side the "moralization" of these terms (their pushing back into conscience, the association of the notion of bad conscience with a deity), and even wrote at the end of the last paragraph as though such a moralization had never taken place; as though with the notion of a divine creditor falling into disuse those notions too were doomed. Unfortunately this is far from being the case. The modern moralization of the ideas of guilt and duty—their relegation to a purely subjective "bad conscience"—represents a determined attempt to invert the normal order of development, or at least to stop it in its tracks. The object now is to close the prospect of final deliverance and make man's gaze rebound from an iron barrier; to force the ideas of guilt and duty to face about and fiercely turn on—whom? Obviously on the "debtor," first of all, who, infested and eaten away by bad conscience, which spreads like a polyp, comes to view his debt as unredeemable by any act of atonement (the notion of "eternal penance"). But eventually the "creditor" too is turned on in the same fashion. Now the curse falls upon man's *causa prima* ("Adam," "original sin," the "bondage of the will"); or upon nature, which gave birth to man and which is now made the repository of the evil principle (nature as the instrument of the devil); or upon universal existence, which now appears as absolute non-value (nihilistic turning away from life, a longing for nothingness or for life's "opposite," for a different sort of "being"—Buddhism, etc.). Then suddenly we come face to face with that paradoxical and ghastly expedient which brought temporary relief to tortured humanity, that most brilliant stroke of Christianity: God's sacrifice of himself for man. God makes himself the ransom for what could not otherwise be ransomed; God alone has power to absolve us of a debt we can no longer discharge; the creditor offers himself as a sacrifice for his debtor out of sheer love (can you believe it?), out of love for his debtor. . . .

By now the reader will have guessed what has really been happening behind all these façades. Man, with his need for self-torture, his sublimated cruelty resulting from the cooping up of his animal nature within a polity, invented bad conscience in order to hurt himself, after the blocking of the more natural outlet of his cruelty. Then this guilt-ridden man seized upon religion in order to exacerbate his self-torment to the utmost. The thought of being in God's debt became his new instrument of torture. He focused in God the last of the opposites he could find to his true and inveterate animal instincts, making these a sin against God (hostility, rebellion against the "Lord," the "Father," the "Creator"). He stretched himself upon the contradiction "God" and "Devil" as on a rack. He projected all his denials of self, nature, naturalness out of himself as affirmations, as true being, embodiment, reality, as God (the divine Judge and Executioner), as transcendence, as eternity, as endless torture, as hell, as the infinitude of guilt and punishment. In such psychological cruelty we see an insanity of the *will* that is without parallel: man's will to find himself guilty, and unredeemably so; his will to believe that he might be punished to all eternity without ever expunging his guilt; his will to poison the very foundation of things with the problem of guilt and punishment and thus to cut off once and for all his escape from this labyrinth of obsession; his will to erect an ideal (God's holiness) in order to assure himself of his own absolute unworthiness. What a mad, unhappy animal is man! What strange notions occur to him; what perversities, what paroxysms of nonsense, what bestialities of idea burst from him, the moment he is prevented ever so little from being a beast of action! . . . All this is exceedingly curious and interesting, but dyed with such a dark, somber, enervating sadness that one must resolutely tear away one's gaze. Here, no doubt, is sickness, the most terrible sickness that has wasted man thus far. And if one is still able to hear—but how few these days have ears to hear it!—in this night of torment and absurdity the cry *love* ring out, the cry of rapt longing, of redemption in love, he must turn away with a shudder of invincible horror. . . . Man harbors too much horror; the earth has been a lunatic asylum for too long.

This should take care, once for all, of the origin of "Our Holy Lord."—A single look at the Greek gods will convince us that a belief in gods need not result in morbid imaginations, that there are nobler ways of creating divine figments—ways which do not lead to the kind of self-crucifixion and self-punishment in which Europe, for millennia now, has excelled. The Hellenic gods reflected a race of noble and proud beings, in whom man's animal self had divine status and hence no need to lacerate and rage against itself. For a very long time the Greeks used their gods precisely to keep bad conscience at a distance, in order to enjoy their inner freedom undisturbed; in other words, they made the opposite use of them that Christianity has made of *its* god. They went very far in that direction, these splendid and lionhearted children, and no less an authority than the Homeric Zeus gives them to understand, now and again, that they make things a little too easy for themselves. "How strange," he says once (the case is that of Aegisthus, a *very* bad case indeed): "How strange that the mortals complain so loudly of us gods! They claim that we are responsible for all their evils. But they are the ones who create their own misery, by their folly, even in the teeth of fate." Yet the reader notices at once that even this Olympian spectator and judge is far from holding a grudge against them or thinking ill of them therefore. "How foolish they are!" he thinks as he watches the misdeeds of mortals; and the Greeks, even during the heyday of their prosperity and strength, allowed that foolishness, lack of discretion, slight mental aberrations might be the source of much evil and disaster. Foolishness, not sin. . . . But even those mental aberrations were a problem. "How can such a thing happen to people like us, nobly bred, happy, virtuous, well educated?" For many centuries noble Greeks would ask themselves this question whenever one of their number had defiled himself by one of those incomprehensible crimes. "Well, he must have been deluded by a god," they would finally say, shaking their heads. This was a typically Greek solution. It was the office of the gods to justify, up to a certain point, the ill ways of man, to serve as "sources" of evil. In those days they were not agents of punishment but, what is nobler, repositories of guilt.

It is clear that I am concluding this essay with three unanswered questions. It may occur to some reader to ask me, "Are you constructing an ideal or destroying one?" I would ask him, in turn, whether he ever reflected upon the price that had to be paid for the introduction of every new ideal on earth? On how much of reality, in each instance, had to be slandered and misconceived, how much of falsehood ennobled, how many consciences disturbed, how many gods sacrificed? For the raising of an altar requires the breaking of an altar: this is a law—let anyone who can prove me wrong. We moderns have a millennial heritage of conscience-vivisection and cruelty to the animals in ourselves. This is our most ancient habit, our most consummate artistry perhaps, in any case our greatest refinement, our special fare. Man has looked for so long with an evil eye upon his natural inclinations that they have finally become inseparable from "bad conscience." A converse effort can be imagined, but who has the strength for it? It would consist of associating all the *unnatural* inclinations—the longing for what is unworldly, opposed to the senses, to instinct, to nature, to the animal in us, all the anti-biological and earth-calumniating ideals— with bad conscience. To whom, today, may such hopes and pretensions address themselves? The *good* men, in particular, would be on the other side; and of course all the comfortable, resigned, vain, moony, weary people. Does anything give greater offense and separate one more thoroughly from others than to betray something of the strictness and dignity with which one treats oneself? But how kind and accommodating the world becomes the moment we act like all the rest and let ourselves go! To accomplish that aim, different minds are needed than are likely to appear in this age of ours: minds strengthened by struggles and victories, for whom conquest, adventure, danger, even pain, have become second nature. Minds accustomed to the keen atmosphere of high altitudes, to wintry walks, to ice and mountains in every sense. Minds possessed of a sublime kind of malice, of that self-assured recklessness which is a sign of strong health. What is needed, in short, is just superb health. Is such health still possible today?

But at some future time, a time stronger than our effete, self-doubting present, the true Redeemer will come, whose surging creativity will not let him rest in any shelter or hiding place, whose solitude will be misinterpreted as a flight from reality, whereas it will in fact be a dwelling *on*, a dwelling *in* reality—so that when he comes forth into the light he may bring with him the redemption of that reality from the curse placed upon it by a lapsed ideal. This man of the future, who will deliver us both from a lapsed ideal and from all that this ideal has spawned —violent loathing, the will to extinction, nihilism—this great and decisive stroke of midday, who will make the will free once more and restore to the earth its aim, and to man his hope; this anti-Christ and anti-nihilist, conqueror of both God and Unbeing—*one day he must come*. . . .

But why go on? I've reached the term of my speech; to continue here would be to usurp the right of one younger, stronger, more pregnant with future than I am —the right of Zarathustra, *impious* Zarathustra. . . .

III

The Compulsions of Guilt

SIGMUND FREUD
Dostoevsky and Parricide

Four facets may be distinguished in the rich personality
of Dostoevsky: the creative artist, the neurotic, the moralist and the sinner. How is one to find one's way in this
bewildering complexity?

The creative artist is the least doubtful: Dostoevsky's
place is not far behind Shakespeare. *The Brothers Karamazov* is the most magnificent novel ever written; the
episode of the Grand Inquisitor, one of the peaks in the
literature of the world, can hardly be valued too highly.
Before the problem of the creative artist analysis must,
alas, lay down its arms.

The moralist in Dostoevsky is the most readily assail-
able. If we seek to rank him high as a moralist on the plea
that only a man who has gone through the depths of sin

From *The Standard Edition of the Complete Psychological
Works of Sigmund Freud,* edited by James Strachey (London:
Hogarth Press, 1961), Vol. XXI. Translated by D. F. Tait,
revised by J. Strachey. "Dostoevsky and Parricide" also appears
as Chapter XXI of *The Collected Papers of Sigmund Freud,*
Volume 5, edited by Ernest Jones, M.D., Basic Books, Inc.,
Publishers, New York, 1959. Reprinted by permission of the
Hogarth Press Ltd., the Institute of Psycho-Analysis, Sigmund
Freud Copyrights Ltd., and Basic Books, Inc.

can reach the highest summit of morality, we are neglect-
ing a doubt that arises. A moral man is one who reacts to
temptation as soon as he feels it in his heart, without
yielding to it. A man who alternately sins and then in his
remorse erects high moral standards lays himself open to
the reproach that he has made things too easy for himself.
He has not achieved the essence of morality, renunciation,
for the moral conduct of life is a practical human interest.
He reminds one of the barbarians of the great migrations,
who murdered and did penance for it, till penance became an actual technique for enabling murder to be done.
Ivan the Terrible behaved in exactly this way; indeed
this compromise with morality is a characteristic Russian
trait. Nor was the final outcome of Dostoevsky's moral
strivings anything very glorious. After the most violent
struggles to reconcile the instinctual demands of the individual with the claims of the community, he landed in
the retrograde position of submission both to temporal
and spiritual authority, of veneration both for the Tsar and
for the God of the Christians, and of a narrow Russian
nationalism—a position which lesser minds have reached
with smaller effort. This is the weak point in that great
personality. Dostoevsky threw away the chance of becoming a teacher and liberator of humanity and made himself one with their gaolers. The future of human civilization will have little to thank him for. It seems probable
that he was condemned to this failure by his neurosis.
The greatness of his intelligence and the strength of his
love for humanity might have opened to him another, an
apostolic, way of life.

To consider Dostoevsky as a sinner or a criminal rouses
violent opposition, which need not be based upon a phi-
listine assessment of criminals. The real motive for this
opposition soon becomes apparent. Two traits are essential in a criminal: boundless egoism and a strong destructive urge. Common to both of these, and a necessary
condition for their expression, is absence of love, lack of an

emotional appreciation of (human) objects. One at once
recalls the contrast to this presented by Dostoevsky—his
great need of love and his enormous capacity for love,
which is to be seen in manifestations of exaggerated kind-
ness and caused him to love and to help where he had a
right to hate and to be revengeful, as, for example, in his
relations with his first wife and her lover. That being so,
it must be asked why there is any temptation to reckon
Dostoevsky among the criminals. The answer is that it
comes from his choice of material, which singles out from
all others violent, murderous and egoistic characters, thus
pointing to the existence of similar tendencies within himself, and also from certain facts in his life, like his passion
for gambling and his possible confession to a sexual
assault upon a young girl.[1] The contradiction is resolved
by the realization that Dostoevsky's very strong destructive instinct, which might easily have made him a criminal, was in his actual life directed mainly against his own
person (inward instead of outward) and thus found expression as masochism and a sense of guilt. Nevertheless,
his personality retained sadistic traits in plenty, which show
themselves in his irritability, his love of tormenting and
his intolerance even towards people he loved, and which
appear also in the way in which, as an author, he treats
his readers. Thus in little things he was a sadist towards

[1] See the discussion of this in René Fülöp-Miller and Friedrich Eckstein, ed., *Der unbekannte Dostojewski* (Munich,
1926). Stefan Zweig (*Three Masters: Balzac, Dickens, Dostoevsky*, trans. Eden and Cedar Paul [New York and London, 1930]) writes: "He was not halted by the barriers of
bourgeois morality; and no one can say exactly how far he
transgressed the bounds of law in his own life or how much
of the criminal instincts of his heroes was realized in himself."
For the intimate connection between Dostoevsky's characters
and his own experiences, see René Fülöp-Miller's remarks in
the introductory section of Fülöp-Miller and Eckstein, ed.,
Dostojewski am Roulette (Munich, 1925), which are based
upon Nikolai Strakhov, *Biographia, pisma i zametki is zapis-
noi knizhki Dostoevskovo* [Biography, Letters and Notes from
Dostoevsky's Notebook] (Petersburg, 1883).

others, and in bigger things a sadist towards himself, in fact a masochist—that is to say the mildest, kindliest, most helpful person possible.

We have selected three factors from Dostoevsky's complex personality, one quantitative and two qualitative: the extraordinary intensity of his emotional life, his perverse innate instinctual disposition, which inevitably marked him out to be a sado-masochist or a criminal, and his unanalysable artistic gift. This combination might very well exist without neurosis; there are people who are complete masochists without being neurotic. Nevertheless, the balance of forces between his instinctual demands and the inhibitions opposing them (plus the available methods of sublimation) would even so make it necessary to classify Dostoevsky as what is known as an 'instinctual character'. But the position is obscured by the simultaneous presence of neurosis, which, as we have said, was not in the circumstances inevitable, but which comes into being the more readily, the richer the complication which has to be mastered by the ego. For neurosis is after all only a sign that the ego has not succeeded in making a synthesis, that in attempting to do so it has forfeited its unity.

How then, strictly speaking, does his neurosis show itself? Dostoevsky called himself an epileptic, and was regarded as such by other people, on account of his severe attacks, which were accompanied by loss of consciousness, muscular convulsions and subsequent depression. Now it is highly probable that this so-called epilepsy was only a symptom of his neurosis and must accordingly be classified as hystero-epilepsy—that is, as severe hysteria. We cannot be completely certain on this point for two reasons —firstly, because the anamnestic data on Dostoevsky's alleged epilepsy are defective and untrustworthy, and secondly, because our understanding of pathological states combined with epileptiform attacks is imperfect.

To take the second point first. It is unnecessary here to reproduce the whole pathology of epilepsy, for it would throw no decisive light on the problem. But this may be said. The old *morbus sacer* is still in evidence as an ostensible clinical entity, the uncanny disease with its incalculable, apparently unprovoked convulsive attacks, its changing of the character into irritability and aggressiveness, and its progressive lowering of all the mental faculties. But the outlines of this picture are quite lacking in precision. The attacks, so savage in their onset, accompanied by biting of the tongue and incontinence of urine and working up to the dangerous *status epilepticus* with its risk of severe self-injuries, may, nevertheless, be reduced to brief periods of *absence*, or rapidly passing fits of vertigo or may be replaced by short spaces of time during which the patient does something out of character, as though he were under the control of his unconscious. These attacks, though as a rule determined, in a way we do not understand, by purely physical causes, may nevertheless owe their first appearance to some purely mental cause (a fright, for instance) or may react in other respects to mental excitations. However characteristic intellectual impairment may be in the overwhelming majority of cases, at least *one* case is known to us (that of Helmholtz) in which the affliction did not interfere with the highest intellectual achievement. (Other cases of which the same assertion has been made are either disputable or open to the same doubts as the case of Dostoevsky himself.) People who are victims of epilepsy may give an impression of dullness and arrested development just as the disease often accompanies the most palpable idiocy and the grossest cerebral defects, even though not as a necessary component of the clinical picture. But these attacks, with all their variations, also occur in other people who display complete mental development and, if anything, an excessive and as a rule insufficiently controlled emotional life. It is no wonder in these circumstances that it has been found impossible to maintain that 'epilepsy' is a single clinical entity. The similarity that we find in the manifest symptoms seems to call for a functional view of them. It is as though a mechanism for abnormal instinctual discharge had been laid down organically, which could be made use of in quite different circumstances—both in the case of disturbances of cerebral activity due to severe histolytic or toxic affections, and also in the case of inadequate control over the mental economy and at times when the activity of the energy operating in the mind reaches crisis-pitch. Behind this dichotomy we have a glimpse of the identity of the underlying mechanism of instinctual discharge. Nor can that mechanism stand remote from the sexual processes, which are fundamentally of toxic origin: the earliest physicians described coition as a minor epilepsy, and thus recognized in the sexual act a mitigation and adaptation of the epileptic method of discharging stimuli.

The 'epileptic reaction', as this common element may be called, is also undoubtedly at the disposal of the neurosis whose essence it is to get rid by somatic means of amounts of excitation which it cannot deal with psychically. Thus the epileptic attack becomes a symptom of hysteria and is adapted and modified by it just as it is by the normal sexual process of discharge. It is therefore quite right to distinguish between an organic and an 'affective' epilepsy. The practical significance of this is that a person who suffers from the first kind has a disease of the brain, while a person who suffers from the second kind is a neurotic. In the first case his mental life is subjected to an alien disturbance from without, in the second case the disturbance is an expression of his mental life itself.

It is extremely probable that Dostoevsky's epilepsy was of the second kind. This cannot, strictly speaking, be proved. To do so we should have to be in a position to insert the first appearance of the attacks and their subsequent fluctuations into the thread of his mental life; and for that we know too little. The descriptions of the attacks themselves teach us nothing and our information about the relations between them and Dostoevsky's experiences is defective and often contradictory. The most probable assumption is that the attacks went back far into his childhood, that their place was taken to begin with by milder symptoms and that they did not assume an epileptic form until after the shattering experience of his eighteenth year —the murder of his father.[2] It would be very much to the point if it could be established that they ceased completely during his exile in Siberia, but other accounts contradict this.[3]

The unmistakable connection between the murder of the father in *The Brothers Karamazov* and the fate of Dostoevsky's own father has struck more than one of his biographers, and has led them to refer to 'a certain modern school of psychology'. From the standpoint of psychoanalysis (for that is what is meant), we are tempted to see in that event the severest trauma and to regard

[2] See René Fülöp-Miller, "Dostojewskis Heilige Krankheit," *Wissen und Leben*, Heft 19–20 (1924), 1184–91. Of especial interest is the information that in the novelist's childhood 'something terrible, unforgettable and agonizing' happened, to which the first signs of his illness were to be traced (from an article by Suvorin in the newspaper *Novoe Vremya*, 1881, quoted in the introduction to Fülöp-Miller and Eckstein, 1925, xlv). See also Orest Miller, "Zur Lebensgeschichte Dostojewskis," in F. M. Dostojewski, *Autobiographische Schriften* (Munich, 1921), 140: "There is, however, another special piece of evidence about Fyodor Mikhailovich's illness, which relates to his earliest youth and brings the illness into connection with a tragic event in the family life of his parents. But, although this piece of evidence was given to me orally by one who was a close friend of Fyodor Mikhailovich, I cannot bring myself to reproduce it fully and precisely since I have had no confirmation of this rumour from any other quarter.' Biographers and scientific research workers cannot feel grateful for this discretion.

[3] Most of the accounts, including Dostoevsky's own, assert on the contrary that the illness only assumed its final, epileptic character during the Siberian exile. Unfortunately there is reason to distrust the autobiographical statements of neurotics. Experience shows that their memories introduce falsifications which are designed to interrupt disagreeable causal connections. Nevertheless, it appears certain that Dostoevsky's detention in the Siberian prison markedly altered his pathological condition. Cf. Fülöp-Miller (1924, 1186).

Dostoevsky's reaction to it as the turning-point of his neurosis. But if I undertake to substantiate this view psychoanalytically, I shall have to risk the danger of being unintelligible to all those readers who are unfamiliar with the language and theories of psycho-analysis.

We have one certain starting-point. We know the meaning of the first attacks from which Dostoevsky suffered in his early years, long before the incidence of the 'epilepsy'. These attacks had the significance of death: they were heralded by a fear of death and consisted of lethargic, somnolent states. The illness first came over him while he was still a boy, in the form of a sudden, groundless melancholy, a feeling, as he later told his friend Soloviev, as though he were going to die on the spot. And there in fact followed a state exactly similar to real death. His brother Andrey tells us that even when he was quite young Fyodor used to leave little notes about before he went to sleep, saying that he was afraid he might fall into this death-like sleep during the night and therefore begged that his burial should be postponed for five days. (Fülöp-Miller and Eckstein, 1925, lx.)

We know the meaning and intention of such deathlike attacks. They signify an identification with a dead person, either with someone who is really dead or with someone who is still alive and whom the subject wishes dead. The latter case is the more significant. The attack then has the value of a punishment. One has wished another person dead, and now one *is* this other person and is dead oneself. At this point psycho-analytical theory brings in the assertion that for a boy this other person is usually his father and that the attack (which is termed hysterical) is thus a self-punishment for a death-wish against a hated father.

Parricide, according to a well-known view, is the principal and primal crime of humanity as well as of the individual. (See my *Totem and Taboo*, 1912–13.) It is in any case the main source of the sense of guilt, though we do not know if it is the only one: researches have not yet been able to establish with certainty the mental origin of guilt and the need for expiation. But it is not necessary for it to be the only one. The psychological situation is complicated and requires elucidation. The relation of a boy to his father is, as we say, an 'ambivalent' one. In addition to the hate which seeks to get rid of the father as a rival, a measure of tenderness for him is also habitually present. The two attitudes of mind combine to produce identification with the father; the boy wants to be in his father's place because he admires him and wants to be like him, and also because he wants to put him out of the way. This whole development now comes up against a powerful obstacle. At a certain moment the child comes to understand that an attempt to remove his father as a rival would be punished by him with castration. So from fear of castration—that is, in the interests of preserving his masculinity—he gives up his wish to possess his mother and get rid of his father. In so far as this wish remains in the unconscious it forms the basis of the sense of guilt. We believe that what we have here been describing are normal processes, the normal fate of the so-called 'Oedipus complex'; nevertheless it requires an important amplification.

A further complication arises when the constitutional factor we call bisexuality is comparatively strongly developed in a child. For then, under the threat to the boy's masculinity by castration, his inclination becomes strengthened to diverge in the direction of femininity, to put himself instead in his mother's place and take over her role as object of his father's love. But the fear of castration makes *this* solution impossible as well. The boy understands that he must also submit to castration if he wants to be loved by his father as a woman. Thus both impulses, hatred of the father and being in love with the father, undergo repression. There is a certain psychological distinction in the fact that the hatred of the father is given up on account of fear of an *external* danger (castration), while the being in love with the father is treated as an

internal instinctual danger, though fundamentally it goes
back to the same external danger.

What makes hatred of the father unacceptable is *fear*
of the father; castration is terrible, whether as a punishment or as the price of love. Of the two factors which re-
press hatred of the father, the first, the direct fear of punishment and castration, may be called the normal one; its
pathogenic intensification seems to come only with the
addition of the second factor, the fear of the feminine attitude. Thus a strong innate bisexual disposition becomes
one of the preconditions or reinforcements of neurosis.
Such a disposition must certainly be assumed in Dostoevsky, and it shows itself in a viable form (as latent homosexuality) in the important part played by male friendships in his life, in his strangely tender attitude towards
rivals in love and in his remarkable understanding of situations which are explicable only by repressed homosexuality,
as many examples from his novels show.

I am sorry, though I cannot alter the facts, if this exposition of the attitudes of hatred and love towards the
father and their transformations under the influence of the
threat of castration seems to readers unfamiliar with
psycho-analysis unsavoury and incredible. I should myself
expect that it is precisely the castration complex that
would be bound to arouse the most general repudiation.
But I can only insist that psycho-analytic experience has
put these matters in particular beyond the reach of doubt
and has taught us to recognize in them the key to every
neurosis. This key, then, we must apply to our author's
so-called epilepsy. So alien to our consciousness are the
things by which our unconscious mental life is governed!

But what has been said so far does not exhaust the consequences of the repression of the hatred of the father in
the Oedipus complex. There is something fresh to be
added: namely that in spite of everything the identification with the father finally makes a permanent place for
itself in the ego. It is received into the ego, but establishes
itself there as a separate agency in contrast to the rest of

the content of the ego. We then give it the name of super-ego and ascribe to it, the inheritor of the parental influence, the most important functions. If the father was hard, violent and cruel, the super-ego takes over those attributes from him and, in the relations between the ego and it, the passivity which was supposed to have been repressed is re-established. The super-ego has become sadistic, and the ego becomes masochistic—that is to say, at bottom passive in a feminine way. A great need for punishment develops in the ego, which in part offers itself as a victim to Fate, and in part finds satisfaction in ill-treatment by the super-ego (that is, in the sense of guilt). For every punishment is ultimately castration and, as such, a fulfilment of the old passive attitude towards the father. Even Fate is, in the last resort, only a later projection of the father.

The normal processes in the formation of conscience must be similar to the abnormal ones described here. We have not yet succeeded in fixing the boundary line between them. It will be observed that here the largest share in the outcome is ascribed to the passive component of repressed femininity. In addition, it must be of importance as an accidental factor whether the father, who is feared in any case, is also especially violent in reality. This was true in Dostoevsky's case, and we can trace back the fact of his extraordinary sense of guilt and of his masochistic conduct of life to a specially strong feminine component. Thus the formula for Dostoevsky is as follows: a person with a specially strong innate bisexual disposition, who can defend himself with special intensity against dependence on a specially severe father. This characteristic of bisexuality comes as an addition to the components of his nature that we have already recognized. His early symptoms of death-like attacks can thus be understood as a father-identification on the part of his ego, which is permitted by his super-ego as a punishment. 'You wanted to kill your father in order to be your father yourself. Now you *are* your father, but a dead father'—the regular mechanism of hysterical symptoms. And further: 'Now your father is killing *you*.' For the ego the death symptom is a satisfaction in phantasy of the masculine wish and at the same time a masochistic satisfaction; for the super-ego it is a punitive satisfaction—that is, a sadistic satisfaction. Both of them, the ego and the super-ego, carry on the role of father.

To sum up, the relation between the subject and **his** father-object, while retaining its content, has been transformed into a relation between the ego and the super-ego —a new setting on a fresh stage. Infantile reactions from the Oedipus complex such as these may disappear if reality gives them no further nourishment. But the father's character remained the same, or rather, it deteriorated with the years, and thus Dostoevsky's hatred for his father and his death-wish against that wicked father were maintained. Now it is a dangerous thing if reality fulfils such repressed wishes. The phantasy has become reality and all defensive measures are thereupon reinforced. Dostoevsky's attacks now assumed an epileptic character; they still undoubtedly signified an identification with his father as a punishment, but they had become terrible, like his father's frightful death itself. What further content they had absorbed, particularly what sexual content, escapes conjecture.

One thing is remarkable: in the aura of the epileptic attack, one moment of supreme bliss is experienced. This may very well be a record of the triumph and sense of liberation felt on hearing the news of the death, to be followed immediately by an all the more cruel punishment. We have divined just such a sequence of triumph and mourning, of festive joy and mourning, in the brothers of the primal horde who murdered their father, and we find it repeated in the ceremony of the totem meal.[4] If it proved to be the case that Dostoevsky was free from his attacks in Siberia, that would merely substantiate the

[4] See *Totem and Taboo* [(1912–13), Section 5 of Essay IV, *Standard Ed.*, 13, 140].

view that they were his punishment. He did not need
them any longer when he was being punished in another
way. But that cannot be proved. Rather does this necessity
for punishment on the part of Dostoevsky's mental
economy explain the fact that he passed unbroken through
these years of misery and humiliation. Dostoevsky's condemnation as a political prisoner was unjust and he must
have known it, but he accepted the undeserved punishment at the hands of the Little Father, the Tsar, as a
substitute for the punishment he deserved for his sin
against his real father. Instead of punishing himself, he
got himself punished by his father's deputy. Here we
have a glimpse of the psychological justification of the punishments inflicted by society. It is a fact that large groups
of criminals want to be punished. Their super-ego demands
it and so saves itself the necessity for inflicting the punishment itself.

Everyone who is familiar with the complicated transformation of meaning undergone by hysterical symptoms
will understand that no attempt can be made here to follow
out the meaning of Dostoevsky's attacks beyond this beginning.[5] It is enough that we may assume that their original
meaning remained unchanged behind all later accretions.
We can safely say that Dostoevsky never got free from
the feelings of guilt arising from his intention of murdering his father. They also determined his attitude in the
two other spheres in which the father-relation is the decisive factor, his attitude towards the authority of the State
and towards belief in God. In the first of these he ended

[5] The best account of the meaning and content of his attacks was given by Dostoevsky himself, when he told his friend
Strakhov that his irritability and depression after an epileptic
attack were due to the fact that he seemed to himself a criminal
and could not get rid of the feeling that he had a burden of
unknown guilt upon him, that he had committed some great
misdeed, which oppressed him. (Fülöp-Miller, 1924, 1188.) In
self-accusations like these psycho-analysis sees signs of a recognition of 'psychical reality', and it endeavours to make the
unknown guilt known to consciousness.

up with complete submission to his Little Father, the Tsar, who had once performed with him in *reality* the comedy of killing which his attacks had so often represented in *play*. Here penitence gained the upper hand. In the religious sphere he retained more freedom: according to apparently trustworthy reports he wavered, up to the last moment of his life, between faith and atheism. His great intellect made it impossible for him to overlook any of the intellectual difficulties to which faith leads. By an individual recapitulation of a development in world-history he hoped to find a way out and a liberation from guilt in the Christ ideal, and even to make use of his sufferings as a claim to be playing a Christ-like role. If on the whole he did not achieve freedom and became a reactionary, that was because the filial guilt, which is present in human beings generally and on which religious feeling is built, had in him attained a super-individual intensity and remained insurmountable even to his great intelligence. In writing this we are laying ourselves open to the charge of having abandoned the impartiality of analysis and of subjecting Dostoevsky to judgements that can only be justified from the partisan standpoint of a particular *Weltanschauung*. A conservative would take the side of the Grand Inquisitor and would judge Dostoevsky differently. The objection is just; and one can only say in extenuation that Dostoevsky's decision has every appearance of having been determined by an intellectual inhibition due to his neurosis.

It can scarcely be owing to chance that three of the masterpieces of the literature of all time—the *Oedipus Rex* of Sophocles, Shakespeare's *Hamlet* and Dostoevsky's *The Brothers Karamazov*—should all deal with the same subject, parricide. In all three, moreover, the motive for the deed, sexual rivalry for a woman, is laid bare.

The most straightforward is certainly the representation in the drama derived from the Greek legend. In this it is still the hero himself who commits the crime. But poetic treatment is impossible without softening and disguise. The naked admission of an intention to commit parricide, as we arrive at it in analysis, seems intolerable without analytic preparation. The Greek drama, while retaining the crime, introduces the indispensable toning-down in a masterly fashion by projecting the hero's unconscious motive into reality in the form of a compulsion by a destiny which is alien to him. The hero commits the deed unintentionally and apparently uninfluenced by the woman; this latter element is however taken into account in the circumstance that the hero can only obtain possession of the queen mother after he has repeated his deed upon the monster who symbolizes the father. After his guilt has been revealed and made conscious, the hero makes no attempt to exculpate himself by appealing to the artificial expedient of the compulsion of destiny. His crime is acknowledged and punished as though it were a full and conscious one—which is bound to appear unjust to our reason, but which psychologically is perfectly correct.

In the English play the presentation is more indirect; the hero does not commit the crime himself; it is carried out by someone else, for whom it is not parricide. The forbidden motive of sexual rivalry for the woman does not need, therefore, to be disguised. Moreover, we see the hero's Oedipus complex, as it were, in a reflected light, by learning the effect upon him of the other's crime. He ought to avenge the crime, but finds himself, strangely enough, incapable of doing so. We know that it is his sense of guilt that is paralysing him; but, in a manner entirely in keeping with neurotic processes, the sense of guilt is displaced on to the perception of his inadequacy for fulfilling his task. There are signs that the hero feels this guilt as a superindividual one. He despises others no less than himself: 'Use every man after his desert, and who should 'scape whipping?'

The Russian novel goes a step further in the same direction. There also the murder is committed by someone else. This other person, however, stands to the murdered man in the same filial relation as the hero, Dmitri; in this other person's case the motive of sexual rivalry is openly admitted; he is a brother of the hero's, and it is a remarkable fact that Dostoevsky has attributed to him his own illness, the alleged epilepsy, as though he were seeking to confess that the epileptic, the neurotic, in himself was a parricide. Then, again, in the speech for the defence at the trial, there is the famous mockery of psychology—it is a 'knife that cuts both ways':[6] a splendid piece of disguise, for we have only to reverse it in order to discover the deepest meaning of Dostoevsky's view of things. It is not psychology that deserves the mockery, but the procedure of judicial enquiry. It is a matter of indifference who actually committed the crime; psychology is only concerned to know who desired it emotionally and who welcomed it when it was done. And for that reason all of the brothers, except the contrasted figure of Alyosha, are equally guilty—the impulsive sensualist, the sceptical cynic and the epileptic criminal. In *The Brothers Karamazov* there is one particularly revealing scene. In the course of his talk with Dmitri, Father Zossima recognizes that Dmitri is prepared to commit parricide, and he bows down at his feet. It is impossible that this can be meant as an expression of admiration; it must mean that the holy man is rejecting the temptation to despise or detest the murderer and for that reason humbles himself before him. Dostoevsky's sympathy for the criminal is, in fact, boundless; it goes far beyond the pity which the unhappy wretch has a right to, and reminds us of the 'holy awe' with which epileptics and lunatics were regarded in the past. A criminal is to him almost a Redeemer, who has taken on himself the guilt which must else have been borne by others. There is no longer any need for one to murder, since *he* has already murdered; and one must be grateful to him, for, except for him, one would have been obliged oneself to murder. That is not kindly pity alone, it is identification

[6] [In the German (and in the original Russian) the simile is 'a stick with two ends'. The 'knife that cuts both ways' is derived from Constance Garnett's English translation. The phrase occurs in Book XII, Chapter X, of the novel.]

on the basis of similar murderous impulses—in fact, a slightly displaced narcissism. (In saying this, we are not disputing the ethical value of this kindliness.) This may perhaps be quite generally the mechanism of kindly sympathy with other people, a mechanism which one can discern with especial ease in this extreme case of a guilt-ridden novelist. There is no doubt that this sympathy by identification was a decisive factor in determining Dostoevsky's choice of material. He dealt first with the common criminal (whose motives are egotistical) and the political and religious criminal; and not until the end of his life did he come back to the primal criminal, the parricide, and use him, in a work of art, for making his confession.

The publication of Dostoevsky's posthumous papers and of his wife's diaries has thrown a glaring light on one episode in his life, namely the period in Germany when he was obsessed with a mania for gambling (cf. Fülöp-Miller and Eckstein, 1925), which no one could regard as anything but an unmistakable fit of pathological passion. There was no lack of rationalizations for this remarkable and unworthy behaviour. As often happens with neurotics, Dostoevsky's sense of guilt had taken a tangible shape as a burden of debt, and he was able to take refuge behind the pretext that he was trying by his winnings at the tables to make it possible for him to return to Russia without being arrested by his creditors. But this was no more than a pretext and Dostoevsky was acute enough to recognize the fact and honest enough to admit it. He knew that the chief thing was gambling for its own sake—*le jeu pour le jeu*.[7] All the details of his impulsively irrational conduct show this and something more besides. He never rested until he had lost everything. For him gambling was a method of self-punishment as well. Time after

[7] 'The main thing is the play itself,' he writes in one of his letters. 'I swear that greed for money has nothing to do with it, although Heaven knows I am sorely in need of money.'

time he gave his young wife his promise or his word of honour not to play any more or not to play any more on that particular day; and, as she says, he almost always broke it. When his losses had reduced himself and her to the direst need, he derived a second pathological satisfaction from that. He could then scold and humiliate himself before her, invite her to despise him and to feel sorry that she had married such an old sinner; and when he had thus unburdened his conscience, the whole business would begin again next day. His young wife accustomed herself to this cycle, for she had noticed that the one thing which offered any real hope of salvation—his literary production —never went better than when they had lost everything and pawned their last possessions. Naturally she did not understand the connection. When his sense of guilt was satisfied by the punishments he had inflicted on himself, the inhibition upon his work became less severe and he allowed himself to take a few steps along the road to success.[8]

What part of a gambler's long-buried childhood is it that forces its way to repetition in his obsession for play? The answer may be divined without difficulty from a story by one of our younger writers. Stefan Zweig, who has incidentally devoted a study to Dostoevsky himself, has included in his collection of three stories *Die Verwirrung der Gefühle* [published in English as *Conflicts*, trans. Eden and Cedar Paul (New York and London, 1927)] one which he calls 'Vierundzwanzig Stunden aus dem Leben einer Frau' ['Four-and-Twenty Hours in a Woman's Life']. This little masterpiece ostensibly sets out only to show what an irresponsible creature woman is, and to what excesses, surprising even to herself, an unexpected experience may drive her. But the story tells far more than

---

[8] 'He always remained at the gaming tables till he had lost everything and was totally ruined. It was only when the damage was quite complete that the demon at last retired from his soul and made way for the creative genius.' (Fülöp-Miller and Eckstein, 1925, lxxxvi.)

this. If it is subjected to an analytical interpretation, it will be found to represent (without any apologetic intent) something quite different, something universally human, or rather something masculine. And such an interpretation is so extremely obvious that it cannot be resisted. It is characteristic of the nature of artistic creation that the author, who is a personal friend of mine, was able to assure me, when I asked him, that the interpretation which I put to him had been completely strange to his knowledge and intention, although some of the details woven into the narrative seemed expressly designed to give a clue to the hidden secret.

In this story, an elderly lady of distinction tells the author about an experience she has had more than twenty years earlier. She has been left a widow when still young and is the mother of two sons, who no longer need her. In her forty-second year, expecting nothing further of life, she happens, on one of her aimless journeyings, to visit the Rooms at Monte Carlo. There, among all the remarkable impressions which the place produces, she is soon fascinated by the sight of a pair of hands which seem to betray all the feelings of the unlucky gambler with terrifying sincerity and intensity. These hands belong to a handsome young man—the author, as though unintentionally, makes him of the same age as the narrator's elder son—who, after losing everything, leaves the Rooms in the depth of despair, with the evident intention of ending his hopeless life in the Casino gardens. An inexplicable feeling of sympathy compels her to follow him and make every effort to save him. He takes her for one of the importunate women so common there and tries to shake her off; but she stays with him and finds herself obliged, in the most natural way possible, to join him in his apartment at the hotel, and finally to share his bed. After this improvised night of love, she exacts a most solemn vow from the young man, who has now apparently calmed down, that he will never play again, provides him with money for his journey home and promises to meet him at the station before the departure of his train. Now, however, she begins to feel a great tenderness for him, is ready to sacrifice all she has in order to keep him and makes up her mind to go with him instead of saying goodbye. Various mischances delay her, so that she misses the train. In her longing for the lost one she returns once more to the Rooms and there, to her horror, sees once more the hands which had first excited her sympathy: the faithless youth had gone back to his play. She reminds him of his promise, but, obsessed by his passion, he calls her a spoilsport, tells her to go, and flings back the money with which she has tried to rescue him. She hurries away in deep mortification and learns later that she has not succeeded in saving him from suicide.

The brilliantly told, faultlessly motivated story is of course complete in itself and is certain to make a deep effect upon the reader. But analysis shows us that its invention is based fundamentally upon a wishful phantasy belonging to the period of puberty, which a number of people actually remember consciously. The phantasy embodies a boy's wish that his mother should herself initiate him into sexual life in order to save him from the dreaded injuries caused by masturbation. (The numerous creative works that deal with the theme of redemption have the same origin.) The 'vice' of masturbation is replaced by the addiction to gambling; and the emphasis laid upon the passionate activity of the hands betrays this derivation. Indeed, the passion for play is an equivalent of the old compulsion to masturbate; 'playing' is the actual word used in the nursery to describe the activity of the hands upon the genitals. The irresistible nature of the temptation, the solemn resolutions, which are nevertheless invariably broken, never to do it again, the stupefying pleasure and the bad conscience which tells the subject that he is ruining himself (committing suicide)—all these elements remain unaltered in the process of substitution. It is true that Zweig's story is told by the mother, not by the son. It must flatter the son to think: 'if my mother only knew what dangers masturbation involves me in, she would certainly save me from them by allowing me to lavish all my tenderness on her own body'. The equation of the mother with a prostitute, which is made by the young man in the story, is linked up with the same phantasy. It brings the unattainable woman within easy reach. The bad conscience which accompanies the phantasy brings about the unhappy ending of the story. It is also interesting to notice how the *façade* given to the story by its author seeks to disguise its analytic meaning. For it is extremely questionable whether the erotic life of women is dominated by sudden and mysterious impulses. On the contrary, analysis reveals an adequate motivation for the surprising behavior of this woman who had hitherto turned away from love. Faithful to the memory of her dead husband, she had armed herself against all similar attractions; but— and here the son's phantasy is right—she did not, as a mother, escape her quite unconscious transference of love on to her son, and Fate was able to catch her at this undefended spot.

If the addiction to gambling, with the unsuccessful struggles to break the habit and the opportunities it affords for self-punishment, is a repetition of the compulsion to masturbate, we shall not be surprised to find that it occupied such a large space in Dostoevsky's life. After all, we find no cases of severe neurosis in which the auto-erotic satisfaction of early childhood and of puberty has not played a part; and the relation between efforts to suppress it and fear of the father are too well known to need more than a mention.[9]

[9] Most of the views which are here expressed are also contained in an excellent book by Jolan Neufeld, *Dostojewski: Skizze zu seiner Psychoanalyse* (Vienna, 1923).

IV

Existential Guilt

MARTIN BUBER

Guilt and Guilt Feelings[1]

At the London International Conference for Medical Psychotherapy of 1948,[2] 'The Genesis of Guilt' was fixed as the theme of the first plenary session. The first speaker, a Hollander, began with the announcement that in his special group the question had been discussed as to whether the genesis of guilt or the genesis of guilt feelings was meant. The question remained unclarified. But in the course of the discussion it was left to the theologians to speak of guilt itself (by which, indeed, they did not actually mean personal guilt, but the original sin of the human race). The psychologists concerned themselves merely with guilt feelings.

This distribution of themes, through which the factual occurrences of guilt in the lives of 'patients', of suffering

---

"Guilt and Guilt Feelings," from *The Knowledge of Man, Selected Essays of Martin Buber,* edited by Maurice Friedman, translated by Maurice Friedman and Ronald Gregor Smith. Copyright © 1965 by Martin Buber and Maurice Friedman. Reprinted by permission of Harper & Row, Publishers.

[1] Trans. by Maurice Friedman.
[2] International Congress of Mental Health, London 1948; *Proceedings of the International Conference on Medical Psychotherapy,* Vol. III.

men, hardly enters into view, is characteristic of most of
what one calls the psychotherapeutic discipline. Only in
the most recent period have some begun to complain that
both in the theory and in the practice of this science the
psychic 'projection' of guilt is afforded room, the real
events of guilt are not. This omission has not been presented and methodologically grounded as such. It has been
treated as a limitation that follows as a matter of course
from the nature of psychology.

Nothing of the kind is self-evident, however; indeed,
nothing of the kind by right exists. Certainly, in the course
of the history of the spirit each science that has detached
itself from a comprehensive context and ensured for itself
the independence of its realm has just thereby severely
and ever more severely limited its subject and the manner
of its working. But the investigator cannot truthfully maintain his relationship with reality—a relationship without
which all his work becomes a well-regulated game—if he
does not again and again, whenever it is necessary, gaze
beyond the limits into a sphere which is not his sphere of
work, yet which he must contemplate with all his power of
research in order to do justice to his own task. For the
psychotherapist this sphere is formed from the factual
course of the so-called external life of his patients and
especially the actions and attitudes therein, and again
especially the patient's active share in the manifold relation between him and the human world. Not only his decisions are included in this share, but also his failures to
come to a decision when, in a manner perceptible to him,
they operate as decisions.

To the valid scientific realm of psychotherapy belong
the 'inner' reactions of the individual to his passive and
active life-experience, the psychic elaboration of the biographical events, whether it takes place in conscious or
in unconscious processes. The relationship of the patient
to a man with whom he stands in a contact that strongly
affects his own life is for the psychologist important as

such only in so far as its effects on the psyche of the patient can serve the understanding of his illness. The relationship itself in its reciprocal reality, the significant actuality of what is happening and has happened between the two men, transcends his task as it transcends his method. He limits himself to those of its inner connections that his work of exploring the mind of the patient makes accessible to him. And yet, if he wishes to satisfy not merely what he owes to the laws of his discipline and their application, but also what he owes to the existence and the need of man, he may, in fact he must, go beyond that realm where an existing person merely relates to himself. He must cast his glance again and again to where existing person relates to existing person—this person, the 'patient', to another living being who is not 'given' to the doctor and who may be completely unknown to him. The psychotherapist cannot include this other person, these other persons in his work. It is not for him to concern himself with them. And yet he may not neglect them in their reality; he must succeed in grasping their reality as adequately as possible in so far as it enters into the relationship between them and his patient.

This state of affairs manifests itself with the greatest intensity in the problem that occupies us here. Within his methods the psychotherapist has to do only with guilt feelings, conscious and unconscious (Freud was already aware of the contradiction that lies in the concept of unconscious feelings). But within a comprehensive service to knowledge and help, he must himself encounter guilt as something of an ontic character whose place is not the soul but being. He will do this, to be sure, with the danger that through his new knowledge the help which he is obliged to give might also be modified so that something uncustomary will be demanded of his method; indeed, he must be ready even to step out of the established rules of his school. But a 'doctor of souls' who really is one—that is, who does not merely carry on the work of healing but enters into it at times as a partner—is precisely one who dares.

The boundaries set by the psychotherapist's method do not, in any case, suffice to explain the negative or indifferent attitude that psychotherapy has so long taken toward the ontic character of guilt. The history of modern psychology shows us that here deeper motives are at work that have also contributed to the genesis and development of the methods. The two clearest examples of it are provided us by the two most noteworthy representatives of this intellectual tendency: Freud and Jung.

Freud, a great, late-born apostle of the enlightenment, presented the naturalism[3] of the enlightenment with a scientific system and thereby with a second flowering. As Freud himself recognized with complete clarity,[4] the struggle against all metaphysical and religious teachings of the existence of an absolute and of the possibility of a relation of the human person to it had a great share in the development of psychoanalytic theory. As a result of this basic attitude, guilt was simply not allowed to acquire an ontic character; it had to be derived from the transgression against ancient and modern taboos, against parental and social tribunals. The feeling of guilt was now to be understood as essentially only the consequence of dread of punishment and censure by this tribunal, as the consequence of the child's fear of 'loss of love' or, at times when it was a question of imaginary guilt, as a 'need for punishment' of a libidinal nature, as 'moral masochism'[5]

[3] Freud himself described psychoanalysts as 'incorrigible mechanists and materialists' (Sigmund Freud, 'Psycho-analysis and Telepathy', in *The Standard Edition of the Complete Psychological Works of Sigmund Freud*, XVIII (London: Hogarth Press, 1955), pp. 177–93.

[4] See, for example, 'A Philosophy of Life', ch. 7 in Freud, *New Introductory Lectures on Psycho-Analysis* (London: Hogarth Press; New York: W. W. Norton, 1933).

[5] Freud, 'The Economic Problem in Masochism', in *Collected Papers* (London: Hogarth Press, 1948), pp. 255–68.

which is complemented by the sadism of the superego. 'The first renunciation of instinctual gratification', Freud stated in 1924, 'is enforced by external powers, and it is this that creates morality which expresses itself in conscience and exacts a further renunciation of instinct.'[6]

Of an entirely different, indeed diametrically opposed, nature is the teaching of Carl Jung, whom one can describe as a mystic of a modern, psychological type of solipsism. The mystical and religio-mystical conceptions that Freud despised are for Jung the most important subject of his study; but they are such merely as 'projections' of the psyche, not as indications of something extrapsychic that the psyche meets. For Freud the structure of the psyche culminates in the superego, which represents, with its censory function, only the authoritative tribunals of family and society; for Jung it culminates or rather is grounded in the self, which is 'individuality in its highest meaning'[7] and forms 'the most immediate experience of the divine which can be grasped at all psychologically'.[8] Jung does not recognize at all any relationship between the individual soul and another existing being which oversteps the limits of the psychic. But to this must be added the fact that the integration of evil as the unification of the opposites in the psyche is put forward as a central motif in the process of 'individuation', of the 'realization of self'.[9] Seen from this vantage point, there is in Jung's panpsychism, as in Freud's materialism, no place for guilt in the ontological sense, unless it be in the relationship of man to himself—that is, as failure in the process of individuation. In fact, in the whole great work of Jung we learn

[6] *Ibid.*, p. 267.

[7] Carl Jung, *Von den Wurzeln des Bewusstseins*, Psychologische Abhandlungen, IX (Zurich: Rascher, 1954), pp. 296 f.

[8] *Ibid.*, p. 300.

[9] Carl Jung, *Von der Wurzeln des Bewusstseins*, Psychologische Abhandlungen, IX (Zurich: Rascher, 1954). For a fuller analysis of Jung, see Martin Buber, *Eclipse of God*, Section 2, 'Religion and Modern Thinking', and 'Supplement: Reply to C. G. Jung', trans. by Maurice Friedman.

nothing of guilt as a reality in the relation between the human person and the world entrusted to him in his life.

With the other psychoanalytic doctrines it stands, in general, much the same. Almost everyone who seriously concerns himself with the problem of guilt proceeds to derive the guilt feelings that are met with in analysis from hidden elements, to trace them back to such elements, to unmask them as such. One seeks the powerful repressions in the unconscious as those that hide behind the phenomena of illness, but not also the live connection the image of which has remained in the living memory, time and again admonishing, attacking, tormenting, and, after each submersion in the river of no-longer-thinking-about-that, returning and taking up its work anew.

A man stands before us who, through acting or failing to act, has burdened himself with a guilt or has taken part in a community guilt, and now, after years or decades is again and again visited by the memory of his guilt. Nothing of the genesis of his illness is concealed from him if he is only willing no longer to conceal from himself the guilt character of that active or passive occurrence. What takes possession of him ever again has nothing to do with any parental or social reprimand, and if he does not have to fear an earthly retribution and does not believe in a heavenly one, no court, no punishing power exists that can make him anxious. Here rules the one penetrating insight—the one insight capable of penetrating into the impossibility of recovering the original point of departure and the irreparability of what has been done, and that means the real insight into the irreversibility of lived time, a fact that shows itself unmistakably in the starkest of all human perspectives, that concerning one's own death. From no standpoint is time perceived so like a torrent as from the vision of the self in guilt. Swept along in this torrent, the bearer of guilt is visited by the shudder of identity with himself. I, he comes to know, I, who have become another, am the same.

I have seen three important and, to me, dear men fall

into long illnesses from their failing to stand the test in the days of an acute community guilt. The share of the psychogenic element in the illness could hardly be estimated, but its action was unmistakable. One of them refused to acknowledge his self-contradiction before the court of his spirit. The second resisted recognizing as serious a slight error he remembered that was attached to a very serious chain of circumstances. The third, however, would not let himself be forgiven by God for the blunder of a moment because he did not forgive himself. It now seems to me that all three needed and lacked competent helpers.

The psychotherapist into whose field of vision such manifestations of guilt enter in all their forcefulness can no longer imagine that he is able to do justice to his task as doctor of guilt-ridden men merely through the removal of guilt feelings. Here a limit is set to the tendency to derive guilt from the taboos of primeval society. The psychologist who sees what is here to be seen must be struck by the idea that guilt does not exist because a taboo exists to which one fails to give obedience, but rather that taboo and the placing of taboo have been made possible only through the fact that the leaders of early communities knew and made use of a primal fact of man as man—the fact that man can become guilty and know it.

Existential guilt—that is, guilt that a person has taken on himself as a person and in a personal situation—cannot be comprehended through such categories of analytical science as 'repression' and 'becoming conscious'. The bearer of guilt of whom I speak remembers it again and again by himself and in sufficient measure. Not seldom, certainly, he attempts to evade it—not the remembered fact, however, but its depths as existential guilt—until the truth of this depth overwhelms him and time is now perceived by him as a torrent.

Can the doctor of souls function here as helper, beyond professional custom and correct methods? May he do so? Is he shown at times another and higher therapeutic goal than the familiar one? Can and may he try his strength, not with conscious or unconscious, founded or unfounded guilt feelings, but with the self-manifesting existential guilt itself? Can he allow himself to recognize, from this stand-point, that healing in this case means something other than the customary, and what it means in this case?

The doctor who confronts the effects on the guilty man of an existential guilt must proceed in all seriousness from the situation in which the act of guilt has taken place. Existential guilt occurs when someone injures an order of the human world whose foundations he knows and recognizes as those of his own existence and of all common human existence. The doctor who confronts such a guilt in the living memory of his patient must enter into that situation; he must lay his hand in the wound of the order and learn: this concerns you. But then it may strike him that the orientation of the psychologist and the treatment of the therapist have changed unawares and that if he wishes to persist as a healer he must take upon himself a burden he had not expected to bear.

One could protest that an existential guilt is only the exception and that it is not proper to frighten the already overburdened therapist with the image of such borderline cases. But what I call existential guilt is only an intensifica-tion of what is found in some measure wherever an authen-tic guilt feeling burns, and the authentic guilt feeling is very often inextricably mingled with the problematic, the 'neurotic', the 'groundless'. The therapist's meth-ods, naturally, do not willingly concern themselves with the authentic guilt feeling which, in general, is of a strictly personal character and does not easily allow itself to be imprisoned in general propositions. It lies essentially nearer to the doctrine and practice to occupy itself with the effects of repressed childhood wishes or youthful lusts gone astray, than with the inner consequences of a man's betrayal of his friend or his cause. And for the patient it is a great relief to be diverted from his authentic guilt feel-ing to an unambiguous neurotic one that, favoured within this category by the school of his doctor, allows itself to be discovered in the microcosmos of his dreams or in the stream of his free associations. To all this the genuine doctor of souls stands opposed with the postulative awareness that he should act here as at once bound and unbound. He does not, of course, desist from any of his methods, which have in fact become adaptable. But where, as here, he becomes aware of a reality between man and man, between man and the world, a reality inaccessible to any of the psychological categories, he recognizes the limits that are set here for his methods and recognizes that the goal of healing has been transformed in this case because the context of the sickness, the place of the sickness in being, has been transformed. If the therapist recognizes this, then all that he is obliged to do becomes more difficult, much more difficult—and all becomes more real, radically real.

I shall clarify this statement through the example of a life history that I have already made use of before, although all too briefly.[10] I select it from among those at my disposal because I was a witness, sometimes more distant, sometimes nearer, to the happenings, and I have followed their sequence. The life course I have in mind is that of a woman—let us call her Melanie—of more intellectual than truly spiritual gifts, with a scientific education, but without the capacity for independent mastery of her knowledge. Melanie possessed a remarkable talent for good comradeship which expressed itself, at least from her side, in more or less erotically tinged friendships that left unsatisfied her impetuous rather than passionate need for love. She made the acquaintance of a man who was on the point of marriage with another, strikingly ugly, but

[10] See my Preface to Hans Trüb's posthumous work, *Heilung aus der Begegnung: Eine Auseinandersetzung mit der Psychologic C. G. Jungs*, ed. by Ernst Michel and Arie Sborowitz (Stuttgart: Ernst Klett Verlag, 1952). This Preface appears in English as 'Healing through Meeting' in Martin Buber, *Pointing the Way*, pp. 93–97.

remarkable woman. Melanie succeeded without difficulty
in breaking up the engagement and marrying the man.
Her rival tried to kill herself. Melanie soon afterwards accused her, certainly unjustly, of feigning her attempt at
suicide. After a few years Melanie herself was supplanted
by another woman. Soon Melanie fell ill with a neurosis
linked with disturbances of the vision. To friends who
took her in at the time, she confessed her guilt without
glossing over the fact that it had arisen not out of a passion, but out of a fixed will.

Later she gave herself into the care of a well-known
psychoanalyst. This man was able to liberate her in a short
while from her feelings of disappointment and guilt and
to bring her to the conviction that she was a 'genius of
friendship' and would find in this sphere the compensation
that was due her. The conversion succeeded, and Melanie
devoted herself to a rich sociality which she experienced
as a world of friendship. In contrast to this, she associated
in general with the men with whom she had to deal in her
professional 'welfare work' not as persons needing her understanding and even her consolation, but as objects to be
seen through and directed by her. The guilt feelings were
no longer in evidence; the apparatus that had been in-
stalled in place of the paining and admonishing heart func-
tioned in model fashion.

Now that is certainly no extraordinary fate. We recognize again the all too usual distress of human action and
suffering, and there can be no talk here of existential guilt
in the great sense of the term. And yet, the guilt feeling
that grew up at that time in the illness and that so fused
with the illness that no one could say which of the two
was the cause and which the effect, had throughout an
authentic character. With the silencing of the guilt feeling there disappeared for Melanie the possibility of reconciliation through a newly won genuine relationship to her
environment in which her best qualities could at the
same time unfold. The price paid for the annihilation of
the sting was the final annihilation of the chance to be-

come the being that this created person was destined to become through her highest disposition.

Again one may raise the objection that it cannot be the affair of the psychotherapist to concern himself about this kind of thing. His task is to investigate malady and to heal it, or rather to help it toward healing, and it is just this that the doctor who had been called in had done. But here lies an important problem. Stated generally, one can formulate it somewhat as follows: Shall a man who is called upon to help another in a specific manner merely give the help for which he is summoned or shall he also give the other help that, according to the doctor's knowledge of him, this man objectively needs?

However, what is the meaning here of the help that one objectively needs? Clearly this, that his being follows other laws than his consciousness. But also quite other ones than his 'unconscious'. The unconscious is still far less concerned than the conscious about whether the essence of this man thrives. Essence—by this I mean that for which a person is peculiarly intended, what he is called to become. The conscious, with its planning and its weighing, concerns itself with it only occasionally; the unconscious, with its wishes and contradictions, hardly ever. Those are great moments of existence when a man discovers his essence or rediscovers it on a higher plane; when he decides and decides anew to become what he is and, as one who is becoming this, to establish a genuine relation to the world; when he heroically maintains his discovery and decision against his everyday consciousness and against his unconscious. Should the helper, can the helper, may the helper now enter into an alliance with the essence of him who summoned him, across this person's conscious and unconscious will, provided that he has really reliably recognized the need of this essence? Is something of this sort at all his office? Can it be his office? Particularly where the helping profession is so exactly circumscribed by principles and methods as in modern psychotherapy? Does not the danger threaten here of a pseudointuitive dilettantism that dissolves all fixed norms?

An important psychologist and doctor of our time, the late Viktor von Weizsaecker, laid down, in very precise language, a sober admonition on this point. There the 'treatment of the essential in man' is simply excluded from the realm of psychotherapy. 'Just the final destiny of man', he writes, 'must not be the subject of therapy.'[11] And my lay insight must concur with this declaration. But there is an exceptional case—the case where the glance of the doctor, the perceiving glance that makes him a doctor and to whom all his methods stand in a serving relation, extends into the sphere of the essence, where he perceives essential lapse and essential need. There, to be sure, it is still denied him to treat 'the essential' in his patients, but he may and should guide it to where an essential help of the self, a help till now neither willed nor anticipated, can begin. It is neither given the therapist nor allowed to him to indicate a way that leads onward from here. But from the watchtower to which the patient has been conducted, he can manage to see a way that is right for him and that he can walk, a way that it is not granted the doctor to see. For at this high station all becomes personal in the strictest sense.

The psychotherapist is no pastor of souls and no substitute for one. It is never his task to mediate a salvation; his task is always only to further a healing. But it is not merely incumbent upon him to interest himself in that need of the patient which has become symptomatically manifest in his sickness—to interest himself in it as far as the analysis conducted according to the therapist's method discloses to him the genesis of this illness. That need is also confided to him which first allows itself to be recognized in the immediacy of the partnership between the patient who is having recourse to the doctor and the doctor who is concerned about the recovery of

[11] *Herztliche-Fragen* (1934), p. 9.

the patient—although occasionally this need remains veiled, even then.

I have already pointed to the fact that the doctor, in order to be able to do this adequately, must for the time being lift himself off the firm ground of principles and methods on which he has learned to walk. One must not, of course, understand this to mean that he now soars in the free ether of an unrestrained 'intuition'. Now too, and only now really, he is obliged to think consistently and to work exactly. And if he may now surrender himself to a more direct vision, it can still only be one that realizes its individual norms in each of its insights—norms that cannot be translated into general propositions. In this sphere of action, too, even though it seems left to his independent direction, the man of the intellectual profession learns that a true work is an affair of a listening obedience.

But in order that the therapist be able to do this, he must recognize just one thing steadfastly and recognize it ever again: there exists real guilt, fundamentally different from all the anxiety-induced bugbears that are generated in the cavern of the unconscious. Personal guilt, whose reality some schools of psychoanalysis contest and others ignore, does not permit itself to be reduced to the trespass against a powerful taboo.

We cannot now content ourselves, however, with allowing this knowledge, which was long under a ban, to be conveyed to us by this or that tradition which is holy to us. It must arise anew from the historical and biographical self-experience of the generation living today. We who are living today know in what measure we have become historically and biographically guilty. That is no feeling and no sum of feelings. It is, no matter how manifoldly concealed and denied, a real knowledge about a reality. Under the schooling of this knowledge, which is becoming ever more irresistible, we learn anew that guilt exists.

In order to understand this properly we must call to mind one fact, no accessory fact but the basic one. Each man stands in an objective relationship to others; the totality of this relationship constitutes his life as one that factually participates in the being of the world. It is this relationship, in fact, that first makes it at all possible for him to expand his environment (*Umwelt*) into a world (*Welt*). It is his share in the human order of being, the share for which he bears responsibility. An objective relationship in which two men stand to one another can rise, by means of the existential participation of the two, to a personal relation; it can be merely tolerated; it can be neglected; it can be injured. Injuring a relationship means that at this place the human order of being is injured. No one other than he who inflicted the wound can heal it. He who knows the fact of his guilt and is a helper can help him try to heal the wound.

One last clarification is still necessary. When the therapist recognizes an existential guilt of his patient, he cannot—that we have seen—show him the way to the world, which the latter must rather seek and find as his own personal law. The doctor can only conduct him to the point from which he can glimpse his personal way or at least its beginning. But in order that the doctor shall be able to do this, he must also know about the general nature of the way, common to all great acts of conscience, and about the connection that exists between the nature of existential guilt and the nature of this way.

In order not to fall into any error here, however, we must bear in mind that there are three different spheres in which the reconciliation of guilt can fulfil itself and between which noteworthy relations often establish themselves. Only one of these spheres, that which we shall designate as the middle one, directly concerns the therapist whom I have in mind.

The first sphere is that of the law of the society. The action begins here with the demand, actually made or latent, which society places on the guilty man according to its laws. The event of fulfilment is called confession of guilt. It is followed by penalty and indemnification. With this sphere the therapist, naturally, has nothing to do. As doctor, an opinion is not even accorded him as to whether the demand of the society is right or not. His patient, the guilty man, may be guilty toward the society or he may not be; its judgment over him may be just or it may not be. This does not concern the doctor as doctor; he is incompetent here. In his relation to the patient this problematic theme can find no admission, with the exception of the unavoidable occupation with the anxiety of the patient in the face of the punishments, the censure, the boycotts of society.

But the third and highest sphere, that of faith, also cannot be his affair. Here the action commences within the relation between the guilty man and his God and remains therein. It is likewise consummated in three events which correspond to the three of the first sphere, but are connected with each other in an entirely different manner. These are the confession of sin, repentence, and penance in its various forms. The doctor as such may not touch on this sphere even when he and the patient stand in the same community of faith. Here no man can speak unless it be one whom the guilty man acknowledges as a hearer and speaker who represents the transcendence believed in by the guilty man. Also when the therapist encounters the problem of faith in the anxiety concerning divine punishment that is disclosed in the patient's analysis, he cannot interfere here—even if he possesses great spiritual gifts —without falling into a dangerous dilettantism.

The middle sphere, as we have said, is one to the sight of which the therapist may lead—up to it, but no farther. This sphere, about which he must *know* for this purpose, we may call that of conscience, with a qualification which I shall shortly discuss. The action demanded by the conscience also fulfils itself in three events, which I call self-illumination, perseverance, and reconciliation, and which I shall define more exactly still.

Conscience means to us the capacity and tendency of man radically to distinguish between those of his past and future actions which should be approved and those which should be disapproved. The disapproval, in general, receives far stronger emotional stress, whereas the approval of past actions at times passes over with shocking ease into a most questionable self-satisfaction. Conscience can, naturally, distinguish and if necessary condemn in such a manner not merely deeds but also omissions, not merely decisions but also failures to decide, indeed even images and wishes that have just arisen or are remembered.

In order to understand this capacity and tendency more exactly, one must bear in mind that among all living beings known to us man alone is able to set at a distance not only his environment[12] but also himself. As a result, he becomes for himself a detached object about which he can not only 'reflect', but which he can, from time to time, confirm as well as condemn. The content of conscience is in many ways determined, of course, by the commands and prohibitions of the society to which its bearer belongs or those of the tradition of faith to which he is bound. But conscience itself cannot be understood as an introjection of either the one authority or the other, neither ontogenetically nor phylogenetically. The table of shalts and shalt-nots under which this man has grown up and lives determines only the conceptions which prevail in the realm of the conscience, but not its existence itself, which is grounded in just that distancing and distinguishing—primal qualities of the human race. The more or less hidden criteria that the conscience employs in its acceptances and rejections only rarely fully coincide with a standard received from the society or community. Connected with that is the fact that the guilt feeling can hardly ever be wholly traced to a transgression against a taboo of a family or of society. The totality of the order that a man knows to be injured or injurable by him transcends to some degree the totality of the parental and social taboos that

12 See Martin Buber, *The Knowledge of Man,* ed. Maurice Friedman (New York: Harper & Row, 1965), pp. 60–68.

bind him. The depth of the guilt feeling is not seldom connected with just that part of the guilt that cannot be ascribed to the taboo-offence, hence with the existential guilt.

The qualification of which I spoke, accordingly, is that our subject is the relation of the conscience to existential guilt. Its relation to the trespassing of taboos concerns us here only in so far as a guilty man understands this trespassing more strongly or weakly as real existential guilt which arises out of his being and for which he cannot take responsibility without being responsible to his relationship to his own being.

The vulgar conscience that knows admirably well how to torment and harass, but cannot arrive at the ground and abyss of guilt, is incapable, to be sure, of summoning to such responsibility. For this summoning a greater conscience is needed, one that has become wholly personal, one that does not shy away from the glance into the depths and that already in admonishing envisages the way that leads across it. But this in no way means that this personal conscience is reserved for some type of 'higher' man. This conscience is possessed by every simple man who gathers himself into himself in order to venture the breakthrough out of the entanglement in guilt. And it is a great, not yet sufficiently recognized, task of education to elevate the conscience from its lower common form to conscience-vision and conscience-courage. For it is innate to the conscience of man that it can elevate itself.

From what has been said it already follows with sufficient clarity that the primeval concept of conscience, if only it is understood as a dynamic one rather than as a static, judging one, is more realistic than the modern structural concept of the superego. The concept of the superego attains only an orienting significance and one, moreover, which easily orients the novice falsely.

If we now wish to speak of actions in the sphere of conscience in this high and strict sense, we do not mean

thereby the well-known synthesis out of the internalization
of censure, torment, and punishment that one customarily
regards as the proper factual content of conscience—that
pressuring and oppressing influence of an inner high court
on an 'ego' that is more or less subject to it. Rather this
tormenting complex has, for our consideration, only the
character of an angelic—demonic intermezzo on which the
high dramatic or tragicomic act of neurosis may follow,
and the whole affair may end with a therapy that passes
for successful. What concerns us here is another possibility, whether it be the true process of healing after the
neurosis, or whether it be without a neurosis preceding it.
It is that possible moment when the whole person who
has become awake and unafraid ascends from the an-
guishing lowland of the conscience to its heights and independently masters the material delivered to him by it.

From this position a man can undertake the threefold
action to which I have referred: first, to illuminate the
darkness that still weaves itself about the guilt despite all
previous action of the conscience—not to illuminate it with
spotlights but with a broad and enduring wave of light;
second, to persevere, no matter how high he may have
ascended in his present life above that station of guilt—
to persevere in that newly won humble knowledge of the
identity of the present person with the person of that
time; and third, in his place and according to his capacity,
in the given historical and biographical situations, to restore the order-of-being injured by him through the relation of an active devotion to the world—for the wounds
of the order-of-being can be healed in infinitely many
other places than those at which they were inflicted.

In order that this may succeed in that measure that is
at all attainable by this man, he must gather the forces
and elements of his being and ever again protect the unity
that is thus won from the cleavage and contradiction that
threaten it. For, to quote myself, one cannot do evil with
his whole soul, one can do good only with the whole

DATE DUE

NOV 09 1994		

Demco, Inc. 38-293

soul.[13] What one must wrest from himself, first, is not yet the good; only when he has first attained his own self does the good thrive through him.

The event of illumination corresponds on the plane of the law to the legal confession of guilt, on the plane of faith to the confession of sin. As a social concept, confession of guilt is naturally the most familiar of the three; what takes place here takes place in public in the legal institutions of society.

The confession of sin is spoken by a man when, seeking reconciliation with God, he directly or indirectly steps before the absolute judgment. That may happen in the chorus of the community, as at the Jewish Day of Atonement, or in the whispers of the confessing man into the ear of the confessor, or even in solitude by those who feel themselves as standing before God and their speech as addressing God: the confessing one is always removed from the anonymous publicity of society, but by no means referred to himself. He has one over against him who receives his confession, answers it, 'forgives' him—for the Jews, in a significant co-operation with him toward whom the confessing one has become guilty.

The matter is otherwise with the first of the three events in the action of the great conscience, the event of illumination. Here a man ventures to illuminate the depths of a guilt which he has certainly recognized as what it is, but not yet in its essence and its meaning for his life. What he is now obliged to do cannot be accomplished in any other place than in the abyss of I-with-me, and it is just this abyss that must be illuminated.

Legal confession of guilt means a dialogue with the representatives of society who rejoin as judges according to the penal law. Religious confession means a dialogue with the absolute divine person who replies in mysterious fash-

[13] Martin Buber, *Good and Evil: Two Interpretations* (New York: Charles Scribner's Sons, paperback, 1961), p. 130. British edition, *Images of Good and Evil* (London: Routledge, 1952).

ion out of his mystery. As for the illumination of essence, it is in its most real moments not even a monologue, much less a real conversation between an ego and a superego: all speech is exhausted; what takes place here is the mute shudder of self-being. But without this powerful wave of light which illuminates the abyss of mortality, the legal confession of guilt remains without substance in the inner life of the guilty man, no matter how weighty its consequences may be, and the religious confession is only a pathetic prattle that no one hears.

We must not fail to recognize that it has become more difficult for the man of our age than any earlier one to venture self-illumination with awake and unafraid spirit, although he imagines that he knows more about himself than did the man of any earlier time. The inner resistance which shows itself here—a deeper one than all that discloses itself to the genetic investigation of the analyst—has found so valid a representation in two of the characteristic forms of the epic literatures of the nineteenth and twentieth centuries that we cannot do better than to turn to them in order to supplement our understanding of the problem. I mean Nikolai Stavrogin in Dostoevski's novel *The Possessed* and Joseph K in Kafka's narrative *The Trial*. In our discussion of this subject, the second of these books, as little as it is comparable to the first in artistic power, must still be the more important because in it the present stage of the human problem of guilt has found expression. But in order to see how this later stage is connected with that which preceded it, we must turn our attention first to Dostoevski.

For our formulation of the question it is necessary to proceed from the complete text of the novel, that which contains the chapter of Stavrogin's confession, later expunged by the author on external grounds, and some related material.

Stavrogin was thought of by Dostoevski as the man on the outermost rim of the age who dissolves the meaning of existence through denying it and who manages to destroy himself through the destruction of all over whom he gets power. In the omitted chapter it is told how Stavrogin visits a holy man and brings to him the record of a confession which he declares he wishes to publish. In it he confesses how he raped a little girl. Later he disavows the confession, evidently because he knows from the reaction of the priest as soon as it has been made that it cannot accomplish what he has expected it to. The content of the confession is true, but the act of making it is fictitious. It has nothing at all to do with Stavrogin's self-illumination, with persevering self-identification, with reconciling renewed relationship with the world. Thus even his 'unfeigned need for a public execution' (as Dostoevski states in explanation) is permeated with the fictitious. What Stavrogin desires is 'the leap'. A fragmentary sketch by Dostoevski informs us unambiguously about this. It says, clearly in this connection, that the priest opposed Stavrogin's intention to publish the confession: 'The high priest pointed out that a leap was not necessary, that the man must rather set himself to rights from within—through long work; only then could he complete the leap. "And would it be impossible to do it suddenly?" Stavrogin asks. "Impossible?" rejoins the priest. "From the work of an angel it would become the work of a devil." "Ah," exclaims Stavrogin, "that I already knew myself."'

Stavrogin 'commits' the confession as he commits his crimes: as an attempt to snatch the genuine existence which he does not possess, but which—nihilist in practice but (in anticipation) existentialist in views—he has recognized as the true good. He is full of 'ideas' (Dostoevski even lends him his own!), full of 'spirit', but he does not exist. Only after Dostoevski's time, only in our own, will this type of man discover the basic nihilism in existential form after he has learned that he cannot attain to existence by the ways corresponding to his kind of person. Only this is now left to him: to proclaim the spiritful *nihil* as

existence and himself as the new man. Stavrogin is not
yet so 'advanced'. All he can do is to kill himself; after all,
the 'demonic' game with ideas, crimes, and confessions—
this game that has a goal—has proved itself powerless.
The decisive moment, excised in the usual version of the
novel as abridged by the author, is precisely the failure
of the confession: Stavrogin has wanted the holy man to
believe in its existential character and thereby help him,
Stavrogin, to existence. But existential confession is possible only as a breaking-through to the great action of
the high conscience in self-illumination, persevering self-
identification, and a reconciling relationship to the world.
This possibility, however, is in Stavrogin's eyes one of two
things: either essentially not accorded to him or destroyed
by him through his life-game. In Dostoevski's own eyes,
however, man is redeemable when he wills redemption
as such and thereby also his share in it—the great act of the
high conscience.

The Possessed was written in 1870, Kafka's *Trial* in
1915. The two books represent two basically different but
closely connected situations of human history from which
their authors suffered: the one the uncanny negative certainty, 'Human values are beginning to shatter', and the
other the still more uncanny uncertainty, 'Do world-
meaning and world-order still have any connection at all
with this nonsense and this disorder of the human world?'
—an uncertainty that appears to have arisen out of that
negative certainty.

Everything in Kafka's book is intended to be uncertain
and indefinite, at times to the point of an absurdity, which
always remains artistically mastered. This court of justice
before which Joseph K is unexpectedly cited because of
an unnamed and to him unknown guilt is at once prosa-
ically real and of ghostly indefiniteness, wild, crude, and
senselessly disordered through and through. But Joseph K
is himself, in all his actions, of hardly less indefiniteness—

merely a different kind—as, charged with guilt, he con-
fusedly carries on day after day a life as directionless as
before. Directionless, that is, except for the one aim he
now pursues, sometimes busily, sometimes incidentally:
namely, that of getting free of the court. To this end he
occupies himself with indefinite advocates, indefinite
women, and other indefinite human instruments in order
that they may provide him, in the face of the peculiar
ways of this peculiar court, with the protection that he
imagines is all he needs. The indefinite guilt with which
he is charged occupies him only in so far as he thinks
from time to time of composing a written defence in the
form of a short description of his life which will explain,
in connection with each more important event, on what
grounds he then acted thus and not otherwise, and
whether he now approves or condemns his manner of
acting at that time. Finally there happens what is reported
in an unfinished chapter: 'From then on K forgot the court.'

All this is not to be called chaotic, for in a chaos is hidden a world that shall emerge out of it; here there is no
trace of a cosmos that wills to come into being. But one
may well call all this taken together—the court, the accused, and the people around him—labyrinthine. The disorder, mounting to absurdity, points toward a secret order,
one, however, which nowhere shows itself except by way
of a hint, which apparently would first become manifest
only if Joseph K did what until the end he does not do—
make 'the confession' that is demanded of him. But he
cannot, as he says, discover the least guilt on account of
which one could accuse him. Indeed, he ends later—
clearly without quite knowing what he is saying—by uttering the presumptuous words that are not proper to any
human mouth: 'I am completely guiltless.' The thread that
leads out of the labyrinth is not to be found in the book;
rather this thread exists only when just that happens
which did not happen, the 'confession of guilt'.

But what can be meant here, under the given presuppositions, by making a confession? This question hovers in a strange, altogether intentional paradox. A well-informed young woman says to Joseph K, leaning on his shoulder, 'One cannot, in fact, defend oneself against this court; one must make the confession. Make it therefore at the first opportunity. Only then is there any possibility of escaping.' And he answers, 'You understand much about this court and about the deceit that is necessary here'. Since Kafka himself says nothing like this, it can only mean that Joseph, who holds himself, in fact, to be 'entirely guiltless', understands that he should make a false confession, and at this moment he does not seem disinclined to do so. Later, however, a painter, who is likewise, as we hear, well-acquainted with the ways of this court, advises him thus: 'Since you are guiltless, it is really possible for you to rely on your innocence.' Note well: In the same speech the same speaker declares that he has never yet witnessed a single acquittal, but immediately afterwards he says that the decisions of the court were not published, that there exist, however, 'legends' of actual acquittals, and that these legends probably contain 'a certain truth'.

In this atmosphere the action moves forward, and it clearly seems as though the accusation and with it the encouragement to confession are a senseless absurdity, as Joseph K has declared them to be in his speech before the court: 'And the meaning of this great organization, gentlemen? It consists in the fact that innocent persons are arrested, and against them a senseless and for the most part, as in my case, inconsequential proceedings are instituted.' Some Kafka interpreters take these words to express the essential message of the book. This position is refuted through the further course of the action and through notes in Kafka's diaries relating to it.

I have in mind the chapter, 'In the Cathedral', in which is told how Joseph K comes by accident into a church and is here addressed by name by a clergyman unknown to him, the prison chaplain, who also belongs to the organization of the court, but does not act by order of the court. This chapter corresponds exactly to the one excised by Dostoevski from *The Possessed*, in which Stavrogin hands over his confession to the high priest (a chapter which Kafka, moreover, could have known only in an incomplete version, not including the text of the confession). In both a priest is the antagonist, in both it is a matter of a confession of guilt; however, in Dostoevski it is furnished undemanded while in Kafka it is demanded. For it is this demand that the chaplain wishes to convey by the information that the case is going badly, since the court holds the guilt to be proved. 'But I am not guilty,' answers K, 'it's a misunderstanding. And, if it comes to that, how can any man be called guilty? We are all simply men here, one as much as the other.' One must listen closely: What is denied here is the ontic character of guilt, the depth of existential guilt beyond all mere violations of taboos. It is just this that Freud wished to deny when he undertook to relativize guilt feeling genetically. And to Joseph K's reply the priest answers, 'That is true', which means: Indeed we are all men, and should not overestimate the difference between men. He continues, however, 'But that's how all guilty men talk', which means: He who is in question gets off by talking about the others, instead of occupying himself with himself.

Now the priest asks, 'What is the next step you propose to take in the matter?' 'I'm going to seek more help', answers K. 'You cast about too much for outside help', he now hears. And when he still will not understand, the chaplain shrieks at him, 'Can't you see two steps in front of you?' He speaks like one who sees a man, still standing there before him, as already fallen. What he wants to say with his words, without directly saying it, is that the verdict, 'into which the proceedings gradually pass over', now stands at hand, and the verdict itself already means death.

And now, as the last and most extreme effort, the chaplain tells the man, for whose soul and destiny he wrestles in one, the parable of the doorkeeper who stands, as one of countless men, 'before the Law', before one of the countless doors leading into the interior of the Law, and of the man who desires entrance here. This man is frightened by the difficulties that await him who dares entrance, according to the information imparted to him by the doorkeeper. He now passes days and years, the entire remainder of his life, sitting sideways before this one out of innumerably many doors, until shortly before his end the keeper discloses to him that this doorway was destined for him alone and now is going to be shut. Joseph K listens to the parable and does not understand it: What then could the man have done to manage to get in? The clergyman does not tell him. Kafka himself, as he records in his diaries, first understood the significance of the story when he read it aloud to his fiancée. On another occasion, he clearly expressed this significance himself in an unforgettable passage in his notebooks: 'Confession of guilt, unconditional confession of guilt, door springing open, it appears in the interior of the house of the world whose turbid reflection lay behind walls.' The confession is the door springing open. It is the true 'breakthrough', by which word Joseph K is falsely accustomed to describe the aspired-for escape from the law.

What does the legal concept of confession of guilt become here? What is so named here is self-illumination, the first and opening event in the action of the great conscience.

Stavrogin makes a confession in words. He describes therein in horrible detail the course of his crime, but both in remembering it and in recording it he remains incapable of self-illumination. He lacks the small light of humility that alone can illuminate the abyss of the guilty self in broad waves. He seeks for some kind of foothold, no matter how meagre; then he gives up and kills himself.

Joseph K makes no confession; he refuses to understand

that it is necessary for him to do so. In distinction from Stavrogin he is not proud; unlike the latter, he does not distinguish himself from other men. But by that very fact, with his, 'We are all simply men here', he escapes the demand to bear into his inner darkness (of which Kafka speaks in his diaries) the cruel and salutary light. He insists that there is no such thing as personal existential guilt. His innermost being knows otherwise—because Kafka, who is closely connected with Joseph K, knows otherwise—but he shuns penetrating to this innermost being until it is too late. At this point Franz Kafka and Joseph K seem to have to part company. Kafka had imparted to him something of his own name, he had given him to bear (as he gave to 'K' in *The Castle*) his own suffering from a senselessly acting environment; with humorous caricature he had endowed him with his own traits. But now in the decisive hour, according to the logic of the fiction, he lets him say, 'How can any man be called guilty?' and lets him lengthily and ingeniously dispute over the story of the doorkeeper, Kafka's most concentrated statement of his life-view, instead of accepting its teaching. As a result, Kafka, who understands the depth of existential guilt, must separate himself at this point from Joseph K.

He attains connection with him again, however, through the fact that soon afterwards, when the executioners are already leading Joseph K to his death, Kafka lets him concentrate himself in a strong, although still rational, self-recollection. He lets Joseph, who now knows that and how the trial is going to end, say to himself, 'I always wanted to snatch at the world with twenty hands, and not for a very laudable motive, either'. Joseph K has recognized that he has projected on the disordered human world only his own disorder. His self-recollection is not, of course, the beginning of a self-illumination, but it is a first step toward it, without the man who does it knowing it. And now, before the end, Kafka may again take the foolish man to his heart, although at the very end, before

the knife falls on Joseph K, Kafka lets the old foolish notions of some still forgotten objections come into his mind.
Perhaps Kafka meant himself by the man whom Joseph
K glimpses at the last standing in a window, 'a man faint
and insubstantial at that distance and at that height': he
wants to help his creature and may not.

It might still be asked how the absurd confusion that
rules in the court is to be reconciled with the justice of the
accusation and the demand. The question places before us
a central problem of Kafka's that we find in the background of this novel and of the related novel *The Castle*,
where an inaccessible power governs by means of a slov-
enly bureaucracy. We can extract the answer from an
important note in Kafka's diary, from the time of the
genesis of *The Trial*, in which he speaks of being occupied
with the biblical figure of the unjust judges. It reads, 'I
find, therefore, my opinion, or at least the opinion that I
have formerly found in me'. Psalm 82, of which he is
clearly speaking here, has as its subject God's judgment
over those 'sons of God', or angels, to whom He had entrusted the regimen over the human world and who had
vilely misused their office and 'judged falsely'. The content
of this late psalm is connected with that of the oriental
myth, elaborated by the Gnostics, of the astral spirits who
fatefully determine the destiny of the world, but from
whose power that man may become free who dedicates
himself to the concealed highest light and enters into rebirth. I have reason to assume that Kafka also knew this
myth at that time.[14] In *The Trial* he modified it, in accord with his own contemplation of the world, through
letting the just accusation of an inaccessible highest judgment be conveyed by a disorderly and cruel court. Only
that man can escape the arm of this court who, out of his
own knowledge, fulfils the demand for confession of guilt
according to its truth through executing the primal con-

[14] I refer to a question concerning this myth that Kafka put
to me at the time of his visit to my house in Berlin in 1911 or
1912.

fession, the self-illumination. Only he enters the interior of the Law.

The destiny of both men, that of Stavrogin and that of Joseph K, is determined by their false relationship to their guiltiness.

Stavrogin, of course, plays with the thought of bearing before him like a banner the confession of his most shameful guilt, but he does not bring forth the greater courage to understand in self-illumination his essential being and the origin of his guilt. His feeling, as he says in his last letter, is 'too weak and too shallow', his wish 'too little strong; it cannot lead me'. He declares himself unable to kill himself, for 'vexation and shame can never exist in me, and consequently no despair'. But immediately thereafter despair overwhelms him and he gives himself up to death.

Joseph K belongs to another, essentially later, more 'advanced' generation. Not merely before the world, but also before himself, he refuses to concern himself with an ostensible state of guilt. He refuses to find and illuminate in himself the cause of this indictment which this questionable society casts on him from somewhere—say, from an invisible, unknowable 'highest court'. Indeed, it now passes as proved, in this his generation, that no real guilt exists; only guilt feeling and guilt convention. Until the last moment he refuses to enter through the door that still stands open and is only apparently shut; thus the verdict overtakes him.

Both Stavrogin and Joseph K have not taken the crucial hour of man upon themselves, and now have lost it.

It is the crucial hour of man of which we speak. For, to use Pascal's language, the greatness of man is bound up with his misery.

Man is the being who is capable of becoming guilty and is capable of illuminating his guilt.

I have illustrated through two examples from epic literature the manifold resistance of the human being against self-illumination. But this inner resistance is entirely different from the patient's struggle, well known to the psychoanalyst, against his efforts to convey from the unconscious into the conscious[15] a repressed state of facts of a guiltlike nature. For the guilt which is in question here is not at all repressed into the unconscious. The bearer of existential guilt remains in the realm of conscious existence. This guilt is not one that allows itself to be repressed into the unconscious. It remains in the chamber of memory, out of which it can at any moment penetrate unexpectedly into that of consciousness, without it being possible for any barriers to be erected against this invasion. The memory receives all experiences and actions without the assistance of man. It may, however, retain the ingredients of what is remembered in such a manner that what ascends into the actual remembering does not enter it in its original character. The existential guilt, therefore, does not enter it as such. Only when the human person himself overcomes his inner resistance can he attain to self-illumination.

The 'opening door' of self-illumination leads us into no place beyond the law, but into the interior of the law. It is the law of man in which we then stand: the law of the identity of the human person as such with himself, the one who recognizes guilt with the one who bears guilt, the one in light with the one in darkness. The hard trial of self-illumination is followed by the still harder, because never ceasing, trial of persevering in this self-identification. But by this is not meant an ever renewed scourging of the soul with its knowledge of its abyss understood as something inevitably allotted to it. What is meant is an upright and calm perseverance in the clarity of the great light.

If a man were only guilty toward himself, in order to satisfy the demanding summons that meets him at the height of conscience, he would only need to take this one

[15] Freud, *A General Introduction to Psychoanalysis* (New York: Liveright, 1920), see Lecture 19.

road from the gate of self-illumination, that of persevering. But a man is always guilty toward other beings as well, toward the world, toward the being that exists over against him. From self-illumination he must, in order to do justice to the summons, take not one road but two roads, of which the second is that of reconciliation. By reconciliation is understood here that action from the height of conscience that corresponds on the plane of the law to the customary act of reparation. In the realm of existential guilt one cannot, of course, 'make reparation' in the strict sense—as if the guilt with its consequences could thereby be recalled, as it were. Reconciliation means here, first of all, that I approach the man toward whom I am guilty in the light of my self-illumination (in so far as I can still reach him on earth) acknowledge to his face my existential guilt and help him, in so far as possible, to overcome the consequences of my guilty action. But such a deed can be valid here only as reconciliation if it is done not out of a premeditated resolution, but in the unarbitrary working of the existence I have achieved. And this can happen, naturally, only out of the core of a transformed relationship to the world, a new service to the world with the renewed forces of the renewed man.

This is not the place to speak of the events in the sphere of faith that correspond to the events in the sphere of the high conscience that we have just discussed. For the sincere man of faith, the two spheres are so referred to each other in the practice of his life, and most especially when he has gone through existential guilt, that he cannot entrust himself exclusively to either of them. Both, the human faith not less than the human conscience, can err and err again. And knowing about this their erring, both —conscience not less than faith—must place themselves in the hands of grace. It is not for me to speak in general terms of the inner reality of him who refuses to believe in a transcendent being with whom he can communicate. I have only this to report: that I have met many men in the course of my life who have told me how, acting from the high conscience as men who had become guilty, they experienced themselves as seized by a higher power. These men grew into an existential state to which the name of rebirth is due.

With all this, I repeat, the psychotherapist in his medical intercourse with his patients has nothing directly to do, not even when he ventures in a particular case to set for himself the goal of an existential healing. The utmost that can be expected of him, as I have said, is only this: that, reaching out beyond his familiar methods, he conduct the patient, whose existential guilt he has recognized, to where an existential help of the self can begin. But to do this, he must know about the reality toward which I have tried to point in this essay.

V

Guilt, Ritual, and Culture

MARGARET MEAD

Some Anthropological Considerations
Concerning Guilt

The contributions which anthropological research has
made to theories of guilt are of several sorts. Most of them,
however, stem directly from the attempts to relate the
findings of psychoanalysis to the findings of anthropologists
working on primitive, exotic, or contemporary modern societies. I shall attempt to intimate briefly the nature and
variety of these approaches, and then devote the bulk of
the paper to the question of guilt as a sanction for positive constructive behavior as it has been developed in
societies in which parents assume the responsibility of rewarding and punishing their children for labeled and
discriminated types of good and bad behavior.

Interpretations of the Form and
Function of Ritual

There are, then, first theories which relate ritual and
ritual idiom of definite cultural groups to psychological

From *Feelings and Emotions,* by M. L. Reymert. Copyright,
1950, McGraw-Hill, Inc. Used with permission of McGraw-Hill
Book Company.

findings upon expiative and appeasing rituals found in individuals, using a knowledge of mechanisms involved in individual rituals of the neurotic to interpret both the history and the function of rituals shared by whole groups. These interpretations may take the form of relating a present ritual (such as the totem meal, in which all members of the group, all initiated males, etc., ceremonially eat an animal normally regarded as sacred and taboo and the mythical ancestor or supernatural relative of the group) to some event in the far-distant past (such as the original killing of the old man of the horde by a group of brothers). This type of interpretation, of which the classical example is Freud's *Totem and Taboo* (5), is more concerned with origin than with function. The ceremony itself is regarded as the datum which is to be explained, and the explanation is found, not in the present behavior of the individuals involved in the ceremony, but in a set of connections which may be traced between the various elements in the ritual. The interpretative statement may then take the form: this ceremony is a ritual expression of killing the father, and the ritual taboos observed the rest of the year, which include respect for and abstention from the totem animal, are a ritual defense against the same act of patricide. Such an analysis may take the further form of being regarded as proof of some earlier social habit, such as deposition and killing of an aging father, very much as a recurrent dream in an adult may be used as evidence of a childhood trauma. The actual historical value of such interpretations is of course low, for just as a fantasied event in the life history of an individual may function in the same way as an event in which other human beings have participated, so ceremonials of this type may be seen also as constructs, as reactive formations to fears or wishes which have at no time in the history of the group ever been acted out. So a ceremony and set of taboos which, when their constituent elements are carefully analyzed, appear to be intelligible as an expression of guilt for which no present

antecedents are found in the life of the contemporary
members of the group which practice it, may be taken as
data on the constructs of some other people who developed the ceremony, but not as data upon any social
events which occurred in their historical past, such as
patricide, regicide, practice of incest, etc.

When speculation about the content of rituals of sacrifice, scapegoating, extravagant group mourning, etc., was
succeeded by field work in which the experience of individuals, both as children and as adults, could be placed
side by side with the ceremonies in which those individuals
participated, it became possible to point out immediate relationships between the child's experience of closeness to
the mother, of castration fears, of frustration of a type
which led to strong hatreds and hostilities, and ceremonies
designed to make amends for the various types of guilt
associated with aroused incestuous or murderous wishes.
The most conspicuous explorations of such relationships,
particularly emphasizing the genetic connections between
the experiences of infancy and early childhood and later
ceremonials, have been made by Geza Roheim (16, 18,
29), who has followed up the earlier interpretations of
Australian ceremonials with analysis of children's games,
methods of child rearing, and dreams of individuals and
has demonstrated striking correspondences between the
inferred affects of the child and the pattern of the ceremonial.

It is possible to emphasize the function that ritual activities have in solving conflicts which are culturally created, either for the whole group or for some members
of the group whose individual experience has developed a
higher degree of self-accusation, feelings of unworthiness,
or sense of deeply disapproved wishes, such as cannibalistic fantasies directed toward parents or siblings. An example of the former type, the solution of an individual
conflict assumed to be engendered in the entire group,
may be found in those mourning ceremonies in which two

souls are distinguished, so that ambivalence toward the dead may take the form of appeasing and warding off the bad soul and tenderly cherishing and providing a comfortable afterlife for the good soul (14). Where emphasis is placed upon the contemporary meaning of a ritual observance for those who actually practice it, it is possible to add to the genetic explanation of the classical psychoanalytic type such further considerations as the effect upon the young child of simultaneously undergoing the interpersonal experiences which appear to arouse the feelings which will need ritual solution. Such occurs, for example, when the young child in Bali simultaneously undergoes the type of teasing from his mother which appears to induce deep hostility and reactive withdrawal, and an oft-enacted ceremonial in which the witch surrogate of the mother is actively attacked by young males who fall down in trance before the magic power of the witch (an assumed surrogate of the mother), and are revived by the magic power of the dragon [an assumed surrogate of the father (1)].

Examples of the relationship between traditional rituals and the experience of selected individuals in a society may be found in witch societies, types of possession and shamanism, the peculiar suicide vows patterns of certain warrior societies among the North American Plains Indians, the custom of hara-kiri among the Japanese, monastic vows and retreats, etc., in which the society keeps alive patterns of behavior, available to those on whom there have been differential pressures, which develop a capacity to make use of the ritual pattern. Any full understanding of the use of such patterns will include a detailed analysis of the way in which the existence of the ritual pattern of atonement or appeasement is communicated to and gives shape to the psychological behavior of the individuals who make use of it, showing to what extent the expressed need of the individual is itself a function of the presence of the ritual. So the practice of ritual confession can be seen as one element in the development of an individual reliance upon confession, whether that confession be of the habitual type practiced in Roman Catholicism, the type of single confession found in ancient Mexico (10), or the confession during sickness of a Manus native (2).

When this type of material is examined from the standpoint of planning for mental health, attention is focused upon the question of to what extent it is necessary to develop ritual solutions of types of guilt which are engendered by various recurrent social practices, such as the extreme individualism of the economic arrangements of each household in modern North America and ritual giving to the Community Chest, the Red Cross, the Hundred Neediest Cases, etc., and to what extent it may be advisable to modify the patterns of interpersonal relationships which give rise to types of guilt which need to be ritually assuaged.

Emphasis upon one type of planned social change or the other will vary as to whether the interest is greater in seeing that the individual pays in psychophysical strain as few prices as possible during childhood and maturity (in which case the recommendation will be to develop a society in which the interpersonal relationships are such that no guilt is aroused to be ceremonially assuaged in social rituals): or, on the other hand, whether attention is directed to the values of a complex culture in which the individual is exposed to a variety of situations arousing profound inadmissible emotions and consequent anxiety and later given a variety of social forms within which to satisfy his complex emotions. But it is important to realize that most of the material on the destructive aspects of exposure to situations arousing strong and forbidden affects comes from the clinical study of the neurotic and psychotic in societies which are changing so rapidly that socially patterned ceremonial solutions for their complex emotional conflicts are not available, except in the work of the individual who is artistically gifted enough to provide his own. This contemporary situation obscures the relationships which may be found in less rapidly changing societies between the arousal of a welter of incestuous and murderous wishes in children and intricate and esthetically satisfying social rituals and artistic forms.

When contemporary forms of social disorganization are observed against a background of the analysis of the imputed psychological content and social function of primitive and exotic ceremonial, it is possible to put new interpretations upon such social phenomena as occur among peoples whose cultures are disintegrating—nativistic cults (26, 31), outbursts of chauvinism, scapegoating, pogroms, lynchings, mass suicides, and mass murders, in which disallowed feelings, which are dealt with either imperfectly or not at all by existing social rituals, reach the level of actual, rather than symbolic acting out (23). From this point of view it is not necessary to assume that the participant in a lynching or a pogrom has more murderous impulses than members of religious groups whose closest approach to ritual killing is participation in a ceremonial blood meal in which the blood is not blood but some surrogate. The only difference may be that in one society the rituals for symbolic expression of the regularly engendered conflicts are present, and in the other they are not.

Most of the types of analysis of social expressions of guilt referred to above are based upon theories concerning very early childhood and upon the way in which the very young child, helpless, dependent, and phrasing his response to others in all-or-none terms, develops fears of his own impulses, fears of the retaliative behavior of others—both impulses and retaliations often being projected into supernatural beings—or other social groups, (11, 28).

Another type of fear has been phrased (3) as the fear of the superego, that is, the internalized representative of the parent who metes out love and punishment to the developing child. This refers to a type of development which occurs in great part after the child has learned to talk and in which the unconscious elements are the result of repression of what has been conscious and verbalized, rather than due to experiences before the mastery of language made it possible for the child to meet interpersonal situations in terms of the processes characteristic of consciousness. The different quality of the unconscious content of guilt based on the preverbal experiences and guilt which may be attributed to the incorporation of parental instruction subsequent to the attainment of language has its counterpart in the levels of social behavior which can profitably be analyzed in terms of these sequential learnings. Ritual, art, myth, are illumined both in interpretation of content and study of their function by reference to these very early infantile situations, while the functioning of moral codes and types of political and social control are illumined by an analysis of type of superego formation and the corresponding moral sanctions in a society.[1]

Types of Superego Formation

When psychoanalytic theory began to develop descriptions of the way in which the child incorporated the image of the rewarding and punishing parent, and so learned to behave *as if* that parent were present in the parent's absence and after the parent's death, contemporaneous examination of primitive cultures revealed the necessity for expanding this description to include a wide variety of methods of moral training and corresponding character structure. These expansions have taken the form of challenging the classical picture of the significance of the strong father and the role of the Oedipus situation in the formation of the superego (12), of comparative studies of the relationships between types of moral sanction and types of social structure (17), of surveys of types of sanction char-

[1] While this seems to be a useful generalization at the present stage of our thinking, recent work on the character structure of prerevolutionary Great Russians suggests that, in certain instances, experiences during the first year of life may provide a definitive basis for attitudes toward authority, without the invocation of regularities of the interpersonal relationships of later childhood (7, 8).

acteristic of an area (27), of attempts in the classification of sanctions as guilt, shame, fear, anger, pride, etc. (20). Each step in this procedure, which has gone on for 25 years, has been tentative, and the need for continuous reformulation has increased rather than abated.

In the present state of the data it appears useful to distinguish between internalized and noninternalized sanctions, whether personal or impersonal, and between those systems in which the parents are the surrogates which result in a sharply focused point of reference. It is necessary to distinguish the degree of focus as a condition leading to internalization between those systems in which the parents are the executors and interpreters of the sanction, on the one hand, and those systems in which the referent is the parents themselves as the approving and disapproving figures and those in which behavior is enjoined in the name of some wider group, the age group, members of one's own or another caste, "the people," "people," "your possible future mother-in-law."[2] Where the parents are both the interpreters and the executors of the system and use as a sanction, "I, your father, or your mother, will punish and reward you in terms of your behavior," we have the classical superego formation with the characteristic features of oedipal solutions incident to contrast or similarity in sex and to the relative weakness or strength of male and female parents. Such an upbringing develops in the child the capacity to feel guilt, to award to the self, either in anticipation of an act not yet performed or retrospectively, in terms of a past act, the type of suffering or reward once given by the parent. Before discussing the cultural setting of this type of character structure further, I wish to sketch in briefly the

[2] The clarification of the role of the parent or parent surrogate in focusing and so internalizing guilt, shame, or pride I owe to discussions with Geoffrey Gorer, while working on problems of Russian character structure in connection with the Studies in Soviet Culture project of the American Museum of Natural History.

other types of sanction with which it may usefully be contrasted.

Where, instead of the parents or parent surrogate as the referents of approval and disapproval, a larger and less individualized group is invoked, it is useful to distinguish a continuum between pride and shame. Shame, for purposes of this classification, may be described as that sanction under which the individual's attention is focused upon possible disapproval from a group, in which the whole quality of the behavior is negative and one acts in fear of a negatively valued response. Here again it is useful to distinguish between those settings in which the negatively valued response is anticipated as coming from a positively valued group, *i.e.*, fear of the immigrant child of the treatment he will receive from American classmates, fear of the disapproval of the gang to which one passionately wishes to belong, fear of the disapproval of the appropriate members of the opposite sex to whose favors one aspires, etc., and those settings in which the negative response is anticipated from a negatively valued group, neighbors who are also spoken of disparagingly, classmates in a school to which one does not wish to go, servants who are seen as prying into the weaknesses of their employers, etc. Where the emphasis is upon the feared negative response, whether from valued or devalued groups, it may still be described as shame, but there will be a great difference in the whole quality of the individual response.

American Indians are predominantly characterized by the use of shame as sanction, with a high incidence of negative valuation of the group to whose judgments behavior was referred. The child was told, "If you do that people won't like you," and in the same breath heard the "people" whose disapproval had been evoked described in carping, depreciating terms. Among American Indians it is possible to find the whole gamut of degrees of internalization, from the high internalization among the Objibway, who may commit suicide from the shame engendered by an unwitnessed event, where despite the verbal reference to the whole group, the child spends a great deal of time in the small family, and the much lower degree of internalization in the Zuñi, where children live in a crowded multifamilial existence where the "people" referred to are actually present and parents invoke masked supernaturals to punish their children while themselves miming the position of being the children's defenders.

Pride may be placed at the other end of the shame-pride continuum, and here the emphasis is upon expected approval from groups who are either negatively or positively evaluated. Just as the maximally strong and emotionally toned shame position may be defined as a fear of disapproval from a negatively valued group instilled in the child by the parent (and accordingly internalized), so the maximum pride position may be defined as an expectation of the approval of a positively valued group, of elders, superiors, similarly inculcated. Somewhere along this continuum we may locate those intermediate situations in which a group of equals, who are neither more nor less positively valued than the self, mete out approval and disapproval, according to the particular situation. This is a situation congruent with an age-mate group, just as the typical guilt-producing setting is the relationship between parent and child and the typical shame and pride settings are the relationship between the self and a society in which such considerations as superiority, inferiority, superordination and subordination, caste, class, etc., are operative. The expressed sanction "No woman will seek you as daughter-in-law" may be qualified as "Even a poor no-count woman won't have you as daughter-in-law" or "If you embroider as well as that, the queen herself will be proud to have you as a daughter-in-law."

We thus have four different situations to take into account: (*a*) the extent to which the parents or other emotionally close highly identified individuals interpret a sanction to the child, whether that be the guilt-producing sanction of "I, the parent will punish you, or reward you," or the interpretative "people will gossip about you" of shame, or "people will applaud and admire you" of pride, and this participation of parents and parent surrogates seems to determine the degree of internalization which occurs, a limited number of figures with whom one has close ties appearing to provide the conditions for incorporation; (b) the type of behavior expected, e.g., whether it is predominantly approval, praise, and reward or disapproval, blame, and punishment; (c) the individual or group to whom principal reference is made, parents, age mates, specific levels, or the whole of society, or their various supernatural and symbolic surrogates, God, angels, the spirits, the village; and (d) the type of valuation placed on the individual or group to whom behavior is referred, as superior, inferior, loved, feared, etc.

Such a systematic statement immediately reveals the dilemma created by our present terminology, based as it is on the one-sided evidence of the clinical consulting room, and a theory more concerned with sinners than with saints. While we may speak of "a decent sense of shame," thus referring to fear of the disapproval of a group whose standards are respected, and a "proper pride," referring to an appropriate concern with the impact of one's behavior on a respected audience, we have no terminology for "good guilt" for the internalized sanctions in the individual who has been praised and loved for good behavior, rather than blamed and punished for bad. Just as we have a word for *trauma*, or an injury to the organism, and no word for a *blessing*, when some strength or sensitivity is added, so we have only a word which emphasizes the fear of punishment or withdrawal of love if and when something wrong is done, and no antonym.

The fourfold classification of contributing social settings above might suggest that all cultures could be placed within it, in the degrees and ways in which "guilt," good and bad, pride, and shame are used as sanctions. But this schematization does not yet represent a closed system on which we may expect to classify all cultures; before elaborating further on the question of guilt, I wish to describe briefly two other types of sanction systems, the Balinese and the Iatmul (21). In Bali, the parent or child nurse invokes desired behavior in the child by mimicking fear of some repellent, frightening, or supernatural object, communicating to the child a sense of shared fear, which remains throughout life in an undifferentiated state for which such terms as internalized or externalized, positive and negative, are almost meaningless. The Balinese remains within the pattern of his highly complex culture and responds to suggestions of deviating from the pattern with withdrawal and to disturbances in the pattern with withdrawal, sometimes even to the point of benign stupor. A withdrawal response to disapproved, out-of-pattern behavior has been communicated to him, at somewhat the same level that British mothers who were frightened during air raids communicated their fear to very young infants whom they held in their arms (4). A fear which is neither verbalized nor rationalized, indiscriminately communicated by all with whom the Balinese child comes in contact, accompanied by no specific punishments or rewards, seems to remain at the same level.

Among the Iatmul we find another type of child rearing, in which the individual learns to control his behavior in lively expectation of openly expressed anger and physical reprisal from others. There is no wide gap in moral or social status between child and parents or between children and other members of the community, no chiefs, no priesthood, no group to whom behavior can be referred, except—after initiation—the opinion of the opposite sex, who are variously invoked on the shame-pride continuum. But the small child is treated, practically from birth, as if he or she were as strong and independent and willful as the adult and as if the only means of control which the adult could exercise was not praise or blame, love or punishment, or the invocation of the opinion or possible reward or punishment of outside groups, but only actual physical force, exercised in false pantomime by a grown man or woman vis-à-vis the child. Children live in a continuous state of alertness, poised to flee blows which must be given with lightning speed ever to fall on a recipient's skin, and in adult life the whole society is organized about the threat and actual event of wrangle and riot between groups conceived of as equally strong. The lack of any system or hierarchical moral control within the individual mirrors and is repeated in the lack of any political control except that exercised by other equally strong groups upon one's own group in the social organization.

I should now like to return to the subject of "guilt, good and bad," in more detail. This type of character structure is characteristic of the English and North American middle class, in which parents differentiate themselves from their children by assuming the moral responsibility of punishing for disapproved acts and rewarding approved acts, in such a way as to encourage the child to take final responsibility for the content of its acts. In Germany (32), on the other hand, there seems strong evidence that the child is rewarded and punished for obedience to authority, rather than encouraged to take personal responsibility for content. Historically this type of character structure which relies on guilt has been identified with the rise of the commercial classes and invoked as a condition of the industrial revolution and the development of modern science and the machine age (30). It has been reviled as the "Puritan" character with an overpreoccupation with conformity and negative good behavior, a concomitant underdevelopment of the impulse life, a tendency to rigidity, intolerance, etc.

It seems worth while to look for a moment at one small primitive community—the pile-dwelling, seafaring Manus people of the Admiralty Islands (13, 15), where the same type of character has been developed among a stone-age people whose religious system consists of guardian ghosts of the last dead male of each household, far from the intricate complexities of the rise of Protestantism and the rise of capitalism. Yet we find a people with a highly internalized guilt structure devoting their whole energies to the pursuit of a moral way of life which will preserve them from ghostly punishment. They are rigidly puritanical, with strong sex taboos, prudish, anxious, driven, with little place for art or impulse expression. Furthermore these people are competent and efficient, learn to handle machines with ease, have well-developed concepts of number, time, and space relationships. They think in terms of the "how" instead of the "why" or "what" and participate responsibly and with ease in the machine civilization of Europeans. They share with Western European and American Protestant middle-class society a preoccupation with the gastrointestinal tract, with taking in and giving out objects, with reciprocal relations between persons, which is congruent with a tendency to treat persons as things and to emphasize the circulation of goods, trade, turnover, activity (24). Their capacity to deal with engines, with machines in general, and with the type of "rational" thinking characteristic of the thought of the late nineteenth and early twentieth centuries in the West may be related to parental insistence upon early moral responsibility in the child and the focusing of the child's attention upon cause-and-effect relationships between his acts and omissions and their consequences. The principal sanction in the society is good and bad guilt, as the child is rewarded and praised for constructive behavior as well as being punished for behavior regarded as wrong.

An examination in detail of the correspondence between the Manus type of character formation and the "Puritan" character of recent centuries in the West suggests that we are dealing with a cultural constellation which involves not only parental upbringing of the child with a strong assumption of moral responsibility, but also the preoccupation with intake and output of food, which is related to a concentration on person-thing rather than person-person relationships, the two together providing an ideal setting for the nineteenth-century view of men and machines. Analysis of the components of this complex, so similar and yet in such contrasting settings, should provide clues as to how to construct a society which retains the positive aspects of this "guilt character" without the emphasis on the gastrointestinal tract which tends to overvalue person-thing relationships and undervalue the individual's relationship to other persons and to his own, reflexly realized inner impulses. It should then be possible to recognize the very great strengths inherent in the character structure which has been developed within our particular historical tradition and to which neither the special preoccupation on the gastrointestinal tract, with its emphasis on objects, nor the negative emphasis on punishment for not sinning rather than reward for positive constructive acts is integral or essential.

It may be appropriate to add a few remarks about the possible biological bases for guilt, in the widest sense in which it has been used throughout this paper, which includes the constructs based on infantile experience and also the introjection of the parental command to feel pride or shame, as well as the particular detailed parental command subsumed under the more special use of the word "guilt" for this type of sanction. Julian Huxley (9) concludes his *Touchstone for Ethics* by invoking the natural dependency situation of the human infant as providing a natural setting for the development of love, and consequently of fear of loss of love, and all its later ramifications, which give a basis for the development of conscience. The formulation follows the psychoanalytic formulation which localizes the genesis of guilt in the nature of the parent-child situation, rather than within the organism viewed alone. Historically, the perpetuation, even in those societies in which artificial feeding is superseding breast feeding, of the old biologically given mother-child nurturing tie has given this development of guilt special, sex-specialized forms, because the female was the original nurturing parent for children of both sexes. This historical form of character formation would be radically altered if society should take the step, made possible by the abandonment of breast feeding, of a pattern of child rearing in which both sexes participated equally. This would introduce such a radical change in character formation that a basic change in the way in which biological potentialities were involved in the genesis of guilt might also be expected.

But we may also consider whether, in addition to the specific nurturing situation, there may not be a biological basis for guilts of another order covered by the conception of the "metaphysical guilt of creatureliness" (6), guilt which arises inevitably from the nature of life and death itself, guilt over the domestication which men endure who become responsible fathers and the pain which women take on who become mothers, guilt over all who have suffered and died as the human race struggled to its present position in the world—a deep guilt which is reactivated by any failure in the individual organism to grow, to attain full sex membership, to use its particular gifts and capacities. Such guilt, such consciousness of a debt to life which can only be paid by living, may be so inherent in the nature of human beings, who live in a culture, that it is ineradicable and will always be both the mainspring of man's spiritual strivings and the guarantee of his humanity.

REFERENCES

1. BATESON, G., and MEAD, M. *Balinese character: A photographic analysis.* Special Publ., New York Academy of Science, 1942, Vol. 2.
2. FORTUNE, R. F. *Manus religion.* Lincoln, Nebraska: Univ. of Nebraska Press, 1965.
3. FREUD, A. *The ego and the mechanisms of defense.* (Translated by Cecil Baines.) New York: International Universities Press, 1946.
4. FREUD, A., and BURLINGHAM, D. Reports for foster parents' plan for war children. 1945–47, mimeographed.
5. FREUD, S. *Totem and taboo.* (Translated by James Strachey.) New York: Norton, n.d.

6. GILBY, T. The genesis of guilt. *Proc. internat. Conf. med. Psychother.*, 1/1, London: Lewis, 1948.

7. GORER, G. Some aspects of the psychology of the people of Great Russia. *Amer. Slavic East European Rev.*, 1949, 8, 155–66.

8. GORER, G., and RICKMAN, J. *The people of Great Russia.* New York: Norton, 1962.

9. HUXLEY, J., and HUXLEY, T. H. *Touchstone for ethics.* New York: Harper, 1947.

10. JOYCE, T. A. *Mexican archaeology.* New York: Hacker, 1969.

11. KUBIE, L. S. Destructive personalities. *Appl. Anthrop.*, 1948, 7, 36–40.

12. MALINOWSKI, B. *Sex and repression in savage society.* New York: Meridian Books, 1955.

13. MEAD, M. *Growing up in New Guinea.* New York: Apollo Editions, 1962.

14. MEAD, M. An ethnologist's footnote to *Totem and taboo. Psychoanal. Rev.*, 1930, 17, 297–304.

15. MEAD, M. An investigation of the thought of primitive children with special reference to animism. *J. R. anthrop. Instit.*, 1932, 62, 173–90.

16. MEAD, M. Review of *The riddle of the sphinx* by Geza Roheim. *Character & Pers.*, 1935, 4, 85–90.

17. MEAD, M. (Ed.). *Cooperation and competition among primitive peoples.* New York: McGraw-Hill, 1937.

18. MEAD, M. The concept of plot in culture. *Trans. N.Y. Acad. Sci.*, 1939, Series II, 2, 24–27.

19. MEAD, M. The arts in Bali. *Yale Rev.*, 1940, 30, 335–47.

20. MEAD, M. Social change and cultural surrogates. *J. educ. Sociol.*, 1940, 14, 92–110. Reprinted in C. Kluckhohn and H. A. Murray (Eds.), *Personality in nature, society, and culture.* New York: Knopf, 1948. Pp. 511–22.

21. MEAD, M. Administrative contributions to democratic character formation at the adolescent level. *J. nat. Assoc. Deans of Women*, 1941, 4, 51–57. Reprinted in C. Kluckhohn and H. A. Murray (Eds.), *Personality in nature, society, and culture.* New York: Knopf, 1948. Pp. 523–30.

22. MEAD, M. The implications of culture change for personality development. *Amer. J. Orthopsychiat.*, 1947, 17, 633–46.

23. MEAD, M. Collective guilt. *Proc. internat. Conf. med. Psychother.* Paper presented August 13, 1948 (3/1). London: Lewis, 1948.

24. MEAD, M. *Male and female: A study of the sexes in a changing world.* New York: Apollo Editions, 1967.

25. MEAD, M. Character formation and diachronic theory. In Meyer Fortes (Ed.), *Social structure: Studies presented to A. R. Radcliffe-Brown.* New York: Russell & Russell, 1963.

26. MOONEY, J. *The ghost-dance religion and the Sioux outbreak of 1890.* Chicago: Univ. of Chicago Press, 1965.

27. PETTITT, G. A. *Primitive education in North America.* Berkeley and Los Angeles: Univ. of California Press, 1946 (*Univ. Calif. Publ. Amer. Archaeol. Ethnol., 43,* No. 1).

28. RICKMAN, J. Guilt and the dynamics of psychological disorder in the individual. *Proc. internat. Conf. med. Psychother.* Paper presented August 12, 1948 (2/3). London: Lewis, 1948.

29. ROHEIM, G. *The riddle of the sphinx.* (Translated by R. Money-Kyrle.) London: Hogarth Press and the Institute of Psycho-analysis, 1934.

30. WEBER, M. *The Protestant ethic and the spirit of capitalism.* (Translated by Talcott Parsons.) New York: Scribner & Sons, 1958.

31. WILLIAMS, F. E. *Orokaiva magic.* New York: Oxford Univ. Press, 1928.

32. *The problem of German authoritarians and aggression* (studies of psychiatric and psychological material accumulated during the Nuremberg trial). A report based upon the work of a preparatory commission organized under the auspices of the International Congress on Mental Health held in London, 1948.

VI

Social Guilt and
Preventive Innocence

GRESHAM M. SYKES and
DAVID MATZA

*Techniques of Neutralization:
a Theory of Delinquency*

In attempting to uncover the roots of juvenile delinquency, the social scientist has long since ceased to search for devils in the mind or stigma of the body. It is now largely agreed that delinquent behavior, like most social behavior, is learned and that it is learned in the process of social interaction.

The classic statement of this position is found in Sutherland's theory of differential association, which asserts that criminal or delinquent behavior involves the learning of (a) techniques of committing crimes and (b) motives, drives, rationalizations, and attitudes favorable to the violation of law.[1] Unfortunately, the specific content of what is learned—as opposed to the process by which it is learned —has received relatively little attention in either theory or

Reprinted from *The American Sociological Review*, Vol. 22 (December 1957), 664–70, by permission of the authors and the American Sociological Association.

[1] E. H. Sutherland, *Principles of Criminology*, revised by D. R. Cressey, Chicago: Lippincott, 1955, pp. 77–80.

research. Perhaps the single strongest school of thought on the nature of this content has centered on the idea of a delinquent sub-culture. The basic characteristic of the delinquent sub-culture, it is argued, is a system of values that represents an inversion of the values held by respectable, law-abiding society. The world of the delinquent is the world of the law-abiding turned upside down and its norms constitute a countervailing force directed against the conforming social order. Cohen[2] sees the process of developing a delinquent sub-culture as a matter of building, maintaining, and reinforcing a code for behavior which exists by opposition, which stands in point by point contradiction to dominant values, particularly those of the middle class. Cohen's portrayal of delinquency is executed with a good deal of sophistication, and he carefully avoids overly simple explanations such as those based on the principle of "follow the leader" or easy generalizations about "emotional disturbances." Furthermore, he does not accept the delinquent sub-culture as something given, but instead systematically examines the function of delinquent values as a viable solution to the lower-class, male child's problems in the area of social status. Yet in spite of its virtues, this image of juvenile delinquency as a form of behavior based on competing or countervailing values and norms appears to suffer from a number of serious defects. It is the nature of these defects and a possible alternative or modified explanation for a large portion of juvenile delinquency with which this paper is concerned.

The difficulties in viewing delinquent behavior as springing from a set of deviant values and norms—as arising, that is to say, from a situation in which the delinquent defines his delinquency as "right"—are both empirical and theoretical. In the first place, if there existed in fact a delinquent sub-culture such that the delinquent viewed his illegal behavior as morally correct,

[2] Albert K. Cohen, *Delinquent Boys*, Glencoe, Ill.: The Free Press, 1955.

we could reasonably suppose that he would exhibit no feelings of guilt or shame at detection or confinement. Instead, the major reaction would tend in the direction of indignation or a sense of martyrdom.[3] It is true that some delinquents do react in the latter fashion, although the sense of martyrdom often seems to be based on the fact that others "get away with it" and indignation appears to be directed against the chance events or lack of skill that led to apprehension. More important, however, is the fact that there is a good deal of evidence suggesting that many delinquents *do* experience a sense of guilt or shame, and its outward expression is not to be dismissed as a purely manipulative gesture to appease those in authority. Much of this evidence is, to be sure, of a clinical nature or in the form of impressionistic judgments of those who must deal first hand with the youthful offender. Assigning a weight to such evidence calls for caution, but it cannot be ignored if we are to avoid the gross stereotype of the juvenile delinquent as a hardened gangster in miniature.

In the second place, observers have noted that the juvenile delinquent frequently accords admiration and respect to law-abiding persons. The "really honest" person is often revered, and if the delinquent is sometimes overly keen to detect hypocrisy in those who conform, unquestioned probity is likely to win his approval. A fierce attachment to a humble, pious mother or a forgiving, upright priest (the former, according to many observers, is often encountered in both juvenile delinquents and adult criminals) might be dismissed as rank sentimentality, but at least it is clear that the delinquent does not necessarily regard those who abide by the legal rules as immoral.

[3] This form of reaction among the adherents of a deviant subculture who fully believe in the "rightfulness" of their behavior and who are captured and punished by the agencies of the dominant social order can be illustrated, perhaps, by groups such as Jehovah's Witnesses, early Christian sects, nationalist movements in colonial areas, and conscientious objectors during World Wars I and II.

In a similar vein, it can be noted that the juvenile delinquent may exhibit great resentment if illegal behavior is imputed to "significant others" in his immediate social environment or to heroes in the world of sport and entertainment. In other words, if the delinquent does hold to a set of values and norms that stand in complete opposition to those of respectable society, his norm-holding is of a peculiar sort. While supposedly thoroughly committed to the deviant system of the delinquent sub-culture, he would appear to recognize the moral validity of the dominant normative system in many instances.[4]

In the third place, there is much evidence that juvenile delinquents often draw a sharp line between those who can be victimized and those who cannot. Certain social groups are not to be viewed as "fair game" in the performance of supposedly approved delinquent acts while others warrant a variety of attacks. In general, the potentiality for victimization would seem to be a function of the social distance between the juvenile delinquent and others and thus we find implicit maxims in the world of the delinquent such as "don't steal from friends" or "don't commit vandalism against a church of your own faith."[5] This is all rather obvious, but the implications have not received sufficient attention. The fact that supposedly valued behavior tends to be directed against disvalued social groups hints that the "wrongfulness" of such de-

[4] As Weber has pointed out, a thief may recognize the legitimacy of legal rules without accepting their moral validity. Cf. Max Weber, *The Theory of Social and Economic Organization* (translated by A. M. Henderson and Talcott Parsons), New York: Oxford University Press, 1947, p. 125. We are arguing here, however, that the juvenile delinquent frequently recognizes *both* the legitimacy of the dominant social order and its moral "rightness."

[5] Thrasher's account of the "Itschkies"—a juvenile gang composed of Jewish boys—and the immunity from "rolling" enjoyed by Jewish drunkards is a good illustration. Cf. F. Thrasher, *The Gang*, Chicago: The University of Chicago Press, 1947, p. 315.

linquent behavior is more widely recognized by delinquents than the literature has indicated. When the pool of victims is limited by considerations of kinship, friendship, ethnic group, social class, age, sex, etc., we have reason to suspect that the virtue of delinquency is far from unquestioned.

In the fourth place, it is doubtful if many juvenile delinquents are totally immune from the demands for conformity made by the dominant social order. There is a strong likelihood that the family of the delinquent will agree with respectable society that delinquency is wrong, even though the family may be engaged in a variety of illegal activities. That is, the parental posture conducive to delinquency is not apt to be a positive prodding. Whatever may be the influence of parental example, what might be called the "Fagin" pattern of socialization into delinquency is probably rare. Furthermore, as Redl has indicated, the idea that certain neighborhoods are completely delinquent, offering the child a model for delinquent behavior without reservations, is simply not supported by the data.[6]

The fact that a child is punished by parents, school officials, and agencies of the legal system for his delinquency may, as a number of observers have cynically noted, suggest to the child that he should be more careful not to get caught. There is an equal or greater probability, however, that the child will internalize the demands for conformity. This is not to say that demands for conformity cannot be counteracted. In fact, as we shall see shortly, an understanding of how internal and external demands for conformity are neutralized may be crucial for understanding delinquent behavior. But it is to say that a complete denial of the validity of demands for conformity and the substitution of a new normative system is improbable, in light of the child's or adolescent's dependency on adults

[6] Cf. Solomon Kobrin, "The Conflict of Values in Delinquency Areas," *American Sociological Review,* 16 (October, 1951), pp. 653–61.

and encirclement by adults inherent in his status in the social structure. No matter how deeply enmeshed in patterns of delinquency he may be and no matter how much this involvement may outweigh his associations with the law-abiding, he cannot escape the condemnation of his deviance. Somehow the demands for conformity must be met and answered; they cannot be ignored as part of an alien system of values and norms.

In short, the theoretical viewpoint that sees juvenile delinquency as a form of behavior based on the values and norms of a deviant sub-culture in precisely the same way as law-abiding behavior is based on the values and norms of the larger society is open to serious doubt. The fact that the world of the delinquent is embedded in the larger world of those who conform cannot be overlooked nor can the delinquent be equated with an adult thoroughly socialized into an alternative way of life. Instead, the juvenile delinquent would appear to be at least partially committed to the dominant social order in that he frequently exhibits guilt or shame when he violates its proscriptions, accords approval to certain conforming figures, and distinguishes between appropriate and inappropriate targets for his deviance. It is to an explanation for the apparently paradoxical fact of his delinquency that we now turn.

As Morris Cohen once said, one of the most fascinating problems about human behavior is why men violate the laws in which they believe. This is the problem that confronts us when we attempt to explain why delinquency occurs despite a greater or lesser commitment to the usages of conformity. A basic clue is offered by the fact that social rules or norms calling for valued behavior seldom if ever take the form of categorical imperatives. Rather, values or norms appear as *qualified* guides for action, limited in their applicability in terms of time, place, persons, and social circumstances. The moral injunction against killing, for example, does not apply to the enemy during combat in time of war, although a captured enemy comes once again under the prohibition. Similarly, the taking and distributing of scarce goods in a time of acute social need is felt by many to be right, although under other circumstances private property is held inviolable. The normative system of a society, then, is marked by what Williams has termed *flexibility;* it does not consist of a body of rules held to be binding under all conditions.[7]

This flexibility is, in fact, an integral part of the criminal law in that measures for "defenses to crimes" are provided in pleas such as nonage, necessity, insanity, drunkenness, compulsion, self-defense, and so on. The individual can avoid moral culpability for his criminal action—and thus avoid the negative sanctions of society —if he can prove that criminal intent was lacking. *It is our argument that much delinquency is based on what is essentially an unrecognized extension of defenses to crimes, in the form of justifications for deviance that are seen as valid by the delinquent but not by the legal system or society at large.*

These justifications are commonly described as rationalizations. They are viewed as following deviant behavior and as protecting the individual from self-blame and the blame of others after the act. But there is also reason to believe that they precede deviant behavior and make deviant behavior possible. It is this possibility that Sutherland mentioned only in passing and that other writers have failed to exploit from the viewpoint of sociological theory. Disapproval flowing from internalized norms and conforming others in the social environment is neutralized, turned back, or deflected in advance. Social controls that serve to check or inhibit deviant motivational patterns are rendered inoperative, and the individual is freed to engage in delinquency without serious damage to his self image. In this sense, the delinquent both has his cake and eats it too, for he remains committed to the dominant normative

[7] Cf. Robin Williams, Jr., *American Society,* New York: Knopf, 1951, p. 28.

system and yet so qualifies its imperatives that violations are "acceptable" if not "right." Thus the delinquent represents not a radical opposition to law-abiding society but something more like an apologetic failure, often more sinned against than sinning in his own eyes. We call these justifications of deviant behavior techniques of neutralization; and we believe these techniques make up a crucial component of Sutherland's "definitions favorable to the violation of law." It is by learning these techniques that the juvenile becomes delinquent, rather than by learning moral imperatives, values or attitudes standing in direct contradiction to those of the dominant society. In analyzing these techniques, we have found it convenient to divide them into five major types.

The Denial of Responsibility. In so far as the delinquent can define himself as lacking responsibility for his deviant actions, the disapproval of self or others is sharply reduced in effectiveness as a restraining influence. As Justice Holmes has said, even a dog distinguishes between being stumbled over and being kicked, and modern society is no less careful to draw a line between injuries that are unintentional, i.e., where responsibility is lacking, and those that are intentional. As a technique of neutralization, however, the denial of responsibility extends much further than the claim that deviant acts are an "accident" or some similar negation of personal accountability. It may also be asserted that delinquent acts are due to forces outside of the individual and beyond his control such as unloving parents, bad companions, or a slum neighborhood. In effect, the delinquent approaches a "billiard ball" conception of himself in which he sees himself as helplessly propelled into new situations. From a psychodynamic viewpoint, this orientation toward one's own actions may represent a profound alienation from self, but it is important to stress the fact that interpretations of responsibility are cultural constructs and not merely idiosyncratic beliefs. The similarity between this mode of justifying illegal behavior assumed by the delinquent and the implications of a "sociological" frame of reference or a "humane" jurisprudence is readily apparent.[8] It is not the validity of this orientation that concerns us here, but its function of deflecting blame attached to violations of social norms and its relative independence of a particular personality structure.[9] By learning to view himself as more acted upon than acting, the delinquent prepares the way for deviance from the dominant normative system without the necessity of a frontal assault on the norms themselves.

The Denial of Injury. A second major technique of neutralization centers on the injury or harm involved in the delinquent act. The criminal law has long made a distinction between crimes which are *mala in se* and *mala prohibita*—that is between acts that are wrong in themselves and acts that are illegal but not immoral—and the delinquent can make the same kind of distinction in evaluating the wrongfulness of his behavior. For the delinquent, however, wrongfulness may turn on the question of whether or not anyone has clearly been hurt by his deviance, and this matter is open to a variety of interpretations. Vandalism, for example, may be defined by the delinquent simply as "mischief"—after all, it may be claimed, the persons whose property has been destroyed can well afford it. Similarly, auto theft may be viewed as "borrowing," and gang fighting may be seen as a private quarrel, an agreed upon duel between two willing parties, and thus of no concern to the community at large. We are not suggesting that this technique of neutralization, labelled the denial of injury, involves an explicit dialectic. Rather, we are arguing that the delinquent frequently, and in a hazy fashion, feels that his behavior does not really

[8] A number of observers have wryly noted that many delinquents seem to show a surprising awareness of sociological and psychological explanations for their behavior and are quick to point out the causal role of their poor environment.

[9] It is possible, of course, that certain personality structures can accept some techniques of neutralization more readily than others, but this question remains largely unexplored.

cause any great harm despite the fact that it runs counter to law. Just as the link between the individual and his acts may be broken by the denial of responsibility, so may the link between acts and their consequences be broken by the denial of injury. Since society sometimes agrees with the delinquent, e.g., in matters such as truancy, "pranks," and so on, it merely reaffirms the idea that the delinquent's neutralization of social controls by means of qualifying the norms is an extension of common practice rather than a gesture of complete opposition.

The Denial of the Victim. Even if the delinquent accepts the responsibility for his deviant actions and is willing to admit that his deviant actions involve an injury or hurt, the moral indignation of self and others may be neutralized by an insistence that the injury is not wrong in light of the circumstances. The injury, it may be claimed, is not really an injury; rather, it is a form of rightful retaliation or punishment. By a subtle alchemy the delinquent moves himself into the position of an avenger and the victim is transformed into a wrong-doer. Assaults on homosexuals or suspected homosexuals, attacks on members of minority groups who are said to have gotten "out of place," vandalism as revenge on an unfair teacher or school official, thefts from a "crooked" store owner—all may be hurts inflicted on a transgressor, in the eyes of the delinquent. As Orwell has pointed out, the type of criminal admired by the general public has probably changed over the course of years and Raffles no longer serves as a hero;[10] but Robin Hood, and his latter day derivatives such as the tough detective seeking justice outside the law, still capture the popular imagination, and the delinquent may view his acts as part of a similar role.

To deny the existence of the victim, then, by transforming him into a person deserving injury is an extreme form of a phenomenon we have mentioned before, namely, the

[10] George Orwell, *Dickens, Dali, and Others,* New York: Reynal, 1946.

delinquent's recognition of appropriate and inappropriate targets for his delinquent acts. In addition, however, the existence of the victim may be denied for the delinquent, in a somewhat different sense, by the circumstances of the delinquent act itself. Insofar as the victim is physically absent, unknown, or a vague abstraction (as is often the case in delinquent acts committed against property), the awareness of the victim's existence is weakened. Internalized norms and anticipations of the reactions of others must somehow be activated, if they are to serve as guides for behavior; and it is possible that a diminished awareness of the victim plays an important part in determining whether or not this process is set in motion.

The Condemnation of the Condemners. A fourth technique of neutralization would appear to involve a condemnation of the condemners or, as McCorkle and Korn have phrased it, a rejection of the rejectors.[11] The delinquent shifts the focus of attention from his own deviant acts to the motives and behavior of those who disapprove of his violations. His condemners, he may claim, are hypocrites, deviants in disguise, or impelled by personal spite. This orientation toward the conforming world may be of particular importance when it hardens into a bitter cynicism directed against those assigned the task of enforcing or expressing the norms of the dominant society. Police, it may be said, are corrupt, stupid, and brutal. Teachers always show favoritism and parents always "take it out" on their children. By a slight extension, the rewards of conformity—such as material success—become a matter of pull or luck, thus decreasing still further the stature of those who stand on the side of the law-abiding. The validity of this jaundiced viewpoint is not so important as its function in turning back or deflecting the negative sanctions attached to violations of the norms. The delinquent, in effect, has changed the subject of the con-

[11] Lloyd W. McCorkle and Richard Korn, "Resocialization Within Walls," *The Annals of the American Academy of Political and Social Science,* 293, (May, 1954), pp. 88–98.

versation in the dialogue between his own deviant impulses and the reactions of others; and by attacking others, the wrongfulness of his own behavior is more easily repressed or lost to view.

The Appeal to Higher Loyalties. Fifth, and last, internal and external social controls may be neutralized by sacrificing the demands of the larger society for the demands of the smaller social groups to which the delinquent belongs such as the sibling pair, the gang, or the friendship clique. It is important to note that the delinquent does not necessarily repudiate the imperatives of the dominant normative system, despite his failure to follow them. Rather, the delinquent may see himself as caught up in a dilemma that must be resolved, unfortunately, at the cost of violating the law. One aspect of this situation has been studied by Stouffer and Toby in their research on the conflict between particularistic and universalistic demands, between the claims of friendship and general social obligations, and their results suggest that "it is possible to classify people according to a predisposition to select one or the other horn of a dilemma in role conflict."[12] For our purposes, however, the most important point is that deviation from certain norms may occur not because the norms are rejected but because other norms, held to be more pressing or involving a higher loyalty, are accorded precedence. Indeed, it is the fact that both sets of norms are believed in that gives meaning to our concepts of dilemma and role conflict.

The conflict between the claims of friendship and the claims of law, or a similar dilemma, has of course long been recognized by the social scientist (and the novelist) as a common human problem. If the juvenile delinquent frequently resolves his dilemma by insisting that he must "always help a buddy" or "never squeal on a friend,"

---

[12] See Samuel A. Stouffer and Jackson Toby, "Role Conflict and Personality," in *Toward a General Theory of Action,* edited by Talcott Parsons and Edward A. Shils, Cambridge: Harvard University Press, 1951, p. 494.

even when it throws him into serious difficulties with the dominant social order, his choice remains familiar to the supposedly law-abiding. The delinquent is unusual, perhaps, in the extent to which he is able to see the fact that he acts in behalf of the smaller social groups to which he belongs as a justification for violations of society's norms, but it is a matter of degree rather than of kind.

"I didn't mean it." "I didn't really hurt anybody." "They had it coming to them." "Everybody's picking on me." "I didn't do it for myself." These slogans or their variants, we hypothesize, prepare the juvenile for delinquent acts. These "definitions of the situation" represent tangential or glancing blows at the dominant normative system rather than the creation of an opposing ideology; and they are extensions of patterns of thought prevalent in society rather than something created *de novo*.

Techniques of neutralization may not be powerful enough to fully shield the individual from the force of his own internalized values and the reactions of conforming others, for as we have pointed out, juvenile delinquents often appear to suffer from feelings of guilt and shame when called into account for their deviant behavior. And some delinquents may be so isolated from the world of conformity that techniques of neutralization need not be called into play. Nonetheless, we would argue that techniques of neutralization are critical in lessening the effectiveness of social controls and that they lie behind a large share of delinquent behavior. Empirical research in this area is scattered and fragmentary at the present time, but the work of Redl,[13] Cressey,[14] and others has supplied a body of significant data that has done much to clarify the theoretical issues and enlarge the fund of supporting evidence. Two lines of investigation seem to be

[13] See Fritz Redl and David Wineman, *Children Who Hate*, Glencoe: The Free Press, 1956.

[14] See D. R. Cressey, *Other People's Money*, Glencoe: The Free Press, 1953.

critical at this stage. First, there is need for more knowledge concerning the differential distribution of techniques of neutralization, as operative patterns of thought, by age, sex, social class, ethnic group, etc. On *a priori* grounds it might be assumed that these justifications for deviance will be more readily seized by segments of society for whom a discrepancy between common social ideals and social practice is most apparent. It is also possible however, that the habit of "bending" the dominant normative system—if not "breaking" it—cuts across our cruder social categories and is to be traced primarily to patterns of social interaction within the familial circle. Second, there is need for a greater understanding of the internal structure of techniques of neutralization, as a system of beliefs and attitudes, and its relationship to various types of delinquent behavior. Certain techniques of neutralization would appear to be better adapted to particular deviant acts than to others, as we have suggested, for example, in the case of offenses against property and the denial of the victim. But the issue remains far from clear and stands in need of more information.

In any case, techniques of neutralization appear to offer a promising line of research in enlarging and systematizing the theoretical grasp of juvenile delinquency. As more information is uncovered concerning techniques of neutralization, their origins, and their consequences, both juvenile delinquency in particular, and deviation from normative systems in general may be illuminated.

VII

Guilt as Social Drama

KENNETH BURKE

On Human Behavior
*Considered "Dramatistically"**

Human conduct, being in the realm of action and end
(as contrasted with the physicist's realm of motion and
position) is most directly discussible in dramatistic terms.
By "dramatistic" terms are meant those that begin in

From *Permanence and Change*, Second Edition (Los Altos,
Calif.: Hermes Publications, 1954). Reprinted by permission of
Hermes Publications, Los Altos, California.

* This is a revised version of a paper that was originally presented in a symposium on "Organizational Behavior," held at
Princeton University in 1951, under the auspices of the Ford
Foundation. The conference concerned the problem of ideal
"models" that might guide the social scientist in his attempts
to discuss human conduct, as it is affected by specific organizations.

Several of the papers approached the problem in mathe-
matical or technological ways (as with the theory of "stochastic
processes," or with the "Cybernetics" approach to such problems). But the present paper was among those that favored the
retaining of an ethical or psychological terminology. It is based
on the assumption that, human behavior being in the realm of
morals, the kind of certainty best obtainable here is "moral
certainty." Abandoning hopes of "scientific prediction," it
believes rather in the "scientifically documented admonitions."
That is, it looks upon historiography purely as a kind of parable

theories of *action* rather than in theories of *knowledge.* Terminologies grounded in the observing of sensory perception would be classed as theories of Knowledge. In the same classification would fall all theories of *conditioning* (which is the lowest form of learning). We do not mean to imply that "scientist" approaches (in terms of knowledge or learning), do not yield good results. On the contrary, such perspectives can contribute many important *modifiers* to the *essential nouns* of human relationship. Also, it often happens that "scientist" perspectives end by adding coordinates which, while not strictly deducible from the basic experiment upon which they are presumably based, do contrive, by a kind of "leap," or *non-sequitur,* to use an experiment of narrower circumference as specious justification for an interpretation of wider circumference.

Man being specifically a symbol-using animal, we take it that a terminology for the discussion of his social behavior must stress symbolism as a motive, if maximum scope and relevancy is required of the terminology.

However, man being generically a biological organism, the ideal terminology must present his symbolic behavior as grounded in biological conditions. (This statement is *not* the same as saying that symbolism is *reducible* to biology. *On the contrary.*)

In this purely biological sense, property is a necessity.

---

or Æsop's fable, as a mere *warning* backed by data, as a reminder that "We should take such-and-such into account, or else . . ."

However, in contrast with a sheerly pluralistic emphasis that might look upon each situation as unique, the attempt here is to consider what should be the over-all terms for naming relationships and developments that, *mutatis mutandis,* are likely to figure in all human association. To this end, the stress is placed upon the motives of Guilt, Redemption, Hierarchy, and Victimage that supplement and modify men's purely natural or biological inclinations. Such social, linguistically grounded motives can be said to "perfect" nature, in a purely *technical* sense.

(The science of "ecology" has to do with the kinds of balance that prevail among biological organisms, considered as members of a sub-verbal, extra-verbal, or non-verbal community. The members of such a community are so interrelated that assimilation, or appropriation, is mutual, as with animals that fertilize the vegetation they feed on.)

Though man as a biological organism requires property in the sheerly biological sense, by reason of his nature as a characteristically symbol-using species he can conceptualize a symbolic analogue. We have particularly in mind his terms for "rights" and "obligations." Biologically, the rudimentary properties of living, such as food and shelter, are not "rights," but "necessities." *Symbolically*, there can be property to which one has, or claims, a "right," though the possessing of it may not be biologically necessary.

The notion of "rights" in nature is a quasi-naturalistic, metaphysical subterfuge for sanctioning in apparently biological terms a state of affairs that is properly discussed in terms specifically suited to the treatment of symbolism as motive. Jeremy Bentham's juristic critique of language was particularly sharp in helping us to realize that "rights" are not in "nature"; rather, like "obligations," they are a result of man-made laws, which depend upon the resources of language for their form.

The function of words is obvious, in the inventing, perfecting, and handing-on of instruments and methods. (Think of a factory or a laboratory planned and managed without the guidance of terms!) But the full rôle of symbols in shaping men's views of such property, or "capital," is not obvious. For once the division of labor and the handing-down of property (with its attendant "rights" and "obligations") have given rise to classes, there must be some "order" among these classes.[1]

[1] Though other animals may manifest the rudiments of language or of tool-using, man's distinctive genius is in his capacity for doing things at one remove, as when he uses words about words and makes tools for making tools.

Such "order" is not just "regularity." It also involves a distribution of *authority*. And such mutuality of rule and service, with its uncertain dividing-line between loyalty and servitude, takes roughly a pyramidal or hierarchal form (or, at least, it is like a ladder with "up" and "down").

Thus the purely *operational* motives binding a society become inspirited by a corresponding condition of *Mystery*. (Owing to their different modes of living and livelihood, classes of people become "mysteries" to one another.) This condition of Mystery is revealed most perfectly in primitive priestcraft, which serves in part to promote cohesion among disparate classes, and in part to perpetuate ways that, while favoring some at the expense of others, may at times thereby endanger the prosperity of the tribe as a whole.

But in a society so complicated as ours, the normal priestly function, of partly upholding and partly transcending the Mysteries of class, is distributed among many kinds of symbol-users (particularly educators, legislators, journalists, advertising men, and artists).

The priestly stress upon Mystery (which attains its grandest expression in the vision of a celestial hierarchy loosely imagined after the analogy of a human social order) becomes secularized and distributed among these other rôles, each of which treats the social Mystery after its fashion. Thus, the educator has his testimonials of academic rank; the legislator has ways of identifying respect for himself with respect for the august body of which he is a member; the artist helps surround a system of social values with "glamor," as he finds tricks that transform the austere religious passion into a corresponding romantic, erotic passion; journalists and advertising men make a good team, since the one group keeps us abreast of the world's miseries, and the other keeps us agog with promises of extreme comfort, the two combining to provide a crude, secular analogue of the distinction between Christus Crucifixus and Christus Triumphans.

In part, the new modes of Mystery are needed because the many new instruments have given the world a strongly secular cast. In part they are needed because the traditionalists of religion come in time to rely upon images surviving from an earlier social order. And while these have their appeal precisely by reason of their remoteness, they must be supplemented by images more in tune with the times.

Though we would stress the element of Mystery arising from the social hierarchy, we must recognize that there are other mysteries, other orders. There are the mysteries of dream, of creation, of death, of life's stages, of thought (its arising, its remembering, its diseases). There are the mysteries of adventure and love. (As property is part natural, part doctrinal, so love is part natural, part courtesy.) We mention such other sources of mystery to guard against the assumption that we are reducing mystery in general to the social mystery in particular. On the contrary, we are saying: The social mystery gains in depth, persuasiveness, allusiveness and illusiveness precisely by reason of the fact that it becomes inextricably interwoven with mysteries of these other sorts, quite as these other mysteries must in part be perceived through the fog of the social mystery.[2]

II. *The Hierarchal Embarrassment*

As Mystery is the obverse expression of the disrelationship among classes, so the reverse expression is Guilt. (One can most readily realize this fact by considering an attitude midway between: Embarrassment. The specialist in

[2] The attempt to treat *social* "rights" as though they were "natural rights" would be a case in point. The social rights were first *ascribed* to nature, and then "derived" from it. Such a mode of sanction could seem persuasive only because "nature" itself was being perceived through a terministic fog that took form by analogy with sociopolitical principles then current.

one field is not "guilty" with regard to the specialist in another field; he is *embarrassed*. He doesn't know exactly how much to question, how much to take on authority, how much to be merely polite about. Indeed, nineteenth-century Russian fiction is evidence enough that, once the principle of disrelation among classes approaches the absolute, even people within a single class approach one another in terms of the embarrassment prevailing through the hierarchy as a whole.)

The most perfect reflection of hierarchal embarrassment is in the theological doctrine of Original Sin. "Original sin" is *categorical* Guilt, one's "guilt" not as the result of any personal transgression, but by reason of a tribal or dynastic inheritance. (It is the equivalent, in the Christian terminology, to the curse laid upon Orestes *before* the murder of his mother, since his sheer membership in the House of Atreus made him a fit tragic offering.) "Tribally," one inherits *status*. For though the concept of "original sin" may seem, in its formal mode of generalization, to fall outside the disrelations of social rank, the "context of situation" prevailing at the time when the idea was so vigorously developed should certainly be considered as an aspect of its meaning, at least in case one can show specifically why it should be.

(Before we continue, perhaps we should pause to make one point clear, lest we take on unnecessary burdens. In thus equating "original sin" with a "hierarchal psychosis," we do not imply that a formal "socializing" of "private property" would resolve the difficulty. We take it for granted that the pyramidal magic is inevitable in social relations, whereby *individuals*, whether rightly or wrongly, become endowed with the attributes of their *office*. "Private property" may change its name and its nature; and surely it can be so modified that it becomes a better fit for a given social situation than it might be otherwise. But whatever name it may go by, even if its name be "no property," it must exist *in function* insofar as a certain cluster of expectancies, rights, material rewards, honors, and the like is normal to such-and-such a person, as distinct from all other persons, who carries out certain responsibilities or obligations duly recognized as such in his society. In this sense, the slogan of "no property" may be rhetorically persuasive in a given historical situation. But it will be made effective only insofar as backed by organizational means that allocate "properties" all along the line.)

For the next step, let us quote from Coleridge ("First Landing-Place, Essay IV," in *The Friend*) a passage where he is discussing the sheer *form* of his exposition:

"Among my earliest impressions I still distinctly remember that of my first entrance into the mansion of a neighboring baronet, awefully known to me by the name of the great house, its exterior having been long connected in my childish imagination with the feelings and fancies stirred up in me by the perusal of the Arabian Nights' Entertainments. Beyond all other objects, I was most struck with the magnificent staircase, relieved at well-proportioned intervals by spacious landing-places, this adorned with grand or showy plants, the next looking out on an extensive prospect through the stately window, with its side-panes of rich blues and saturated amber or orange tints; while from the last and highest the eye commanded the whole spiral ascent with the marble pavement of the great hall; from which it seemed to spring up as if it merely used the ground on which it rested. My readers will find no difficulty in translating these forms of the outward senses into their intellectual analogies, so as to understand the purport of The Friend's landing-places, and the objects I proposed to myself, in the small groups of essays interposed under this title between the main divisions of the work."

Coleridge is here discussing the series of stages in his exposition. He is idealizing the procedure somewhat, since his actual presentation is much more rambling at times than this version would suggest. But for our purposes, the important thing to note is how explicitly he equates his dialectical method with the image of a staircase which is itself clearly equated with the principle of social distinction. The thought gives us glimpses into the ways in which even purely formal devices, such as the Platonic dialectic so characteristic of Coleridge, can be socially infused, in the total action of the person using it, though technically or operationally such a spirit could be ignored, and even unnoticed.

We could trace further tie-ups. For instance, consider Coleridge's vigorous way of including the Arabian Nights in this same motivational cluster (an emphasis reënforced by a footnote describing the fascination that the book had for him as a child, and the "mixture of obscure dread and intense desire" the sight of it aroused in him, as he hesitated to touch it "till the morning sunshine had reached and nearly covered it"). Here we glimpse ways of showing how the strongly hierarchal magic of these stories, by similarly appealing to his childhood sense of wonder, secondarily added to the magic of the staircase. Since Coleridge himself, in *Table Talk*, talks of the Arabian Nights in connection with his most famous poem, *The Ancient Mariner*, we could proceed to strengthen inferences as to the social motives behind the imagery of the "supernatural" in this poem. But we shall be content, rather, to show by another citation how "celestial" motives can add their powers to the same motivational cluster. We refer to a passage from *Anima Poetæ* (selections from Coleridge's notebooks), a passage in connection with which the editor (Ernest Hartley Coleridge) quoted portions of the paragraph we have already cited:

"The progress of human intellect from earth to heaven is not a Jacob's ladder, but a geometrical staircase with five or more landing-places. That on which we stand enables us to see clearly and count all below us, while that or those above us are so transparent for our eyes that they appear the canopy of heaven. We do not see them, and believe ourselves on the highest."

III. *Hierarchy, Bureaucracy, Order*

It may be thought that, by the "hierarchal motive," we are merely offering a synonym for some such term as "prestige." In one sense, yes, since any term implying emulation can serve the purposes. But our concern is not so much with any one term, as with the question of *companion-terms*. Too often, the argument over some one term conceals the really important matter: the way in which (with the given terministic system) the one term is *modified* by *other terms*.

In an early work (*Attitudes Toward History*), when talking about man as a political animal, we featured the term, "bureaucracy." Or, more accurately, "bureaucratization." It was matched by an antithetical term, "the imaginative." That is, there were said to be plans or purposes, somewhat vaguely conceived in the imagination; and by the forming and use of organizational devices, these "imagined" ends were carried out, with varying degrees of success and varying degrees of public acquiescence.

The notion had a degree of relevance. It also had its metaphysics. We now see that the pattern was essentially idealistic. We have in mind Royce's formula for idealism, in its view of the world as the incarnating of a god, the bringing of a god down to earth. In sum: In the Idealist perspective, there is pure Spirit, Idea, Ideal, Purpose; this Idea attains its mediation, or materialization (incarnation, embodiment) in the temporal order (of "nature" and "history"). In this sense, historiography would be the vision of a god descended to earth, made manifest in the flesh. (We are paraphrasing Royce.) And seen from that point of view, our formula, "the bureaucratization of the imaginative," was a further secularization of idealistic metaphysics, which was itself a partial secularizing of a theological doctrine.

The idealism could in turn be modified in the direction of pragmatism by a secondary consideration. Thus, as *idealism* could be said to have universalized, cosmologized, the relation between an original purpose and its corresponding embodiment in physical and human materials, so *pragmatism* would note how the particular choice of materials and methods in which to embody the ideal gives rise to conditions somewhat at variance with the spirit of the ideal. (We called such eventualities "unintended by-products.") And out of these unforeseen conditions, there arises the need for a redefinition of aim. Hence, where idealism stresses the mediatory step from end to means, (from purpose to agency) pragmatism stresses rather the step from agency to purpose (as it derives ends from the nature of the available means).

And since enterprises of either sort necessarily involved the acceptance or rejection of Authority, or some otherwise qualified relation to Authority, we constructed a terminology with relation to Symbols of Authority.

Bureaucracy and Hierarchy obviously imply each other. Logically, you can't have a Hierarchy without, by the same token, having a Bureaucracy (in the sense of "organization"). But you might, conceivably, have a Bureaucracy without a Hierarchy. That is: there does not seem to be any logical contradiction in the idea of *organized collaboration among absolute equals.* But unless, in practice, authority is at least delegated, organized behavior as we know it becomes impossible. Such authority may be in many ways modified. But its absolute elimination in any feasible enterprise of any scope is beyond our knowledge and imagination.

The practical need of an authoritative ladder in official organization is matched (in art and in the scientific laboratory) by the notion of *steps.* Unless processes *proceed in a "proper" order,* their nature as efficacies is impaired. But whether the enterprise be authoritative in the social sense or successful in the natural sense, in either realm there is necessarily a mode of "order" that is not merely *regular* but *ordinal* (with canons of first, second, third, etc.—canons ranging from absolutes in pope and king, down to purely pragmatic conveniences in *some moments* of *localized* free enterprise).

IV. *The "Two Great Moments"*

In the three preceding sections, we observed: (1) Man's specific nature as a symbol-using animal transcends his generic nature as sheer animal, thereby giving rise to property, rights, and obligations of purely man-made sorts; (2) the necessary nature of property in a complex social order makes for the "embarrassments" of social mystery in men's relations to one another, thereby giving rise to attitudes that pervade areas of thought not strictly germane to it; (3) the terms "Bureaucracy," "Hierarchy," and "Order" all touch upon this realm of social mystery, because of their relation to Authority, and to canons of Propriety. We are now ready for the statement that we consider basic to our thesis. We cite Coleridge, *Aids to Reflexion:*

"The two great moments of the Christian Religion are, Original Sin and Redemption; that the ground, this the superstructure of our faith."

This paper is based on the assumption that a purely social terminology of human relations (conceived in terms of the conditions that mark organized efforts, and of the typical responses to such conditions) can not do better than to hover about that accurate and succinct theological formula, *as we watch always for ways of locating its possible secular equivalents.*

Basically, the pattern proclaims a principle of *absolute* "guilt," matched by a principle that is designed for the corresponding absolute cancellation of such guilt. And this cancellation is contrived by *victimage,* by the choice of a sacrificial offering that is correspondingly absolute in the perfection of its fitness. We assume that, insofar as the "guilt" were but "fragmentary," a victim correspondingly "fragmentary" would be adequate for the redeeming of such a debt, except insofar as "fragmentation" itself becomes an "absolute" condition.

In brief, given "original sin," (tribal, or "inherited" guilt), it follows, by the ultimate logic of symbols, that the compensatory sacrifice of a ritually perfect victim would be the corresponding "norm." Hence, insofar as the religious pattern (of "original sin" and sacrificial redeemer) is adequate to the "cathartic" needs of a human hierarchy (with the modes of mystery appropriate to such a hierarchy) it would follow that the promoting of social cohesion through victimage is "normal" and "natural."

We are here discussing the problem in its widest aspects. As regards particular cases, the particular choice of "fragmentary" scapegoats may be even fantastically and morbidly irrelevant. (Obvious drastic recent example: the Hitlerite promoting of social cohesion through the choice of the Jew, considered generically, as "perfect" ritual offering.) But we are suggesting that, if the great pyramidal social structure of medieval Europe found its ultimate expression in a system of moral purgation based on the two "moments" of "original sin" and "redemption," it would seem to follow that the "guilt" intrinsic to hierarchal order (the only kind of "organizational" order we have ever known) calls correspondingly for "redemption" through *victimage*.

We are *not* saying that such *should* be the case. We are simply saying that, as regards Coleridge's statement about the two essential "moments" of Christian doctrine, such *is* the case, in the great religious and theological doctrine that forms the incunabula of our culture (and so secondarily the incunabula of the scientific or technological views that are now so characteristic a part of it).

It so happens that the present writer felt the logic of this pattern with a new intensity when he was considering, not our society at all, but a purely literary problem with relation to Greek tragedy: the problem of "catharsis" (upon which Aristotle's *Poetics* laid stress in his definition of tragedy, though the pages in which he explained his ideas have been lost, except for a few references in the *Politics* where he says that his main treatment is in the *Poetics*).

We take it that Greek tragedy, being a typically civic ceremony, was designed for the ritual resolving of civic tensions (tensions that, in the last analysis, are always referrible to problems of property). And, noting that in tragedy (as also in Aristophanic comedy) the principle of victimage plays so essential a rôle, we began to ask ourselves whether human societies could possibly cohere without symbolic victims which the individual members of the group share in common.

We are offering the proposition that, as with Coleridge's two "moments," here is the very centre of man's social motivation. And any scheme that shifts the attention to other motivational areas is a costly error, *except insofar as its insights can be brought back into the area of this central quandary.*

Asking ourselves, then, how Greek tragedy produced "catharsis" (a stylistic cleansing of the audience) by the imitation of victimage designed to arouse such emotions as pity and terror, we began to see how "normal" the ways of victimage are. They may be used crudely. Hitlerism is an insultingly clear example of their crude usage. But considering *both* the rationale behind the doctrinal placement of the Crucifixion, *and* the pattern of Greek tragedy (nor should we forget the other great line from which the doctrines of our culture are derived, in this instance the lore of *Azazel*), we began to ask how profound the motive of victimage might be. That is: Insofar as all complex social order will necessarily be grounded in some kind of property structure, and insofar as all such order in its divisive aspects makes for the kind of social malaise which theologians would explain in terms of "original sin," is it possible that rituals of victimage are the "natural" means for affirming the principle of social cohesion above the principle of social division?

v. The "Perfecting" of Victimage

In one sense, we are here but rediscovering a platitude. For everyone recognizes as "natural" or "normal" the practical politicians' ways of temporarily shelving differences among themselves insofar as they can form alliances defined by the sharing of an enemy in common. Then are we, at this late date, but rediscovering some possible Machiavellian uses of the "scapegoat principle"!

The "scapegoat principle" (as used by priesthoods and rhetoricians, and as studied by anthropologists and theorists of political behavior) is certainly involved here. And it should obviously have a prominent place in *any* terminology of social motivations, even if we were but reviewing what is generally known about it. (The mere fact that it is a platitude should not rob it of its high place in a terminology of human and organizational behavior.) But we have a further step in mind here, thus:

Many people with a naturalist or positivist cast of mind look upon the ritual scapegoat as a mere "illusion." They recognize its use as "natural" in the sense that savages, children, political spell-binders, story-writers, and the like spontaneously use such devices, even without any need to be schooled in such usage. Indeed, the need is on the other side: For the spreading of a *naturalistic* lore that will immunize mankind to this *natural* weakness.

Such people usually seem to feel that the cultivating of the scientific mind in general protects against susceptibility to the attempt to solve practical problems by the use of ritualistic (symbolic) victims. But insofar as such a tendency does recur, they seem to assume that the problem is solved by fragmentation. In effect, they would keep the devil on the run by making him legion. That is, they say in effect: Let one fragment of the curative victim be in the villain of a Grade B motion picture, let another fragment be in a radio fool, another in the corpse of a murder mystery, another in the butchery of a prizefight, another in a hard-fought game, another in the momentary flare-up of a political campaign, another in a practical joke played on a rival at the office, another in weeding the garden or ferociously rubbing out a cigarette butt, etc., etc. Insofar as our civilization is marked by great diversity in both labor and leisure, it is fragmentary—and to this extent, there would seem to be something curative in a victimage correspondingly fragmentary.

But there is also a sense in which the condition of fragmentation itself might be felt to need an over-all cure. Fragmentation makes for triviality. And although there are curative elements in triviality, (elements fervently sought, as is evident in the current radio "gag-writer's" cult of the explosive "yak") they can add up to a kind of organized inanity that is socially morbid. The whole aggregate of petty fragmentary victimage may thus require a "total" victim, if it in turn is to be cured.

Now, if people were truly devout in the full religious sense of the term, there should be no difficulty here. For in the pious contemplation of a perfect sacrificial *universal* god, there might be the elements of wholeness needed to correct the morbidities of fragmentation. And the basic structure of such a myth has the classic purity of the ritual sacrifices in Greek tragedy (as contrasted with the loss of such simplicity in dramas where the catharsis of victimage is obscured by a tangle of intrigue).

However, we say as much, not by way of a plea for the religious myth as such, but rather to point up the great temptation confronting a social order which is in its very texture so obviously inclined to materialistic, operational, administrative, technological emphases (as attested by the range and proportion of topics even in its *Sunday* newspapers!). And as regards religion itself, we must consider how its pacific, evangelical aspects come to retreat behind its militant, organizational aspects.

But as we are not pleading for religion, neither are we

attacking it. In referring to the curative totality of the perfect sacrifice, as modified by the predominantly secular nature of modern civilization, we would suggest that the kind of victimage most "natural" to such a situation would be some variant of the Hitlerite emphasis (which put the stress upon the idea of a total cathartic *enemy* rather than upon the idea of a total cathartic *friend*).

Here was an apparent absolute means of redemption: through the sacrifice of a speciously "perfect" victim, the material embodiment of an "idealized" foe.

But our stress upon "totality" of enmity as a cure for the malaise of fragmentation should not be allowed to conceal our major point: That "order" *as such* makes for a tangle of guilt, mystery, ambition ("adventure") and vindication that infuses even the most visible and tangible of material "things" with the spirit of the order through which they are perceived. In this sense, man as symbol-using animal must perceive even his most "animalistic" traits dimly through the symbolic fog arising from the social order of which he is a part. Thus, empiricist, naturalist, positivist, behaviorist, operationalist, and psychologistic views of man's organizational behavior must of necessity but add to the illusion, as regards man's ultimate motives in society, by giving a specious reality to the purely non-symbolic aspect of material property (in things and methods).

The laboratory or the office is as much inhabited by a spirit, a *genius loci*, as any temple (a spirit in turn related to a wider order and deriving authority from it). And unless such a motive is conceived essentially in terms of pyramidal structure (with its corresponding modes of guilt and redemption), it is hard to see how one can get a wholly relevant terminology for the charting of social behavior. Thus, as with theology, an ideal terminology should be dramatistic rather than operational. And while recognizing the tremendous motivational importance of all the new properties which modern technology has produced, and the importance of techniques for the management of these, the ideal terminology must be designed, first of all, to perceive how man's relation to his properties is *symbolically* constituted.

VI. *Variants of Victimage*

Here would be the sort of considerations that would seem to follow from our Dramatistic emphasis:

Along with a search for the modes of vindication by victimage, look for a variant, in possible secularized equivalents of "mortification." To quote from an article published elsewhere, "Thanatopsis for Critics: A Brief Thesaurus of Deaths and Dyings" (*Essays in Criticism,* October 1952):

"If there are social burdens to which one resigns oneself, if there are social barriers which one conscientiously seeks not to want to cross, such moralistic confinements placed upon ambition and trespass are 'sacrificial' in attitude. They reach their ultimate in ascetic disciplines aimed at the programmatic 'mortifying' of the senses. A gallant excess of self-control thus becomes organized into a strategy for living, that attains its grand rationale in a cult of the 'dying life.' Its antithesis is celebrated hugely in Rabelais' rules for the Abbey of Thelema, headed in the slogan, *fais ce que vouldras. . . .*

"Mortification is a scrupulous and deliberate clamping of limitation upon the self. Certain requirements for the maintaining of a given social order attain their counterparts in the requirements of an individual conscience; and when the *principle* of such requirements is scrupulously carried to excess, you get 'mortification.' (For instance, if conditions of private property call forth corresponding ideals of monogamistic love, and if the carrying-out of such ideals, to be scrupulously complete, requires that one should not trespass upon the property of another's wife, then by the rules of 'mortification' one should voluntarily punish whatever 'senses' are thought to make such trespass seem desirable.)"

Such modes of thinking are institutionalized in vows of chastity willingly taken for reasons of piety. But it seems likely that psychogenic illnesses can often be disguised variants of the same motive, though without the conscious code of discipline; for they would be, as it were, the carrying-out of judgments pronounced, willy-nilly, against the self.

"Crime" would be a similar order of motives, but inclining to the "homicidal" rather than the "suicidal" slope. Consider the typical reversal of motives (often noted by criminologists) whereby the *attitude* of criminality precedes the *actual* committing of a crime, so that the crime is in effect the translating of a vague, unreal, and even mysterious sentiment into the conditions of something really here and now. (There is a sense in which crime can even be considered more "normal" and "healthy" than is the case when the sense of criminality eats like an acid into the conscience, producing instead a world of sheer fantasy.)

All told, we are suggesting that the relation is like that between "original sin" and "actual sin" ("original sin" corresponding to the uneasiness or categorical "guilts" implicit in the social order; and the temptation to "actual sin" being a kind of casuistry for the reduction of such generic motives to individual criminal impulses with regard to unlawful encroachment upon property and persons). We are suggesting that, under certain conditions, the *categorical* motive may serve as the matrix for a corresponding *personal* motive. That is: insofar as the notion of an absolute generic or "tribal" guilt is not adequately matched by a correspondingly absolute means of cancellation, crime becomes another partial "solution." Indeed, it even provides a kind of "unity," in that, for the hunted or undetected criminal, danger is "everywhere." (Consider the "mystery" of crime in Dostoevsky.)

Similarly warfare, in its nature as "imagery" (a nature reënforced by the pronouncedly pyramidal design of military hierarchy) can readily be so much more "cathartic" in its promises than in its deliveries. The dialectic of antithesis contributes spontaneously to the imagining of an enemy so "perfectly" suited to his ritual rôle that by his sacrifice all evils would be redeemed. And the false promises arising from his imputed cathartic rôle explain why, although such motives can add to the intensity with which a war is pursued (by making it "holy"), they are a costly encumbrance not only to peaceful international relations but even to the intelligent planning for military defence.

Most in need of study, but hardest of all to study, or even to discern, are the ways whereby the very existence of a hierarchy encourages undue acquiescence among persons otherwise most competent to be its useful critics. This condition probably results much less from over-caution or obsequiousness than from the network of "proprieties" that spontaneously accumulate about a given order. This explicit and methodical study of the "hierarchal psychosis" is needed, if those in authority would guard against the natural tendency to protect their special interests in ways that ultimately impair those interests by bringing the society as a whole into disarray.

A variant of this difficulty is to be seen in the tendency to encourage the teaching of humanistic studies wastefully. A mere glance at a typical list of doctoral theses is enough to make clear the kind of elegant irrelevancies (with question mark after the "elegant") that are still being encouraged. This adds up to a vast subsidizing of inaccuracy such as might have been welcomed in less exacting times, but is almost insupportable now. The purpose seems to be to teach the acquiring of insignia so full of false promises that they are questionable even as insignia.

VII. *"Perfection" as a Motive*

When considering such a notion as the "redemption of guilt," one might note what Bentham would call the "archetypal image" here: the satisfying of a debtor by the paying of a ransom. Next, in line with such thinking generally, one might note how a society's material means of livelihood provide analogies for the building of purely "spiritual" concepts and ideas. And in this respect, one might deem it enough to show how the conception of guilt and redemption reflected certain present or past habits of the society with regard to the exchange of material property.

While not denying the fertility of such speculations, and their relevance for certain purposes, we would remind the reader that the present "Dramatistic" treatment requires the addition of an important intermediate step between the "material" field from which the image is borrowed and the "spiritual" field to which it is applied as a "fiction." This intermediate step involves a kind of "perfecting" or "absolutizing" of the notion or relation from which the analogy is borrowed.

"Implicit" in the notion of a ransomed debt there is a kind of "logical conclusion" or "ultimate reduction." That is: in the idea of an act of trade as such, there lurks as it were the question: "What would be the *most perfect act* of trade, the 'tradiest' trade, or 'trade of trades'?" As soon as some act is brought within the realm of symbols, there is such an end-of-the-line speculation vibrant within the terms for it. The logic of symbolic resources drives towards its fullness in a universal definition. (And this purely technical impulse of symbolism, manifested logically in the demand for definition, is manifested morally and politically in the mind's spontaneous concern with the problems of "justice.")

Then, individual acts ("fragmentary" acts) can be conceived, not just "after the analogy of such-and-such," but *in terms of a corresponding perfection*. The theological notion of God as the *ens perfectissimum* is perhaps the ultimate formulation of the "logic of ultimates" implicit in symbolism.

So, when we encounter "fragmentary" terms got by translating the visible and tangible into their corresponding "fictions," we should not seek for their persuasiveness merely in the seeming "naturalness" of the analogy (as with the anthropomorphic notion that God, like Shakespeare's Shylock, wants vindictive satisfaction for default in a bargain). Rather, we should watch to disclose ways whereby "ultimate" motivations come to be implicit even in the world of contingencies.

Thus, when searching "socio-anagogically" for the "spirit" in *things*, we may begin with simple correspondences. We may note that regulated grass on a college campus, besides its nature as sheer grass, has a social rôle as insignia, standing for a certain order of promises and distinctions connected with the discharging of certain moral and academic obligations. But all such direct correspondences add up to a *principle* of hierarchal order that, by reason of its nature as a principle, is "perfect," an "ultimate" (hence, *technically* equatable with "God," whereat social distinction can become subtly interwoven with divinity, perhaps to the disadvantage of our ideas about divinity, but certainly to the advantage of our ideas about social distinction).

The "perfection" of a secular enemy is the clearest observable instance of ways whereby the intermediate absolutizing step is involved. Given the vast complexities of the modern world, it would be hard to find a "perfect" material victim for any of our ills. But because the *principle* of a "perfect" victim is so implicit in the very concept of victimage, and because men have so "natural" or spontaneous a desire for a "perfect" view of their discomforts, they are eager to tell themselves of victims so thoroughgoing that the sacrifice of such offerings would bring about a correspondingly thoroughgoing cure. The "fragmentary" nature of the enemy thus comes to take on the attributes of an absolute.

The hierarchal psychosis (interweaving the social order with the motives of guilt, wonder, adventure, catharsis, and victimage) arises so spontaneously from the social order, it would seem that a free society should emphasize in its secular educational methods the kinds of observation that make the building of hierarchal magic most difficult. The "efficient" coordinating of such magic seems to go best with dictatorship. Yet as evidence of the way in which hierarchy arises even in the questioning of it: Note that, on principle, science is against such kinds of "mystery"; yet also note that, necessarily, there is the same categorical value placed upon rank and office in scientific and technological hierarchies as elsewhere.

Indeed, the proper educational approach to the motives of hierarchy should not, as now, vacillate between "mystification" and "unmasking," between the journalistic "build up" and the compensatory "character assassination," but should aim at the kinds of contemplation and sufferance that are best adapted to the recognition and acceptance of a social form inevitable to social order.

In the short run, "mystification" may seem to be the best way of promoting social cohesion. But it has been so often misused in history by the defenders of special sinister interests, we clearly see its limitations, as regards the long run. Similarly, in a world wholly "unmasked," no social cohesion would be possible. (However, there is usually an element of deception here. While leading you to watch his act of destruction at one point, the "unmasker" is always furtively building at another point, and by his prestidigitation he can forestall accurate observation of his own moves.)

Fluctuation between one extreme and the other seems to be the usual way in which society considers individual persons enacting rôles in the social order (and, at times of radical upset, certain of the categorical rôles themselves undergo such fluctuation). But might it not be possible that, were an educational system designed to that end, this very fluctuancy could be intelligently stabilized, through the interposing of method?

VIII

Guilt and Awareness

ROLLO MAY

*The Meaning of the
Oedipus Myth*

Our thesis is that symbols and myths are an expression
of man's unique self-consciousness, his capacity to transcend the immediate concrete situation and see his life in
terms of "the possible," and that this capacity is one
aspect of his experiencing himself as a being having a
world. We shall inquire how symbols and myths do this,
through the myth of Oedipus.

The story of Oedipus is a myth rather than a symbol,
but the two are very closely related. *Symbols* are specific
acts or figures, while *myths* develop and elaborate these
symbols into a story which contains characters and several
episodes. The myth is thus more inclusive. But both symbol and myth have the same function psychologically; they
are man's way of expressing the quintessence of his experience—his way of seeing his life, his self-image, and his
relations to the world of his fellow men and of nature—
in a total figure which at the same moment carries the
vital meaning of this experience. The myth of Adam is

From *Review of Existential Psychology and Psychiatry*, Vol. I
(1961). Reprinted by permission of the author and *Review of
Existential Psychology and Psychiatry*.

thus not just a tale of a man in paradise who eats an apple in disobedience to a command, but a story by which we confront the profound problem of the birth of human consciousness, the relation of man to authority, and moral self-knowledge in the sense symbolized by "the tree of the knowledge of good and evil." Thus true myths and symbols, so long as they retain their original power, always carry an element of ultimate meaning which illuminates but reaches beyond each individual man's concrete experience.

The Oedipus myth is particularly useful for our inquiry since it is central both in psychoanalysis and literature. It is basic to the thinking and theoretical system of Freud, and is present in practically all other schools of psychoanalytic thought as well. Freud took it as a picture of the sexual attraction between the child and the parent of the opposite sex: the child experiences guilt thereby, fear of the parent of whom he is the rival, and, illustrated most clearly in the situation of boys, he then suffers castration anxiety. Other schools, like Adler's, deny the instinctual aspect of the Oedipal conflict and see it rather as a power struggle between child and parent; the neo-Freudian cultural schools likewise tend to view it, as does Fromm, in terms of the conflict with authority vested in the parent. In general it is accepted in American thought along the lines made popular by Freud, that the little boy wants to have sexual relations with and marry his mother, has concurrently the desire to kill and put out of the way his rival, the father, and experiences all the conflicts of repression, anxiety, and guilt inherent in such a situation.

But there is a radical and very important difference between the approach of Freud to this myth and the meaning it is given in this country, including that by most orthodox psychoanalysts. Freud presupposed a view of the infant as destructive and driven by cannibalistic desires; the "innocence of the child consists of weakness of limb." For Freud, therefore, the Oedipus myth was genuinely tragic. But in this country we have an almost opposite attitude toward the infant, a Rousseauesque attitude. The baby is essentially social, is called an "angel" by doting parents and viewed, at least potentially, as an angel if only society—and these all-important mothers and fathers who, in the heyday of this attitude, tried to discharge their impossibly heavy task by tiptoeing around on pins and needles when they weren't frantically reading books on child care—does not frustrate the little angel's needs for nourishment too much. The significant point here is that Freud's emphasis on the genuine tragedy in the Oedipus myth was wiped out; the external form of the concept was kept, but its central meaning was lost. Recently, one of the leading theorists of the orthodox psychoanalytic school remarked that the Oedipus myth only showed the "vicissitudes of the family relationship." Certainly it shows much more than that. This illustrates how the tragic aspects of Freud's theories—aspects which saved Freud from succumbing to the mechanistic implications inherent in his dynamics—are the first things thrown overboard when Freudianism crosses the Atlantic.

We believe that Freud's tragic view was closer to the truth, but that he was in error in interpreting the myth literalistically. One consequence of this literalistic interpretation was that the healing aspects of the myth are left out. We propose to demonstrate here that the myth transcends the literalistic problems of sex and aggression. Its tragic locus lies rather in the individual's self-consciousness, his struggles with his fate, in self-knowledge and self-consciousness.

When we read the actual drama of Oedipus, let us say as it comes to Freud and to us from the pen of Sophocles,[1]

[1] To the argument that we are taking Sophocles' "drama," and that the myth itself does have the "content" of killing the father and marrying the mother, I would rejoin that the myth of Adam has the content of eating an apple against a commandment. Then Anatole France could rightly remark, *"Tant de bruit pour une pomme"* (So much noise over one apple). But everyone would agree that such a literalistic, fundamentalistic interpretation does not at all do justice to the profound truths

we are surprised to see that it has nothing to do with conflicts about sexual desire or killing the father as such. These are all done long in the past when the drama begins. Oedipus is a good king ("the mightiest head among us all," he is called) who has reigned wisely and strongly in Thebes and has been for a number of years happily married to Queen Jocasta. The only issue in the drama is whether he will recognize what he has done. The tragic issue is that of seeing the truth about one's self; it is the tragic drama of the passionate relation to truth. Oedipus' tragic flaw in his wrath against his own reality.

Thebes is suffering under a plague as the curtain rises. Word has been brought from the oracle that the plague will be lifted only when the murderer of King Laius is discovered. Oedipus calls the old blind seer, Tiresias, and thereupon proceeds a gripping and powerful unfolding, step by step, of Oedipus' self-knowledge, an unfolding replete with rage, anger at the truth and those who are its bearers, and all other aspects of man's most profound struggle with recognition of his own reality. Tiresias' blindness seems to symbolize the fact that one can more insightfully grasp *inner* reality about human beings—gain *in*-sight—if one is not so distracted by the impingement of external details.

Tiresias at first refuses to answer Oedipus' questioning as to who is the guilty one with the words,

> "How terrible it is to know . . .
> Where no good comes from knowing! Of these matters
> I was full well aware, but let them slip me. . . ."

and meaning of the Adam myth. If we are to take the Oedipus myth literalistically, as a portrayal of the growing boy's attachment to his mother, Oedipus would precisely not have had this toward Jocasta, for he was thrown out on the hillside to die as an infant before he scarcely saw his mother; his "Oedipus" would have expressed itself with the Queen of Corinth, who raised him. I wish by this illustration of the *reductio ad absurdum* of the literalistic interpretation to indicate that we must always go beyond such interpretations and ask the meaning of the myth. Sophocles does this, and I think in a way faithful to the inner consistency and truth of the myth.

In response to Oedipus' new demands and threats, he continues,

> "Let me go home; . . .
> So shalt thou bear thy load most easily. . . ."
> "Ye
> Are all unknowing; my say, in any sort,
> I will not say, lest I display my sorrow."

The drama then unfolds as the progressive revelation of Oedipus to himself, the source from which the truth proceeds being not Oedipus himself but Tiresias, as Professor Paul Ricoeur of the Sorbonne has indicated. The whole gamut of psychoanalytic reactions like "resistance" and "projection" are exhibited by Oedipus as, the closer he gets to the truth, the more violently he fights against it. He accuses Tiresias of planning to betray the city; is this why he will not speak? The seer replies,

> "I will not bring remorse upon myself
> and upon you. Why do you search these matters?"

Then in a burst of angry projection Oedipus accuses Tiresias of having killed Laius himself. And when Oedipus is finally told the truth by the goaded seer, that he himself is the murderer of his father, Oedipus turns upon Tiresias and Creon with the charge that these words are inventions, part of their strategy to take over the state. These forms of behavior, termed "resistance" and "projection," are an understandable part of every man's bitter struggle against the impossibly heavy and painful burden of responsibility in learning the truth about himself and of enduring the revolutionary impact on his self-image and identity. The former, resistance, is an acting-out of the conviction "I cannot bear to admit it is I, so I will not see it!" The latter, projection, is a way of crying out "If it is true, it is somebody else; not I! not I!"

Jocasta tries to persuade Oedipus not to place any weight on the seer's accusation:

> "Listen and learn, nothing in human life
> Turns on the soothsayer's art."

But then, as he begins to sense that some portentous mystery surrounds his birth, she, the mother whom he has married, now herself becomes aware of the terrible knowledge that awaits him. She tries desperately to dissuade him:

> ". . . But why should men be fearful,
> O'er whom Fortune is mistress, and fore-knowledge
> Of nothing sure? Best take life easily,
> As a man may. For that maternal wedding,
> Have no fear; for many men ere now
> Have dreamed as much; but he who by such dreams
> Sets nothing, has the easiest time of it."

When he still proclaims his resolve to face the truth whatever it may be, she cries,

> "Don't seek it! I am sick, and that's enough . . .
> Wretch, what thou art O mightst thou never know!"

It is fascinating to note here that Jocasta, in saying one should not take dreams—or myths or symbols—too seriously, is sharing the viewpoint we see in many textbooks of psychology. Her words above also express the concept of "adjustment" in psychotherapy, an emphasis which tends always to creep into psychology and psychoanalysis precisely because of the anxiety and radical upheaval that goes with pursuing fully the truths about one's self. Jocasta here enunciates the principle of acceptance of reality *without* the passionate, tragic relation to truth.

Interestingly enough, this emphasis in this myth and many others is identified with the *feminine* principle. The mother or wife, the conserving biological function, is blamed for the tendency to hold the man back from the creative breaking through to truth. This tendency for the man to see the woman as the bearer of the temptation to "take life easily as a man may," the temptress leading him to turn against the possibilities of his emerging "better self," has been commented upon by C. G. Jung and Otto Rank in their depth-psychological studies of creativity.

The most fruitful single line of explanation of this, in my judgment, is Rank's idea that all growth is a series of birth experiences and that every new view of truth or the creative act in life is a step in breaking out of the womb and gaining greater individuation. I would add that, since the original breaking out is from the actual womb of the mother, every subsequent act is a re-enactment both of fighting against the mother, who now represents one's own fear of moving ahead, and an expression of anger and hostility at her for having ejected one in the first place.

Oedipus is not dissuaded, but insists that he must know what he is and where he came from. He must know and accept his own reality and his fate:

> "I will not hearken—not to know the whole,
>   Break out what will, I shall not hesitate . . ."

The old shepherd who rescued the infant Oedipus from death on the mountainside is finally brought, the one man who can provide the final link in the fateful story. "O, I am at the horror, now, to speak!" the shepherd cries. And Oedipus answers, "And I to hear. But I must hear—no less."

When Oedipus does learn the final, tragic truth, he cuts out his eyes. It is significant that he is not *castrated*, nor does he castrate himself; he cuts out his eyes, the organ of *seeing*. (The tendency to call this a "symbolic castration" would miss the whole point, and would be another example of using a theory, *e.g.* the primacy of sexual prototypes, as a procrustean bed on which to force the data.) His punishment is then *exile*, first self-imposed but later, as in Colonus, imposed by Creon and the state. The tragedy has now come full circle: he was originally exiled, when he was a few days old, on his father's order; and his life at last ends again in exile. The exile is a fascinating symbolic act from our modern psychoanalytic viewpoint, for we have much data to indicate that the greatest threat and greatest cause of anxiety for Western man in the middle of the twentieth century is not castration but *ostracism,* the terrible situation of being thrown out of the group. Many a contemporary man castrates himself or permits himself to be castrated because of fear of being exiled if he doesn't. He renounces his power and conforms under the greater threat and peril of ostracism.

We now turn to the drama which follows and which reveals the healing, integrative aspects of the Oedipus myth, namely *Oedipus at Colonus.* So far as I know, this drama is never mentioned in psychoanalytic literature at all, an amazing fact in itself. One reason for its neglect is that discussion of the integrative functions of myths in general tends to be omitted in psychoanalysis. But, more specifically, a consequence of the literalistic interpretation of the myth as having to do with sex and killing the father requires that we stop when these are worked through, punishment meted, and the situation accepted, as at the conclusion of *Oedipus Tyrannus.* But viewing the myth as the presentation of man's struggle in self-knowledge to know the reality about his own being, we must indeed go on, as Sophocles does, to see how a man comes to terms with the meaning of these acts. This subsequent drama is Oedipus' stage of reconciliation with himself and with his fellow men in the persons of Theseus and the Athenians, and it is a reconciliation with the ultimate meaning in his life. "For the gods who threw you down sustain you now," as his daughter Ismene phrases it. In some ways this drama is more significant than the first; and since it was written by Sophocles when he was an old man—eighty-nine—it can be supposed to contain the wisdom of his old age as well.

One theme we find in the old Oedipus' meditation at Colonus is *guilt*—the difficult problem of the relation of ethical responsibility to self-consciousness. Is a man guilty if the act was unpremeditated, done unknowingly? In the course of his probing, old Oedipus has come to terms with

his guilt. He defends himself indignantly against the
brash accusations of Creon:

"If then came into the world—as I did come—
In wretchedness, and met my father in fight,
And knocked him down, not knowing that I killed him
Nor whom I killed—again, how could you find
Guilt in that unmeditated act? . . .

As for my mother—damn you, you have no shame,
Though you are her own brother,—

But neither of us knew the truth; and she
Bore my children also— . . .
While I would not have married her willingly
Nor willingly would I ever speak of it."

Again, about his father he cries out that he has

"A just extenuation.
                                This:
I did not know him; and he wished to murder me.
Before the law—before God—I am innocent!"

It is clear that Oedipus accepts and bears his responsibility; but he insists that the delicate and subtle interplay of conscious and unconscious factors (as we could
call them) always makes any legalistic or pharisaic imputation of guilt inaccurate and wrong. It is a truism since
Freud that the problem of guilt is as much within the
heart as within the act. The play holds that the sins of
meanness, of avarice, and the irreverence of Creon and
Polyneices are "no less grave than those sins of passion
for which Oedipus was punished; that in condemning
them to the merciless justice soon to descend, Oedipus
acts thoroughly in accord with a moral order which his
own experience has enabled him to understand."

In angry, vehement words, Oedipus refuses the tricky
proposal of the cruel Creon, the present dictator of Thebes,
who tries to get the exiled king to return by using
Antigone as hostage; and Oedipus refuses likewise the
entreaty of his son, Polyneices, though he knows the de-

struction of Thebes will result. Oedipus' maturity does
not at all include the virtue of forgiveness of enemies, a
later, Christian idea he would no doubt have scorned.
Nevertheless, the play does point toward a conclusion
emphasized by modern existential psychologists, that because of this interplay of conscious and unconscious
factors in guilt and the impossibility of legalistic blame,
we are forced into an attitude of acceptance of the universal human situation and a recognition of the participation
of every one of us in man's inhumanity to man. The words
to Oedipus from the hero, King Theseus, who exhibits
no inner conflict at all, are nevertheless poignant:

> ". . . for I
> Too was an exile. . . .
> I know I am only a man; I have no more
> To hope for in the end than you have."

Another theme in this integrative drama is the power
of Oedipus—now that he has suffered through his terrible
experiences and come to terms with them—*to impart
grace*. As he himself says to the natives who find him
with his daughter in the grove at Colonus,

> "For I come here as one endowed with grace,
> By those who are over Nature; and I bring
> Advantage to this race . . ."

Theseus accepts this: "Your presence, as you say, is a
great blessing." This capacity to impart grace, assumedly,
is connected with the maturity and other emotional and
spiritual qualities which result from the courageous confronting of his shattering experiences. Says Oedipus,

> "One soul, I think, often can make atonement
> For many others, if it be devoted. . . ."

But there is also a clear symbolic element to make the
point of his grace unmistakable: the oracle has revealed
that his body after death will ensure victory to the land

and the ruler which possess him. The mere "presence" of his body has this power.

A last emphasis we mention in the outworking of the myth is *love*. The messenger who came back to the people to report the marvelous manner of Oedipus' death states that in his last words to his daughters he said,

> ". . . And yet one word
> Frees us of all the weight and pain of life:
> That word is love."

But Oedipus does not at all mean love as the absence of aggression or the strong affects of anger. His sharp and violent temper, present at the crossroads where he killed his father years before and exhibited in his sharp thrusts with Tiresias, is still much in evidence in this last drama, unsubdued by suffering or maturity. The fact that Sophocles does not see fit to remove or soften Oedipus' aggression and his anger—the fact, that is, that the "aggression" and the "angry affects" are not the "flaws" he has old Oedipus get over—lends support to our thesis above that the aggression involved in killing the father is not the central issue of the dramas. Oedipus' maturity is not at all a renouncing of passion to come to terms with society, not at all a learning to live "in accord with the reality requirements of civilization." It is a reconciliation with himself, with special persons he loves, and the religious meaning of his life.

Love, thus, is not the opposite of anger or aggression. Old Oedipus will love only those he chooses to love: his son, who has betrayed him, asks for mercy and remarks, "Compassion limits even the power of God," but Oedipus will have none of it. The love, rather, he bears his daughters, Antigone and Ismene, and the love they have shown him during his exiled, blind wanderings is the kind of love he chooses to bless.

Robert Fitzgerald, translator, writes in his notes to the play, "It should be remembered that one of Oedipus' distinguishing qualities was, in the first place, his intelligence. He saved Thebes once by solving the riddle of the Sphinx. He saved the city again by solving with furious persistence the riddle of his own birth. And in this play we see once more the working of that intellect, driving this time toward a transcendence of the purely human." I think Fitzgerald is wrong here in calling this "intelligence," though obviously he is right in his general emphasis. This saving quality of Oedipus goes quite beyond intellectual functions; his solving the riddle of the Sphinx (the word "Sphinx" means "one who binds fast") is much more what we would call "in-sight" and sensitivity than it is the purely rational functions. I believe the term "self-consciousness," in the special way we have used it in this paper to refer to man's capacity for self-knowledge and self-transcendence (rather than in the strictly Cartesian sense of consciousness), is what Fitzgerald is referring to. It is, incidentally, an intriguing psychological implication in the dramas as a whole that *that particular man* who lives through his aggressive potentialities, who does not shrink from standing against his father and consummating the sexual drives in his assertive way, is just the man who solves the riddle and knows the answer, "man," and the one who, experiencing his tragic fate, goes on to be a bearer of grace and salvation for others.

Finally, describing Oedipus' miraculous death and burial, the messenger says,

> "But some attendant from the train of Heaven
> Came for him; or else the underworld
> Opened in love the unlit door of earth.
> For he was taken without lamentation,
> Illness or suffering; indeed his end
> Was wonderful if mortal's ever was."

This touching and beautiful death of a great character is magnificent as Sophocles presents it dramatically. As *Oedipus Tyrannus* is the drama of the "unconscious," the struggle to confront the reality of the dark, destructive forces in man, *Oedipus at Colonus* may be said to be the drama of consciousness, the aspect of the myth which is concerned with the search for meaning and reconciliation. Both together comprise the myth of man confronting his own reality, a confronting that is possible and inevitable by the unique structure of self-consciousness.

IX

Politics, Guilt, and Theory

A. Purification and Change

ROGER W. SMITH

The Political Meaning of Unconscious Guilt

Modern political science finds some degree of power everywhere, yet many people feel increasingly powerless; guilt is a universal experience, yet political science has almost entirely ignored it. I am not presently concerned with why guilt has been an excluded problem; even poverty, until a few years ago, was left to the economists.[1] Nor do I wish to raise in general terms the question of the relevance of guilt to politics. I will, instead, focus on one type of guilt, "unconscious guilt," inquiring into its political meaning. The term comes from Freud, yet the essential idea of unconscious guilt goes back to antiquity. In both cases, it is offered as an explanation of individual and

Reprinted with permission from the *Political Science Quarterly*, LXXXIII, (December 1968), pp. 505–15.

[1] Our tradition of political analysis, as Hannah Arendt has pointed out, tends "to exclude from articulate conceptualization a great variety of authentic political experiences, among which we need not be surprised to find some of an even elementary nature." *The Human Condition* (Garden City, N.Y., n.d.), p. 215.

collective behavior. If we are to believe Freud, this type of explanation is doubly important to us today, for the increasing sense of guilt in modern society is largely unconscious.[2] Unconscious guilt, however, is not really an explanation; it is, at bottom, a metaphor of reconstruction, a weapon of war in the struggle to shape political society.

It would seem reasonable to begin by asking how one recognizes an unconscious sense of guilt. As it turns out, one must begin with a different question: *who*, in fact, recognizes an unconscious sense of guilt? The citizen in modern society, laboring, according to Freud, under a heavy burden of unconscious guilt, does not recognize it; he only feels a "sort of uneasiness or discontent for which other motivations are sought."[3] The patient does not recognize this sense of guilt either. "As far as the patient is concerned this sense of guilt is dumb; it does not tell him he is guilty; he does not feel guilty, he feels ill."[4] Freud seems to suggest, however, that the "pale criminal" or "criminal from a sense of guilt," can, in fact, partially recognize his unconscious guilt.[5] This type of criminal, Freud tells us, does not feel guilty because he commits crimes; rather he commits crimes because he suffers from an oppressive pre-existing sense of guilt which he cannot account for. Like Joseph K. in Kafka's *Trial*, he feels condemned, but does not know what his offense is. In order to account for his sense of condemnation and gain relief from doubt he subsequently commits a crime, fastening "this unconscious sense of guilt on to something real and

[2] Freud, *Civilization and Its Discontents*, trans. Joan Riviere (London, 1930), Chap. 8.

[3] *Ibid.*, p. 124. Hereafter all citations of Freud's books refer to the *Standard Edition of the Complete Psychological Works of Sigmund Freud* (*SE*), ed. James Strachey (London, 1955–64); all citations of his essays refer to the *Collected Papers* (*CP*), ed. Ernest Jones (New York, 1959).

[4] *The Ego and the Id*, SE, XIX, pp. 49–50.

[5] "Some Character-Types Met With in Psycho-Analytic Work," *CP*, 4, pp. 342–44.

immediate."[6] Having earlier stressed the criminal's "pre-existing sense of guilt," Freud suddenly confesses that "the pre-existence of the guilty feeling had of course to be demonstrated by a whole succession of other manifestations and effects."[7] Citizen, patient, pale criminal—all are equally blind. Those who suffer from the malady of unconscious guilt are those least likely to know it. Only the analyst, in fact, can detect unconscious guilt; he thus becomes, in Freudian political theory, indispensable to society.

How does Freud decide that a person or society is suffering from an unconscious sense of guilt? He temporarily suspends the problem of feelings, turning instead to the problem of overt consequences. Freud believes that he then describes the consequences; what he does, of course, is interpret them. Indeed, one of the problems in relying on his case histories is that "what passes for description in the Freudian method is already judgment."[8] Nevertheless, the assumptions that form the backbone of his interpretation stand out clearly. He assumes that a person or society has an objective interest, even though they may not know what it is. If there are consequences which seem to Freud contrary to those interests, the consequences are interpreted as self-imposed punishment. What lies behind punishment, in the Freudian imagination, is some kind of guilt.[9] If the person or society inflicts punishment on itself without knowing why, then there must be an unconscious sense of guilt present. Freud now begins to use the terms "unconscious sense of guilt" and "need for punishment" as interchangeable concepts.[10] The problem, then,

6 *The Ego and the Id*, SE, XIX, p. 52.
7 "Some Character-Types . . . ," *CP*, 4, p. 342.
8 Philip Rieff, *Freud: The Mind of the Moralist* (Garden City, N.Y., 1961), p. 321.
9 We shall see that this is also the classical view.
10 See, for example, *Civilization and Its Discontents*, SE, XXI, p. 135, and "The Economic Problem in Masochism," *CP*, 2, p. 263.

is to find the precise basis for this self-destructive behavior. One engages, therefore, in a historical recollection
—psychoanalysis—in an effort to locate and make conscious
the sense of guilt which has previously been unrecognized. Thus, in the guise of recollecting guilt, the analyst
leads us into accepting guilt. Whether we are made to
accept a private guilt, such as hatred of the father, or a
public guilt, such as racial discrimination, in the eyes of
the analyst the result is an abatement of our self-destructive
behavior.[11] Innocence, defined as conformity with our
true interests, is subsequent to guilt made conscious.
The metaphor of reconstruction has surfaced.

The reconstructive nature of Freud's metaphor becomes clearer if we look at the opposite of unconscious
guilt, an unconscious sense of indignation (nemesis) or
need to punish. If, as Freud believes, society is becoming
increasingly repressive, if man is being harnessed more and
more to a societal yoke contrary to his deepest impulses,
then a basis is laid for man to turn on society in indignation. Viewed in this way, the "pale criminal" acts not from
a pre-existing sense of guilt, but from a pre-existing sense
of indignation; he commits crimes not in order to pro-
voke punishment, but in order to punish society for its
crimes against him. In this perspective, apathy, disrespect,
and violence all become means of social sabotage, aimed
at punishing society, perhaps ultimately at dissolving society altogether.[12] The destruction of society would, indeed, be only a form of judicial murder. The raw material for this perspective comes, of course, almost entirely

[11] This suggests that there are "public" analysts and "private"
analysts. Fromm is an example of the first, Freud of the second.
A systematic comparison of how the two types of analysts
use the concept of unconscious guilt needs to be made.

[12] The contemporary crisis of authority may be in part a
crisis of "inverted nemesis," that is, indignation directed not
at the demands, policies, and values of a particular society, but
against society itself.

from Freud.[13] Yet Freud will have none of it; like Locke, he is a conservative maker of revolutions. Freudian man, for all his apparent aggressiveness and unkind thoughts, seldom acts against authority; aggression always seems to be turned inward.[14] Nemesis appears to Freud, unlike Durkheim, as a metaphor for *dissolution;* to punish *others* is not a way of maintaining the standards of society, it is a way of gratifying our aggressive instincts under the guise of expiation.[15] Freud fears the "honest criminal lurking behind the pious neurotic."[16] Society must be changed, not destroyed.

In a late work, *Moses and Monotheism,* Freud adds a biological portico to the façade of recollected guilt.[17] The result is that the weakness of unconscious guilt as a social explanation becomes obvious; at the same time Freud's struggle to develop a convincing metaphor of reconstruction becomes more explicit. Freud assumes in this phase of his work that the sins of the fathers are unconsciously "known" to the children, and taken over as their own, "independently of direct communication and of the influence of education by the setting of an example."[18] In

[13] Freud expresses sorrow at the fact that man is inescapably a being who lives in society. Man can attain happiness only within society, Freud says, but still it "would perhaps be preferable" if the individual could avoid "integration in, or adaptation to, a human community." *Civilization and Its Discontents, SE,* XXI, p. 140. Although saddened by the human condition, the "reality principle" made him accept it. Ironically, however, Freud may have contributed to the emergence of what he would have rejected, inverted nemesis.

[14] *Ibid.,* Chap. 8.

[15] *Totem and Taboo, SE,* XIII, p. 72.

[16] Rieff, p. 353.

[17] *Moses and Monotheism* (1934–38), despite Freud's thesis that Moses was an Egyptian, is the most Hebraic work Freud ever wrote. His assumptions about punishment, the sins of the fathers, and the solidarity of the group, go back, however, to the earliest Hebrew traditions; he ignores Job, Isaiah, and the later development of Hebrew thought.

[18] *Moses and Monotheism, SE,* XXIII, p. 99. The problem of tradition, and consequently the relation between individual

effect, Southern children, who had never seen or heard of slavery, would still be unconsciously "aware" of the evils of slavery and would feel guilty about it; German children, born well after the Nazi period and kept in a total informational vacuum, would still know and feel guilty for the horrors of nazism. How can this be? Freud argues that memory is inherited genetically; children get guilty consciences the same way they get blue eyes or curly hair. For the "memory traces of the experiences of our ancestors"—especially the repressed guilt, which etches more deeply the more it is repressed—are transmitted to the descendants.[19] If we accept this assumption, Freud tells us, then "we have bridged the gulf between individual and group psychology: we can deal with peoples as we do with an individual neurotic."[20] We can then talk in social terms about the "return of the repressed"— that is, the appearance of symptoms which indicate a "need for punishment"—after a period of "latency"—the relative quiet following the repression of the original guilt.[21] Thus, any problem which society experienced could be explained as the result of an unconscious sense of guilt, due to the fathers having sinned even centuries earlier. The analyst would become a historian of guilt, seeking parallels between the past and the present, showing a people that it has fallen short of its real interests today because of what was done yesterday.

If, of course, we deny Freud's assumption that memory is inherited, we can no longer treat individual and social psychology as identical. Moreover, there would then seem to be no inherent reason why the children must feel guilt in the present for what their fathers did centuries

---

and social psychology, had bothered Freud for a long time. See, for example, *Group Psychology and the Analysis of the Ego* (1921) and the last pages of *Totem and Taboo* (1913).

[19] *Moses and Monotheism*, SE, XXIII, pp. 99–101.

[20] *Ibid.*, p. 100.

[21] *Ibid.*, pp. 66–92, 124–27.

ago. In short, if we reject Freud's major assumption, we see that unconscious guilt does not explain anything, that it is still a metaphor of reconstruction, the theorist's device for altering society.

In the hands of a skilled artist like Freud, the metaphor of unconscious guilt can take on a great deal of persuasive power. The appeal of the metaphor comes not only from art, however, but from its solid grounding on the psychological fact that most of us are, like Freud, "friends of Job"; in affliction we see punishment, behind punishment lies guilt. Psychoanalysis, Freud points out, merely confirms "the habitual pronouncement of the pious: we are all miserable sinners."[22] The political objections to the idea of unconscious guilt, however, seem to me to be even more compelling. Suffering and punishment, as Job well knew but Freud seems to forget, are not equivalent notions. Nor can one equate all forms of anxiety—the uneasiness of modern man, for example—with a sense of guilt. These, of course, are fallacies on the part of Freud, but they are more than that. They are part of the machinery necessary to carry out the central implication of Freud's political thought—the reconstruction of society by an elite. Felt discontent, anxiety, and suffering can be channeled into a sense of guilt, which can, in turn, be used to alter society.[23] If, however, one sets up a notion of objective interest, one can go beyond the pain men feel to the pain they do not know. A distinction between false consciousness and genuine consciousness becomes necessary and in effect creates the basis for the domination of society

[22] *Totem and Taboo, SE,* XIII, p. 72.
[23] The twin brother of this technique is utilized by Lenin. In order to make a revolution, he seeks to harness discontent and convert it into indignation against the political system. See *What Is to Be Done?* (New York, 1929), especially p. 75. The techniques of guilt and nemesis have long been familiar to theologians.

by an elite.[24] A "need for punishment" is present whenever the analyst chooses to find it; the "mysteries of state"
take on a psychoanalytic cast, a new royalty is born. It is
true, of course, that not all acts will be interpreted as punishment—though any given act could be.[25] This only means
that the elite can reconstruct society at will, molding it
to fit the pattern approved by the elite.

The citizen, who has now become a patient, can be expected, however, to offer resistance to the treatment of
his unconscious maladies. "Patients," Freud laments, "do
not easily believe what we tell them about an unconscious
sense of guilt."[26] Rather they hold fast "to the more obvious explanation that treatment by analysis is not the right
remedy. . . ."[27] Freud finally comes to the conclusion, in
Civilization and Its Discontents, that since society will
not see that it is sick, and would resist treatment in any
case, the only hope for society lies in its being coerced into
receiving therapy.[28] Elsewhere Freud notes that therapy
is, in essence, interminable.[29]

The terminology may be different, but classical Greek
thought expresses the idea of unconscious guilt even more
clearly than Freud does. By treating guilt as pollution,
and therefore objective, the Greeks avoid Freud's confusion between individual and social psychology; at the
same time they avoid Freud's conceptual difficulty which
emerges with the phrase, "unconscious feeling." The
formal pattern of the classical unconscious guilt and the

[24] The problem recurs in a vivid fashion in Marxism, but
the distinction between the two types of consciousness is implicit in any form of elitism.
[25] One of the "unconstitutional" features of the concept of
unconscious guilt is its lack of conceptual limits; methodologically it is a blank check.
[26] "The Economic Problem in Masochism," *CP,* 2, p. 263.
[27] *The Ego and the Id, SE,* XIX, p. 50.
[28] *Civilization and Its Discontents, SE,* XXI, p. 144.
[29] "Analysis Terminable and Interminable," (1937), *CP,* 5,
pp. 316–57.

Freudian unconscious sense of guilt are, however, almost identical. The analyst detects illness; he determines that the illness is due to a sense of guilt which the patient (individual or society) has hidden from itself; he announces the means of relief (further analysis); and then proceeds, through an elaborate process of discovery (prolonged analysis), to a precise determination of what has produced the sense of guilt. Making the sense of guilt conscious will not wholly solve the problem of illness, but it makes the problem (the political one) more amenable to solution. Compare with this the pattern found in *Oedipus Rex*.[30] Thebes is in the grip of plague; fields are barren, animals sterile, women suffer "barren agonies of birth," the city reeks with the smell of death. The chorus cries out, "From the fire and pain of pestilence save us and make us clean." They discover, with the help of Apollo (through the Delphi oracle), that the plague is due to the presence of a murderer in their midst. To gain relief from the plague they must find the murderer and drive him from their soil. Then begins the process of discovery. Who, precisely, is the polluted one? Oedipus announces that if the guilty person will give himself up, his only punishment will be banishment; otherwise, horrible curses and the brand of shame will be placed upon him, and he will suffer all his life.

Granted then that unconscious guilt follows the same formal pattern in classical thought that it does in Freud's thought, one may still ask whether the functions are the same. Did the Greeks, for example, utilize, as I have argued Freud implicitly did, the idea of unconscious guilt as a means of changing and restructuring society? I suggest that they did, that the crisis of pestilence was also an opportunity, an opportunity to topple rulers, banish one's political opponents, and change the form of regime. The process of purification was an integral part of classical politics.

[30] All quotations from *Oedipus Rex* come from *Sophocles: The Theban Plays*, trans. E. F. Watling (Baltimore, 1947).

The outcome of purification was by no means certain; no one could accurately predict where the blame for pollution would fall. It was to one's political advantage, therefore, to control the machinery for uncovering hidden guilt. Aristotle mentions a case in which a court, "selected from the nobility," passed a verdict which declared that a sacrilege had been committed: "thereupon, the bodies of the guilty were removed from the tombs, and their family was exiled. . . ."[31] In this way, Cleisthenes could be banished, not as a dangerous radical, but as a man stained by the pollution of his ancestors. Control of the initial verdict, however, was not enough. The city had to be purified through special rites known only to prophets and healers, men like Epimenides of Crete, who cleansed Athens of the sacrilege mentioned above.[32] Only through careful selection and coaxing could one avoid the danger that the prophet might discover a different source of pollution from that formally announced.

The classical use of unconscious guilt for political purposes can be confirmed, too, by way of a powerful exception, the tragedy of Oedipus. Oedipus is willing to accept the verdict of the blind prophet, Teiresias, until the prophet names him as the murderer. As a political man, Oedipus understands the selectivity that goes into uncovering the guilt which lies behind plague. He now suspects Creon of hand-picking the prophet in order to gain the throne. Teiresias, whom moments before Oedipus had praised lavishly, becomes a "pedlar of fraudulent magical tricks, with eyes wide open for profit, but blind in prophecy." Oedipus initially suspects, then, that his tragedy is a political one, that he is about to be toppled in the name of unconscious guilt. He then discovers that his

[31] Aristotle, *Constitution of Athens,* translated and edited by K. von Fritz and E. Kapp in *Constitution of Athens and Related Texts* (New York, 1950), 1, 1.

[32] Epimenides possesses a knowledge of the mysteries of purification; he is prophet and healer. The family resemblance with Freud is strong.

tragedy is personal rather than political, that he is indeed
polluted and no one else can take his place in banishment.
Oedipus had looked through political eyes to no avail;
he blinds himself in his anguish at the personal.

Given the political nature of unconscious guilt, an as-
signment of blame followed by banishment did not put
an end to the matter. It signaled, rather, the beginning of
the struggle for return to power and influence. The living
might be driven out, the bones of the dead taken up; still,
Thucydides notes, the "cursed ones" would try to return.
In one case a faction was driven out several times over
a number of years; "for all that," Thucydides reports,
"they came back afterwards, and their descendants are
still in the city."[33] In another case,[34] Aristotle reports that
one faction managed to overthrow the existing tyranny,
"for it could hardly be denied that it was the Alcmeonidae
who played the most important part in the overthrow of
the tyrants, since they almost incessantly made political
trouble for them." Yet no sooner had the tyranny been
overthrown than the leader of the Alcmeonidae, Cleisthenes, was attacked by the aristocrats for being "among
those who were under a curse." As a result, seven hundred
Athenian families—supporters of Cleisthenes—were expelled as accursed. Cleisthenes, nevertheless, managed to
become ruler by promising the common people a democratic regime. The curse was, in effect, politically neutralized. Some years later, however, Sparta, on the grounds
that it was concerned for the honor of the gods, ordered
Athens to expel the Alcmeonidae. But, as Thucydides tells
it,

they also knew that Pericles . . . was connected with the curse
on his mother's side, and they thought that his banishment
would materially advance their designs on Athens. Not that
they really hoped to succeed in procuring this; they rather

[33] Thucydides, *The Peloponnesian War*, trans. R. Crawley
(New York, 1951), Bk. I, 126–27.
[34] Aristotle, 20, 1–4.

thought to create a prejudice against him in the eyes of his countrymen from the feeling that the war [which Sparta was seeking a pretext for] would be partly caused by his misfortune.[35]

Unconscious guilt had become a weapon in international politics, a means of provoking war while weakening the opponent's ability to fight.

Unconscious guilt is not an explanation; it is a metaphor to induce political change. No two versions of this metaphor, though, will be identical; style, content, and purpose will vary. The marks of the theorist remain in Freud's version; the heavier hand of the politician is visible in the classical approach. Freud is potentially more radical than the Greeks: he can create disease at will; they must wait for nature to provide opportunity in the form of plague. Freud thinks he is dealing with sickness, not with politics. Classical thought also does not adequately distinguish politics from nature; the Greeks have discovered, however, that the gods can be appeased by expiating the sins of one's opponents. Freud sees the citizen as a patient who must be forced to accept his guilt; the Greeks are content to awaken nemesis against their opponents. As for the ends or purposes which lie behind the use of the metaphor, these will vary with the elite, faction, or theorist. The concrete implications of the notion are therefore open to specification in each case; the concept tends to take on the characteristics of its master. At bottom, however, the general implication of any concept of unconscious guilt is that politics is yoked to the notion of disease. What is a remedy for illness is at the same time a metaphor for the reconstruction of society. The diversity of political society is transformed,

[35] Thucydides, Bk. I, 126–28. The Athenians responded by ordering the Spartans to drive out those under a similar curse in Sparta.

consequently, into the polarity of the therapeutic community. Clothed in medicinal style, the "well" henceforth dab at the wounds of the "disabled."[36]

[36] There is, it seems to me, much truth in Philip Rieff's contention that, in the age of Freud, the "hospital is succeeding the church and the parliament as the archetypal institution of Western culture" (p. 390). Ironically, Freud's triumph in the public domain coincides with increasing professional criticism. The sons slay the father only to have him resurrected by society.

B. The Mark of Cain

DONALD CLARK HODGES

Fratricide and Fraternity

But Cain quarrelled with his brother Abel, and when they
were out in the open country, Cain attacked his brother Abel
and killed him. Then the Eternal asked Cain, "Where is your
brother Abel?" "How do I know?" said Cain; "am I a shepherd
to my brother?"[1]

The question "Am I my brother's keeper?" is a clue to the
psychological meaning of the gospel of fraternity. The
biblical view is not only that all men are brothers in the
abstract but that each man is a potential shepherd to his
neighbor. The Bible also suggests that all men are accomplices in fratricide, as the maltreatment of one's brother,
along with disobedience to the Father, are the two original sins of mankind. The two Christian commandments,
the sum of "the law and the prophets," exhort men to
love God and to love one's neighbor as one's self. Whatever the First Commandment means, the guilt of fratricide
received its strongest and clearest expression in the Second
Commandment. The story of Cain and Abel is a prototype
of all the biblical stories having to do with the strife of
brothers: the issue between Isaac and Ishmael, Jacob and

From *The Journal of Religion*, Vol. 38 (October 1958). Copyright 1958 by The University of Chicago. Reprinted by permission of the author and The University of Chicago Press.
[1] James Moffatt (trans.), *The Bible* (New York: Harper &
Bros., 1935), Gen. 4:8–9.

Esau, and Joseph and his brothers. Because of the Bible's preoccupation with the theme of fratricide, the meaning of its ethic of love should be understood as a reaction to the tendency of brothers to quarrel and to take advantage of one another.

Contrary to Freud, who interpreted the biblical ethic as an expression of deep-seated parricidal anxieties, there are grounds for believing that the gospel of neighborliness is primarily a reaction to the guilt of fratricide. In the following essay I try to show that an ethics of fraternity is a reaction to man's feelings of ambivalence toward his brothers and brother-substitutes. Within Freud's theory of the origin of moral valuations there are the germs of a fratricentric as well as a patricentric ethics and grounds for tracing the former to fratricidal instead of parricidal guilt. It is my intention to explore some of these insights in the hope of clarifying the relationship between fratricide and fraternity.

The Sources of Guilt

The two principal forms of morality were characterized by Bergson, in *The Two Sources of Morality and Religion,* as the "closed" and the "open." Bergson's genealogy of these two forms of moral valuation was based upon a purely psychological distinction between instinct and feeling.[2] Instinct gives rise to the customs of the group; feeling liberates man's capacity for individuality. That the "closed" and "open" moralities are useful classifications of moral valuations is amply supported by the history of moral doctrines but that these doctrines are generated in independence of a social context and from separate faculties of mind is seriously open to question. There is much more evidence for Freud's genealogy of moral values from a sense of guilt, the principal form of guilt being of a par-

[2] Bergson, *The Two Sources of Morality and Religion* (Garden City, N.Y.: Doubleday & Co., 1953), p. 39.

ricidal nature and inclining men to submission to the authority of the group. There is also another kind of guilt, that of fratricide, to which Freud attached some importance but failed to develop in detail; and there is evidence that it rather than Bergson's "feeling" is the ultimate ground of an "open" morality.

These two principal types of morality are more adequately characterized by their social relations of affection and subordination than by their degree of stability or emancipation from established forms. Although a "closed" morality is conservative, its conservatism is an effect rather than a cause of the subordination of the individual to the group. The term "community ethics" is a more apt designation of this type of morality. Although an "open" morality is a morality of rebellion, the latter is also an effect rather than a cause. Moral rebellion against the authority of the community is primarily a means of succoring the miserable and oppressed, so that the term "fraternity ethics" is a more adequate expression than "open" morality for this kind of ethics.

Parricidal guilt, according to Freud, lies at the origin of all community ethics, even the most primitive. The three fundamental taboos of primitive society are the prohibitions against eating the totem animal, incest, and fratricide. The first prohibition is a reflection of parricidal guilt, the totem animal being a symbolical substitute for the father of the primal horde. The second taboo is a reflection of parricidal guilt in preserving the command of the deified father not to touch the women of the horde, who belonged exclusively to the father. The third taboo is also a reflection of parricidal guilt to the extent that the primal father sought to maintain order among his sons. However, it also reflects, according to Freud, the practical need of the brothers to get along with one another. The third taboo was gradually transformed into the taboo against killing in general, from which emerged the even more general prohibition against taking advantage of our neighbor and the rational codes of ethics of more mature and civilized societies.

Freud argued that primitive or totemic morality is partly based upon the expiation which parricidal guilt demands and partly upon the necessities of living in society.[3] Whereas the sparing of the totem animal rested entirely upon emotional motives and repressed parricidal guilt, the prohibition against fratricide had primarily a practical and even a rational foundation. Once the father was removed, each of the brothers was in a position not only to take his place but to be reduced once again to servitude. In the fight of each against all, the brothers would have perished, which led Freud to conjecture that there was nothing left for the brothers, if they wanted to live together, but to erect the prohibition against fratricide. As a result, Freud offers us, in *Totem and Taboo* and *Moses and Monotheism*, not a single but a dual source of moral values. What he failed to do was to correlate the rational ethics, which emerged as a result of the taboo against fratricide, with fratricidal as well as parricidal guilt.

Freud failed to give an adequate account of man's sense of practical necessity, which he used to explain the emergence of "higher" rational values. There are different types of rationality which have their source in different kinds of emotional complexes. Freud made the mistake of assuming that man's social and moral reason gives rise to a single ethics common to all rational creatures. However, there are at least two types of rational ethics, each founded upon reason and practical necessity as well as a sense of guilt. They differ inasmuch as a community ethics can be traced to parricidal guilt; a fraternal ethics, to a different emotional complex. Although Freud made a distinction between the first two taboos of totemism, which correspond to the oedipal fantasies of the child, and the third taboo against fratricide, from which a different kind of

[3] Sigmund Freud, "Totem and Taboo," *The Basic Writings of Sigmund Freud*, trans. and ed. A. A. Brill (New York: Random House, 1938), p. 919.

moral code developed, he did not pursue it far enough. He assumed that violation of the taboo against fratricide engenders the same kind of guilt as violation of the taboos that are directly expressive of the oedipal wishes. It is true that a sense of guilt is a source of values in both cases; however, it is questionable whether it is the same kind of guilt.

Although Freud suggested the possibility that the brother-clan may have experienced internal difficulties, he failed to take seriously the possibility of a new kind of guilt engendered by fratricide more bloody and vindictive than the primal parricide. It is somewhat unlikely that social necessity, and the remorse consequent upon the primal crime, could alone have led the brothers to combine to outlaw fratricide. It is difficult to understand how social necessity could have prompted union, considering that the women could have been divided among the stronger of the brothers, who might then have gone their separate ways. Much more plausible is the hypothesis that the taboo aganst fratricide was primarily the result of a sense of guilt over and above that incurred for parricide. This would explain the tendency of a higher religion like Christianity to be expressive of the guilt of fratricide as well as parricide and to raise the murdered son to the dignity of a father-god.

As parricidal guilt is the result of ambivalent feelings toward the father and his substitutes, fratricidal guilt is the result of mixed feelings of love and hate toward the brother or neighbor. Feelings of love for the brother or neighbor, combined with envy of his lot, are not always so intolerable that either feeling has to be repressed. Respect for the brother or equal is seldom as intense as reverence for the superior power of the father and his political and economic substitutes. The guilt of fratricide is not so deeply rooted in the personality as that of parricide. The greater burden of parricidal guilt is explained by the greater dependence upon the father and by the lesser opportunity to express successfully resentment against him. Because there is less reason to fear a brother and more opportunity to resent him, fratricidal guilt is more likely to be conscious than parricidal guilt.

Yet it is a mistake to reduce the guilt of fratricide to an expression of parricidal guilt. Although the guilt of fratricide is, to a large extent, the product of violating paternal authority or the authority of a father-substitute, the son has ambivalent affections not only for the father but for the brothers as well. The ambivalent attitude of brothers is the result of their identification as "victims" of paternal oppression and their rivalry for the authority and privileges of the father. The sense of guilt, according to Freud, is ultimately traceable to feelings of ambivalence, but there is a different kind of guilt depending upon whether ambivalence is felt toward the father or the brothers. Although man's first guilt can be traced to feelings of ambivalence toward the father, the second major source of guilt feelings arises in relation to one's brothers or neighbors.

A major distinction between a community ethics and an ethics of fraternity is their respective attitudes toward authority. As a result of repressed feelings of hostility toward the father, the individual is conscious only of a deep-seated loyalty to and reverence for authority, manifesting itself in a system of moral values which subordinates the value of the individual to the superior power of the father or his political and economic substitutes. The guilt of parricide is the most powerful source of social regimentation and cohesion. A community ethics is the guardian of the civilized values of peace and order and of the principle of the general welfare against the tyranny of special interests. Yet it is also the most subtle and refined form of patriarchal authority, as the community is represented by a ruling class which enjoys special privileges. These are euphemistically termed "inducements" to superior service to the community, although they are acquired by an authority analogous to that which a father enjoys over his sons.

In sharp contrast, repressed hostility toward the brother generates the wish to be a good neighbor, to cease taking advantage of the weak, and to come to the aid of the unfortunate. There results an ethic which subordinates the value of the community to the role of an instrument in the service of individual needs. The guilt of fratricide is the primary source of rebellion against the authority of the community and the interests of a social elite, which justifies its privileges by its services to the community. As a result of fratricidal guilt, anxiety is experienced not in violation of authority but in serving it in order to advance one's own interests. A fraternal ethics, far from representing the authority which a father exercises over his sons, represents the absence of authority and the relationship of equality which the sons enjoy among themselves.

Instead of a uniform sense of guilt as the source of moral values, Freud has given us, implicitly if not explicitly, two sources of morality which serve as the basis for two different systems of moral valuation. Besides a patricentric or "master" morality, to use Nietzsche's expression, there is a fratricentric morality of brotherliness and two different kinds of guilt corresponding to the violations of each. Those forms of authority which, to a large extent, have effected a reconciliation of the moral claims of fathers and sons, as, for example, liberalism, socialism, and democracy, are the expressions not so much of a different kind of moral code as a compromise of the two original species of moral valuation.

Oedipus and Polyneices

It is somewhat surprising that in his perusal of Greek tragedy Freud did not light upon what, for the lack of a better name, might be called the Polyneices complex. Polyneices, the elder of Oedipus' two sons, combined with his brother Eteocles to banish the blind Oedipus from Thebes. Afterward, rivalry between the brothers for the throne culminated in Eteocles gaining the support of the citizens and ousting Polyneices. Resentful and jealous of the privileges of his younger brother, Polyneices raised seven armies to march against Thebes. The struggle between father and sons, which led to the displacement of the father by the sons, culminated in a death struggle between the brothers for the privileges which had formerly been the exclusive prerogative of the father. Each of the sons sought to usurp the authority of the father, and neither was content with less than the father's share. The result was a struggle between the brothers that was a hundred times more bloody than the feud between the older and younger generations. By the Polyneices complex is to be understood, then, the wish for the death of the brother combined with the wish to take the place of the father.

The Polyneices complex is the heir of the Oedipus complex and a natural development out of it. Oedipus himself expresses the unconscious wish to depose the father in order to become the father. His son Polyneices, having deposed Oedipus with the help of his brother, finds in the latter a rival for the throne. The wish to take the place of the father, which is at the root of parricide, is also the motivation to fratricide. Whereas in the Oedipus situation it is necessary to kill the father in order to become like him, in the Polyneices situation it is necessary to kill the brother in order to achieve the same result. In a sense, the struggle between the generations, as the child matures, is displaced by the strife of brothers, which in highly organized societies takes the form of a struggle between social classes. As the aim of both complexes is the same, Freud tended to confuse fratricidal with parricidal guilt. However, as these guilt feelings are directed toward different classes of human beings, namely, superiors and peers, it is a mistake to ignore this fundamental difference.

According to Freud, it is the taboo against fratricide which contains within itself the seeds of rationality and constitutes the basis of a community ethics. The prohibition against killing in general was interpreted by him as a maxim of the general welfare. On the other hand, a fraternal ethics was regarded as an irrational expression of excessive and depressed hostility toward the father. The only rational ethic, according to Freud, is a community ethics, which emerges as a result of man's faculty of reason and the passing of the oedipal complex. Freud believed that with growth to maturity man's powers of rational thinking tend to displace his dread of external authority and an irrationally motivated superego. However, he failed to perceive the authoritarian character of a community ethics and its expression of unresolved parricidal guilt. Instead of regarding the taboo against fratricide as an expression of fratricidal guilt, he interpreted it as a result of emancipation from purely parricidal guilt. The primitive taboo against fratricide is susceptible of a dual interpretation. As an expression of parricidal guilt it may be regarded as the original source of community ethics; but as an expression of fratricidal guilt it is the source of a different kind of ethics, which is no less rational than the former.

Freud acknowledged the historic significance of the oedipal complex by tracing the origin of moral codes to a "sort of . . . social contract," outlawing fratricide together with incest and the killing of the totem animal.[4] But he did not attach the same significance to the emotional complex of Oedipus' two sons. In his analyses of great works of literature he focused almost entirely upon the parricidal theme. Yet *Hamlet,* like the Oedipus sequence, can be read psychoanalytically in a way which neither Freud nor Ernest Jones considered.[5] Hamlet's first shock is not the thought of incest between mother and uncle but the usurpation of the throne by fratricide—the horror of brother against brother. The ghost is more to Hamlet than a father; what the ghost reveals is fratricide, which is what is rotten

[4] Freud, *Moses and Monotheism,* trans. Katherine Jones (New York: Vintage Books, Inc., 1955), p. 104.
[5] Philip Rieff, "The Meaning of History and Religion in Freud's Thought," *Journal of Religion,* XXXI, No. 2 (April, 1951), p. 128.

in the state of Denmark. Besides the images of the parricidal theme in the regicide characters of the drama, there are the images of the fratricide theme—the sons of Oedipus, Joseph and his brothers, Cain and Abel, Arthur and his knights, the Trojan peers, the *Niebelungen*—which are equally significant to an analysis of the primitive sense of guilt.[6]

The Biblical Treatment of Fratricide

The unconscious guilt experiences of higher cultures are only partly the product of parricidal anxieties. They are nurtured by the existence of exploitative classes and national rivalries, which destroy the sense of brotherhood and make the longing for a brother and for comradeship one of the unconscious longings of civilized man. As the guilt of fratricide, when universalized, becomes the guilt of social status, a sense of social injustice tends to become the principal factor in man's consciousness of guilt.[7] The Bible bears a strange and eloquent testimony to this fact. Although there is an apparent rationalization of a primal parricide in the Old Testament, its recurrent theme is the hatred, jealousy, and deception of brothers.

The struggle between Cain and Abel reflects the conflict between pastoral nomads and sedentary agriculturists, which is the key to much of the history of the ancient Middle East. The Old Testament narratives are attempts to appease guilt experiences having their origin in the strife of brothers. Noah's curse upon Canaan, like God's curse upon Cain, may be interpreted as an unconscious effort at self-justification by the Hebrews, confronted with the intense guilt which must have weighed upon them as they exterminated the Canaanite tribes. The guilt of the He-

[6] *Ibid.*, p. 127.
[7] For a more thorough account of the guilt of fratricide and its relation to social status see Lewis Feuer, *Psychoanalysis and Ethics* (Springfield, Ill.: Charles C Thomas, 1955), Part II, chaps. 3–4, pp. 78–86.

brews is projected upon the divine will, by means of which they are freed from the responsibility for the inequality of peoples. The issue between Isaac and Ishmael, Jacob and Esau, and Joseph and his brothers illustrates the importance of the strife of brothers and helps to explain inequalities among the Hebrew tribes themselves. As in the case of Job and his friends, guilt is imputed to those who are disfavored by fortune. Each generation reiterates not only the struggle between fathers and sons but the even more pernicious strife of brothers. The biblical evidence, besides confirming Freud's thesis of the primal origins of guilt, suggests the view that fratricide is also a primary generative component of the social sense of sin.

The importance of fratricide for an understanding of the biblical view was first clearly emphasized by St. Augustine. Not only was the founder of the earthly city a fratricide, but this archetype of crime repeated itself in the foundation of Rome, the city which was destined to be the head of the earthly city.[8] The murder of Abel by Cain prefigured the slaying of Remus by Romulus. The principal difference is that the struggle between Cain and Abel illustrates the hatred between brothers belonging to different cities, that of God and that of men, whereas the quarrel between Romulus and Remus shows how the earthly city is divided against itself.[9] The city of man is characterized by the rivalry of brothers, each seeking to gain the lion's share for himself, while uniting in common enmity against the city of God. Cain's slaying of Abel was also a prototype of the Jews' slaying of Christ—the shepherd of men prefigured by Abel, the shepherd of sheep.[10] The record of history, according to St. Augustine, consists of a series of crimes, motivated by the desire for earthly glory and requiring transgression against the brother.

[8] St. Augustine, *The City of God*, trans. Marcus Dods (New York: Random House, 1950), Book xv, chap. 5.

[9] *Ibid.*

[10] *Ibid.*, chap. vii.

Judaism and Christianity, according to Freud, are proof of the correlation between an intensified sense of guilt and a highly developed ethical system. He correctly assumed that the burden of guilt and original sin, from which Christianity sought to release men, had a social origin. However, he was mistaken in overrating the importance of parricide, as compared with fratricide, in the origination of such guilt. The perception which dawned with St. Paul was not "It is because we killed God the Father that we are so unhappy" but rather "It is because we killed his Son, our brother." That the Son became a God may be explained by ambivalent feelings toward him: love and gratitude for the fraternal equality which he represented and reverence for the symbols of paternal authority which he opposed. It was only by Christ's expiating the crime of Cain against Abel, Joseph's brothers against Joseph, Ishmael against Jacob, and, generally speaking, man against his neighbor that man's sense of guilt could be appeased, so that the crime that is expiated by blood is not murder of the father, Adam, but of the symbolical brother, Abel.

The fact that the Hebrews outshone other peoples in their defense of the oppressed is correlated with their hostility to earthly images of the father and to existing father substitutes, which led them to uphold tyrannicide as righteous. Fratricide is a major crime in the biblical view because it seeks to restore despotic and paternal rule. The monotheistic God of the Bible expresses the "longing for a father" who has no earthly representative. Disillusioned with earthly kingdoms and national rivalries, the Hebrew "longing for the father" could best find expression in the worship of such a God. Considering the fear of freedom, and the ideology of passive suffering characteristic of oppressed groups everywhere, the explanation of Hebrew defiance of social and political domination is that the Hebrews were not merely an oppressed class but an oppressed people. As a nation they maintained their love of independence and hatred for authority throughout successive periods of captivity. Their preoccupation with fratricide is explained by their heritage of the traditions of the brother-clan and their experience of oppression at the same time.

It is a mistake to conceive of the biblical sense of guilt as primarily parricidal, for it expresses an unconscious load of guilt that is also fratricidal. The guilt of fratricide is immeasureably strengthened and raised to the level of parricidal guilt, inasmuch as Father and Son are one, and fraternity is a major commandment of both. The obligation to love one's neighbor as one's self is, in the New Testament, contingent upon a love of God: the neighbor should be loved not only as one's self but after the example of God's love for men. Feelings of hostility toward the brother are symbolical of hostility toward the Father, while mistreatment of the neighbor is a form of ingratitude toward God. Although the concept of "original guilt" refers not to the slaying of Abel by Cain but to Adam's rebellion against the "Lord" and "Sire" of creation, these two kinds of guilt fused with the identification of the Father and the Son of man. The figure of the human Christ evokes feelings of fratricidal rather than parricidal guilt; however, by his identity with the Father he is also a symbol of reconciliation with the latter. In the Christian view fratricidal and parricidal guilt merge in the belief that the Son is no less important a figure than the Father, that they are essentially one, and that a crime against one is a crime against the other.

The Sense of Fraternity

The effect of fratricidal guilt is to inhibit aggressive tendencies toward one's neighbors and comparative equals, so that it is the source of an ethic of brotherly love. Considering the images of the fratricidal theme which crowd the pages of the Old Testament, the primal question of such an ethic is not "Am I my father's son?"

but "Am I my brother's keeper?"[11] The taboo against killing a brother is the primitive source, according to Freud,
of the commandment against killing one's enemies. In its
most spiritualized form it is the formula of the golden
rule. Yet the guilt of fratricide is less a source of social
cohesion than of rebellion against social authority. It is a
gospel not of peace but of war against tyranny and injustice in whatever form. As communities are founded
upon force and are designed to make special privilege possible, according to Freud, with the possible exception of
totemic society all societies are opposed in practice to
brotherly love. Although feelings of brotherly love are
necessary as a social cement, the practice of fraternity
would lead to the dissolution of the class system and the
abolition of man's inhumanity to man.

Unlike a "closed" morality, which would subordinate
the individual to the group, an "open" morality is a morality of rebellion against social pressure and domination.[12]
An "open" morality is fratricentric in orientation in stress-
ing the dignity and equal value of each and every individual. Its principle is not the greatest happiness altogether but equal regard for each. "What should we do,"
asks Bergson, "if we heard that for the common good, for
the very existence of mankind, there was somewhere a
man, an innocent man, condemned to suffer eternal torment?"[13] We would not be treating him as a brother if
we were to continue living at his expense. The brother
upholds the rights and dignity of all his brothers, without
bias or favoritism toward any. An ethic of fraternity is
incompatible with the involuntary sacrifice of individuals
for the sake of the community. Whereas the values of a
community ethics are the disguised imperatives of the
class system, the sense of fraternity is incompatible with
unfairness toward one's fellow men.

11 Rieff, *op. cit.*, p. 128.
12 Cf. Bergson, *op. cit.*, pp. 75–76.
13 *Ibid.*

A fratricentric-oriented morality is diametrically opposed to the ethics of social organization. In place of adult loyalty to the community and its welfare, it upholds the dignity of the individual or the "flesh-and-blood" member of the community. The adult expression of infantile submission to and adoration of the father is sociolatry—reverence for the industrial and political system which degrades the individual to a cog in a machine. Sociolatry gives the illusion of brotherliness without its spirit: the brother esteems others as persons, not as representatives of a particular group; the brother will not forsake his neighbor in need, whereas the citizen will. Sociolatry is the form that patriarchy assumes in a period in which the general literacy of the people and universal education have enabled a majority to participate in the organs of domination and administration in the state. Such participation, however, is inconsistent with an ethic of brotherly love. As the function of all social organization, given men's predatory tendencies, is to use authority as an instrument of class oppression, the sharing of political power is seldom if ever a means to human brotherhood.

The imperatives of community ethics are the imperatives of a class system. However disguised, they imply scorn of inferiors, which exaggerates the sense of guilt and weighs grimly upon members of the upper classes.[14] This explains why movements of social reform proceed, as a rule, from members of the ruling classes rather than from below. Liberal social movements have been fed by a need to assuage the guilt of social status. An ethic of brotherly love helps to alleviate man's burden of fratricidal guilt by attempting to remove the principal sources of oppression. Based upon guilt feelings toward one's fellow beings, it seeks to compensate for the injustices of a community ethics, which sacrifices the individual for the sake of the whole but benefits primarily the ruling classes.[15]

[14] Feuer, *op. cit.*
[15] *Ibid.*

A fratricentric-oriented morality presupposes a revolution in morals that is reminiscent of Nietzsche's "Jewish inversion of values." In most respects similar to Nietzsche's conception of "slave morality," it differs from the latter in sanctioning tyrannicide and rebellion against injustice, insofar as they lie within the power of unfortunate and oppressed groups. Whoever would be a brother to his neighbor but is forced to earn his livelihood in menial employment is obliged to resent the privileges which he cannot share. The postponement of vengeance to the hereafter is justified only under circumstances in which justice cannot be effectively realized on earth. Whereas the Old Testament seeks after an earthly justice, the New Testament leaves to God the judgment of men—an expression of man's longing for justice in this life but inability to achieve it by his own agency.

The Sermon on the Mount is a model of defeatism and a sufficient justification for Nietzsche's epithet of "slave morality." The meaning of voluntary poverty is in part a defensive reaction against tax-gatherers and economic drudgery. Excessive taxation and economic exploitation, when they cannot be abolished by open rebellion, are best combated by an ethic which gives no thought for the morrow and exhorts to vagrancy instead of toil. "Look at the wild birds; they sow not, they reap not, they gather nothing in granaries, and yet your heavenly Father feeds them. Are you not worth more than birds?"[16] The exhortation to become a suffering servant, to help your enemies instead of cursing them, and to suffer without resisting evil are expressions of a fratricentric morality in a situation of despair; just as the exhortation to return evil for evil, "an eye for an eye, a tooth for a tooth," are expressions of the same ethic under conditions of hope. The New Testament, like the Old, is an expression of underlying resentment against a social system which sacrifices the neighbor to the general welfare. It is noteworthy that

16 Moffatt (trans.), op. cit., Matt. 6:26.

Christ was condemned by the high priests and Pharisees in the interests of the Jewish community. Caiaphas, who was high priest that year, said, "You do not understand it is in your own interests that one man should die for the People, instead of the whole nation being destroyed."[17]

A fratricentric morality encourages love of tyrants, oppressors, and exploiters only when they cannot be effectively hated. Even the New Testament is full of repressed hatred in consigning the rich and powerful to perdition and in obliging them to wear an economic hair shirt and to experience guilt for whatever privileges they may enjoy at the expense of the less fortunate. Whereas the "younger brothers" have no recourse but to submit to authority as a means of sharing in the common good, the "older brothers" must voluntarily surrender all unjust prerogatives if they are to be forgiven by the Father. Schopenhauer fittingly explains this masochism of the privileged classes by the exceptionally heavy burden of fratricidal guilt, which their more sensitive members are bound to suffer.[18] Although a rarity, there are persons of considerable income who deny themselves even the most elementary pleasures and comforts in order to distribute their money to those who need it the most. Such persons seek to compensate for their special privileges by trying to strike a balance between their own condition and the less fortunate situation of others. A sense of guilt may lead them to take as much interest in the lives of others as their own, to doubt their right to inherited property, to question the higher salary which their professional experience and education commands, and to feel every service from others and every luxury a reproach.[19] Unlike a community ethics, which serves to maintain such privileges, an ethics

[17] *Ibid.*, John 11:50.
[18] Schopenhauer, "The World as Will and Idea," *Schopenhauer Selections* (New York: Charles Scribner's Sons, 1941), Book III, p. 265.
[19] *Ibid.*, p. 264.

of brotherly love obliges a ruling class to surrender them and to adopt the habits of asceticism.

Such an ethic is impracticable not because it would lead to universal poverty but because it goes counter to the inclinations of men. The biblical ethic obliges the rich to sell all they have and give to the poor; yet it also acknowledges that "You have always the poor beside you."[20] Fratricidal guilt, according to Freud, tends to be deficient for two reasons: it is usually too weak to restrain men from the crime of fratricide or from taking advantage of the weak and it is seldom strong enough to arouse men to rebellion against tyranny and injustice. Because men do not have the same reverence for their equals as for their superiors in knowledge and power, they are less capable of repressing their aggressiveness against their neighbors. They are also more likely to succeed in dominating a brother than in displacing the father and his political or economic substitutes. The oppression of the weak and unfortunate does not arouse the same indignation and moral loathing as disloyalty or sedition in violation of social and political authority. As reverence for the brother is generally weak by comparison with that felt for the father and the symbols of paternal authority, there is less motivation for resisting the exploitation of brother by brother. Although the latter culminates in the regime of class oppression and the rule of colonial by imperial peoples, it is easier to feel indifference toward one's equals and inferiors than to surrender unjust privileges obtained at their expense.

The average citizen wants to exercise authority yet loathes the idea of taking advantage of his brothers. The typical "bourgeois" desires to attain financial security and to practice charity toward his neighbor—goals which are incompatible and generative of a sense of guilt. The experience of fratricidal guilt is usually resolved by sublimating his sense of compassion for others. Since he does

[20] Moffatt (trans.), *op. cit.*, John 12:8.

not really deny himself but gives only from his surplus, he tends to deny the existence of a conflict between self and other love. He assuages his sense of guilt by giving to charity what others give, a percentage of his income which is conventionally regarded as sufficient to the fulfilment of his duty as a citizen. Most men "follow the leader" instead of the rebel in their manner of resolving fratricidal guilt. Torn between love of neighbor and envy of his lot, the typical "bourgeois" seeks constantly to improve his own standard of living rather than to succor the needy.

It is only the more obvious substitutes for fratricide that are punishable by law, so that the social system is insufficient to restrain men from injustice toward their neighbors. Lacking an external punitive agency, the only other measure of protection is the intensification of man's sense of fratricidal guilt. What restrains the sons from repeating the excesses of the father is not their load of parricidal guilt, which is diminished by their assumption of the parent role, but the spiritualization of the taboo against fratricide and its internalization in the superego. If crimes against the brother were legally punished by the civil authorities, there would be less reason to intensify man's sense of fratricidal guilt. Under existing circumstances, however, his burden of fratricidal guilt is in defect of the injustices which he either tolerates in others or perpetrates himself. The laws of society are the expression of a community ethics, so that crimes against the neighbor can be restrained only by an appeal to some other authority. As the masses of men are moved less by reason than by religion, the biblical ethic of fraternity is one of man's principal defenses against the injustices of a social system which tolerates unneighborliness for the sake of the general welfare.

X

Radical Evil

HANNAH ARENDT

Total Domination

The concentration and extermination camps of totalitarian
regimes serve as the laboratories in which the fundamental
belief of totalitarianism that everything is possible is being
verified. Compared with this, all other experiments are
secondary in importance—including those in the field of
medicine whose horrors are recorded in detail in the trials
against the physicians of the Third Reich—although it is
characteristic that these laboratories were used for experiments of every kind.

Total domination, which strives to organize the infinite
plurality and differentiation of human beings as if all of
humanity were just one individual, is possible only if each
and every person can be reduced to a never-changing
identity of reactions, so that each of these bundles of reactions can be exchanged at random for any other. The
problem is to fabricate something that does not exist,
namely, a kind of human species resembling other animal
species whose only "freedom" would consist in "preserving

the species."[1] Totalitarian domination attempts to achieve this goal both through ideological indoctrination of the elite formations and through absolute terror in the camps; and the atrocities for which the elite formations are ruthlessly used become, as it were, the practical application of the ideological indoctrination—the testing ground in which the latter must prove itself—while the appalling spectacle of the camps themselves is supposed to furnish the "theoretical" verification of the ideology.

The camps are meant not only to exterminate people and degrade human beings, but also serve the ghastly experiment of eliminating, under scientifically controlled conditions, spontaneity itself as an expression of human behavior and of transforming the human personality into a mere thing, into something that even animals are not; for Pavlov's dog, which, as we know, was trained to eat not when it was hungry but when a bell rang, was a perverted animal.

Under normal circumstances this can never be accomplished, because spontaneity can never be entirely eliminated insofar as it is connected not only with human freedom but with life itself, in the sense of simply keeping alive. It is only in the concentration camps that such an experiment is at all possible, and therefore they are not only *"la société la plus totalitaire encore réalisée"* (David Rousset) but the guiding social ideal of total domination in general. Just as the stability of the totalitarian regime depends on the isolation of the fictitious world of the movement from the outside world, so the experiment of total domination in the concentration camps depends on sealing off the latter against the world of all others, the world of the living in general, even against the outside world of a country under totalitarian rule. This isolation explains

[1] In the *Tischgespräche* (Bonn, 1951), Hitler mentions several times that he "[strives] for a condition in which each individual knows that he lives and dies for the preservation of his species" (p. 349). See also p. 347: "A fly lays millions of eggs, all of which perish. But the flies remain."

the peculiar unreality and lack of credibility that characterize all reports from the concentration camps and constitute one of the main difficulties for the true understanding
of totalitarian domination, which stands or falls with the
existence of these concentration and extermination camps;
for, unlikely as it may sound, these camps are the true
central institution of totalitarian organizational power.

There are numerous reports by survivors.[2] The more
authentic they are, the less they attempt to communicate
things that evade human understanding and human experience—sufferings, that is, that transform men into "un-
complaining animals."[3] None of these reports inspires
those passions of outrage and sympathy through which
men have always been mobilized for justice. On the contrary, anyone speaking or writing about concentration
camps is still regarded as suspect; and if the speaker has
resolutely returned to the world of the living, he himself
is often assailed by doubts with regard to his own truth-
fulness, as though he had mistaken a nightmare for
reality.[4]

[2] The best reports on Nazi concentration camps are David
Rousset, *Les Jours de Notre Mort,* Paris, 1947; Eugen Kogon,
Der SS-Staat, Munich, 1946; Bruno Bettelheim, "On Dachau
and Buchenwald" (from May 1938 to April 1939), in *Nazi
Conspiracy* (Washington, 1946), VII, 824 ff. For Soviet con-
centration camps, see the excellent collection of reports by
Polish survivors published under the title *The Dark Side of the
Moon* (New York, 1947); also David J. Dallin and Boris I.
Nicolaevsky, *Forced Labor in Russia* (New Haven, 1947),
though their reports are sometimes less convincing because
they come from "prominent" personalities who are intent on
drawing up manifestos and indictments.

[3] *The Dark Side of the Moon;* the introduction also stresses
this peculiar lack of communication: "They record but do not
communicate."

[4] See especially Bruno Bettelheim, *op. cit.* "It seemed as if I
had become convinced that these horrible and degrading experiences somehow did not happen to 'me' as subject but to 'me'
as an object. This experience was corroborated by the statements of other prisoners. . . . It was as if I watched things happening in which I only vaguely participated. . . . 'This cannot

This doubt of people concerning themselves and the reality of their own experience only reveals what the Nazis have always known: that men determined to commit crimes will find it expedient to organize them on the vastest, most improbable scale. Not only because this renders all punishments provided by the legal system inadequate and absurd; but because the very immensity of the crimes guarantees that the murderers who proclaim their innocence with all manner of lies will be more readily believed than the victims who tell the truth. The Nazis did not even consider it necessary to keep this discovery to themselves. Hitler circulated millions of copies of his book in which he stated that to be successful, a lie must be enormous—which did not prevent people from believing him as, similarly, the Nazis' proclamations, repeated *ad nauseam*, that the Jews would be exterminated like bedbugs (*i.e.*, with poison gas), prevented anybody from *not* believing them.

There is a great temptation to explain away the intrinsically incredible by means of liberal rationalizations. In each one of us, there lurks such a liberal, wheedling us with the voice of common sense. The road to totalitarian domination leads through many intermediate stages for which we can find numerous analogies and precedents. The extraordinarily bloody terror during the initial stage of totalitarian rule serves indeed the exclusive purpose of defeating the opponent and rendering all fur-

---

be true, such things just do not happen.' . . . The prisoners had to convince themselves that this was real, was really happening and not just a nightmare. They were never wholly successful."

See also Rousset, *op. cit.*, p. 213. ". . . Those who haven't seen it with their own eyes can't believe it. Did you yourself, before you came here, take the rumors about the gas chambers seriously?

"No, I said.

". . . You see? Well, they're all like you. The lot of them in Paris, London, New York, even at Birkenau, right outside the crematoriums . . . still incredulous, five minutes before they were sent down into the cellar of the crematorium. . . ."

ther opposition impossible; but total terror is launched only
after this initial stage has been overcome and the regime
no longer has anything to fear from the opposition. In this
context it has been frequently remarked that in such a
case the means have become the end, but this is after all
only an admission, in paradoxical disguise, that the category "the end justifies the means" no longer applies, that
terror has lost its "purpose," that it is no longer the means
to frighten people. Nor does the explanation suffice that
the revolution, as in the case of the French Revolution, was
devouring its own children, for the terror continues even
after everybody who might be described as a child of the
revolution in one capacity or another—the Russian factions,
the power centers of party, the army, the bureaucracy—
has long since been devoured. Many things that nowadays
have become the specialty of totalitarian government are
only too well known from the study of history. There have
almost always been wars of aggression; the massacre of
hostile populations after a victory went unchecked until
the Romans mitigated it by introducing the *parcere sub-
jectis;* through centuries the extermination of native peoples went hand in hand with the colonization of the Amer-
icas, Australia and Africa; slavery is one of the oldest
institutions of mankind and all empires of antiquity were
based on the labor of state-owned slaves who erected their
public buildings. Not even concentration camps are an invention of totalitarian movements. They emerge for the
first time during the Boer War, at the beginning of the
century, and continue to be used in South Africa as well
as India for "undesirable elements"; here, too, we first find
the term "protective custody" which was later adopted
by the Third Reich. These camps correspond in many respects to the concentration camps at the beginning of
totalitarian rule; they were used for "suspects" whose offenses could not be proved and who could not be sentenced by ordinary process of law. All this clearly points
to totalitarian methods of domination; all these are ele-

ments they utilize, develop and crystallize on the basis of
the nihilistic principle that "everything is permitted,"
which they inherited and already take for granted. But
wherever these new forms of domination assume their au-
thentically totalitarian structure they transcend this principle, which is still tied to the utilitarian motives and self-
interest of the rulers, and try their hand in a realm that
up to now has been completely unknown to us: the realm
where "everything is possible." And, characteristically
enough, this is precisely the realm that cannot be limited
by either utilitarian motives or self-interest, regardless of
the latter's content.

What runs counter to common sense is not the nihilistic
principle that "everything is permitted," which was already contained in the nineteenth-century utilitarian conception of common sense. What common sense and
"normal people" refuse to believe is that everything is
possible.[5] We attempt to understand elements in present
or recollected experience that simply surpass our powers
of understanding. We attempt to classify as criminal a
thing which, as we all feel, no such category was ever
intended to cover. What meaning has the concept of murder when we are confronted with the mass production of
corpses? We attempt to understand the behavior of
concentration-camp inmates and SS-men psychologically,
when the very thing that must be realized is that the
psyche *can* be destroyed even without the destruction of
the physical man; that, indeed, psyche, character, and
individuality seem under certain circumstances to express
themselves only through the rapidity or slowness with
which they disintegrate.[6] The end result in any case is
inanimate men, *i.e.*, men who can no longer be psychologically understood, whose return to the psychologically
or otherwise intelligibly human world closely resembles
the resurrection of Lazarus. All statements of common

[5] The first to understand this was Rousset in his *Univers
Concentrationnaire,* Paris, 1946.
[6] Rousset, *op. cit.,* p. 587.

sense, whether of a psychological or sociological nature, serve only to encourage those who think it "superficial" to "dwell on horrors."[7]

If it is true that the concentration camps are the most consequential institution of totalitarian rule, "dwelling on horrors" would seem to be indispensable for the understanding of totalitarianism. But recollection can no more do this than can the uncommunicative eyewitness report. In both these genres there is an inherent tendency to run away from the experience; instinctively or rationally, both types of writer are so much aware of the terrible abyss that separates the world of the living from that of the living dead, that they cannot supply anything more than a series of remembered occurrences that must seem just as incredible to those who relate them as to their audience. Only the fearful imagination of those who have been aroused by such reports but have not actually been smitten in their own flesh, of those who are consequently free from the bestial, desperate terror which, when confronted by real, present horror, inexorably paralyzes everything that is not mere reaction, can afford to keep thinking about horrors. Such thoughts are useful only for the perception of political contexts and the mobilization of political passions. A change of personality of any sort whatever can no more be induced by thinking about horrors than by the real experience of horror. The reduction of a man to a bundle of reactions separates him as radically as mental disease from everything within him that is personality or character. When, like Lazarus, he rises from the dead, he finds his personality or character unchanged, just as he had left it.

Just as the horror, or the dwelling on it, cannot affect a change of character in him, cannot make men better or worse, thus it cannot become the basis of a political community or party in a narrower sense. The attempts to build up a European elite with a program of intra-European

[7] See Georges Bataille in *Critique*, January, 1948, p. 72.

understanding based on the common European experience
of the concentration camps have foundered in much the
same manner as the attempts following the first World
War to draw political conclusions from the international
experience of the front generation. In both cases it turned
out that the experiences themselves can communicate no
more than nihilistic banalities.[8] Political consequences
such as postwar pacifism, for example, derived from the
general fear of war, not from the experiences in war. Instead of producing a pacifism devoid of reality, the insight into the structure of modern wars, guided and mobilized by fear, might have led to the realization that the
only standard for a necessary war is the fight against conditions under which people no longer wish to live—and
our experiences with the tormenting hell of the totalitarian
camps have enlightened us only too well about the possibility of such conditions.[9] Thus the fear of concentration
camps and the resulting insight into the nature of total
domination might serve to invalidate all obsolete political
differentiations from right to left and to introduce beside
and above them the politically most important yardstick
for judging events in our time, namely: whether they serve
totalitarian domination or not.

In any event, the fearful imagination has the great advantage to dissolve the sophistic-dialectical interpretations
of politics which are all based on the superstition that
something good might result from evil. Such dialectical
acrobatics had at least a semblance of justification so long
as the worst that man could inflict upon man was murder.
But, as we know today, murder is only a limited evil. The

[8] Rousset's book contains many such "insights" into human
"nature," based chiefly on the observation that after a while the
mentality of the inmates is scarcely distinguishable from that
of the camp guards.

[9] In order to avoid misunderstandings it may be appropriate
to add that with the invention of the hydrogen bomb the whole
war question has undergone another decisive change. A discussion of this question is of course beyond the theme of this
book.

murderer who kills a man—a man who has to die anyway —still moves within the realm of life and death familiar to us; both have indeed a necessary connection on which the dialectic is founded, even if it is not always conscious of it. The murderer leaves a corpse behind and does not pretend that his victim has never existed; if he wipes out any traces, they are those of his own identity, and not the memory and grief of the persons who loved his victim; he destroys a life, but he does not destroy the fact of existence itself.

The Nazis, with the precision peculiar to them, used to register their operations in the concentration camps under the heading "under cover of the night (*Nacht und Nebel*)." The radicalism of measures to treat people as if they had never existed and to make them disappear in the literal sense of the word is frequently not apparent at first glance, because both the German and the Russian system are not uniform but consist of a series of categories in which people are treated very differently. In the case of Germany, these different categories used to exist in the same camp, but without coming into contact with each other; frequently, the isolation between the categories was even stricter than the isolation from the outside world. Thus, out of racial considerations, Scandinavian nationals during the war were quite differently treated by the Germans than the members of other peoples, although the former were outspoken enemies of the Nazis. The latter in turn were divided into those whose "extermination" was immediately on the agenda, as in the case of the Jews, or could be expected in the predictable future, as in the case of the Poles, Russians and Ukrainians, and into those who were not yet covered by instructions about such an over-all "final solution," as in the case of the French and Belgians. In Russia, on the other hand, we must distinguish three more or less independent systems. First, there are the authentic forced-labor groups that live in relative freedom and are sentenced for limited periods. Secondly, there are the concentration camps in which the human material is

ruthlessly exploited and the mortality rate is extremely
high, but which are essentially organized for labor purposes. And, thirdly, there are the annihilation camps in
which the inmates are systematically wiped out through
starvation and neglect.

The real horror of the concentration and extermination
camps lies in the fact that the inmates, even if they happen to keep alive, are more effectively cut off from the
world of the living than if they had died, because terror
enforces oblivion. Here, murder is as impersonal as the
squashing of a gnat. Someone may die as the result of
systematic torture or starvation, or because the camp is
overcrowded and superfluous human material must be
liquidated. Conversely, it may happen that due to a shortage of new human shipments the danger arises that the
camps become depopulated and that the order is now
given to reduce the death rate at any price.[10] David Rousset called his report on the period in a German concentration camp *"Les Jours de Notre Mort,"* and it is indeed
as if there were a possibility to give permanence to the
process of dying itself and to enforce a condition in which
both death and life are obstructed equally effectively.

It is the appearance of some radical evil, previously unknown to us, that puts an end to the notion of developments and transformations of qualities. Here, there are

---

[10] This happened in Germany toward the end of 1942, where-
upon Himmler served notice to all camp commandants "to
reduce the death rate at all costs." For it had turned out that
of the 136,000 new arrivals, 70,000 were already dead on
reaching the camp or died immediately thereafter. See *Nazi
Conspiracy*, IV, Annex II.—Later reports from Soviet Russian
camps unanimously confirm that after 1949—that is, when Stalin
was still alive—the death rate in the concentration camps,
which previously had reached up to 60 per cent of the inmates,
was systematically lowered, presumably due to a general and
acute labor shortage in the Soviet Union. This improvement
in living conditions should not be confused with the crisis of
the regime after Stalin's death which, characteristically enough,
first made itself felt in the concentration camps. Cf. Wilhelm
Starlinger, *Grenzen der Sowjetmacht*, Würzburg, 1955.

neither political nor historical nor simply moral standards but, at the most, the realization that something seems to be involved in modern politics that actually should never be involved in politics as we used to understand it, namely all or nothing—all, and that is an undetermined infinity of forms of human living-together, or nothing, for a victory of the concentration-camp system would mean the same inexorable doom for human beings as the use of the hydrogen bomb would mean the doom of the human race.

There are no parallels to the life in the concentration camps. Its horror can never be fully embraced by the imagination for the very reason that it stands outside of life and death. It can never be fully reported for the very reason that the survivor returns to the world of the living, which makes it impossible for him to believe fully in his own past experiences. It is as though he had a story to tell of another planet, for the status of the inmates in the world of the living, where nobody is supposed to know if they are alive or dead, is such that it is as though they had never been born. Therefore all parallels create confusion and distract attention from what is essential. Forced labor in prisons and penal colonies, banishment, slavery, all seem for a moment to offer helpful comparisons, but on closer examination lead nowhere.

Forced labor as a punishment is limited as to time and intensity. The convict retains his rights over his body; he is not absolutely tortured and he is not absolutely dominated. Banishment banishes only from one part of the world to another part of the world, also inhabited by human beings; it does not exclude from the human world altogether. Throughout history slavery has been an institution within a social order; slaves were not, like concentration-camp inmates, withdrawn from the sight and hence the protection of their fellow-men; as instruments of labor they had a definite price and as property a definite value. The concentration-camp inmate has no price, because he can always be replaced; nobody knows to whom he belongs, because he is never seen. From the point of view of normal society he is absolutely superfluous, although in times of acute labor shortage, as in Russia and in Germany during the war, he is used for work.

The concentration camp as an institution was not established for the sake of any possible labor yield; the only permanent economic function of the camps has been the financing of their own supervisory apparatus; thus from the economic point of view the concentration camps exist mostly for their own sake. Any work that has been performed could have been done much better and more cheaply under different conditions.[11] Especially Russia, whose concentration camps are mostly described as forced-labor camps because Soviet bureaucracy has chosen to dignify them with this name, reveals most clearly that forced labor is not the primary issue; forced labor is the normal condition of all Russian workers, who have no freedom of movement and can be arbitrarily drafted for work to any place at any time. The incredibility of the horrors is closely bound up with their economic uselessness. The Nazis carried this uselessness to the point of open anti-utility when in the midst of the war, despite the shortage of building material and rolling stock, they set up

[11] See Kogon, *op. cit.*, p. 58: "A large part of the work exacted in the concentration camps was useless, either it was superfluous or it was so miserably planned that it had to be done over two or three times." Also Bettelheim, *op. cit.*, pp. 831–32: "New prisoners particularly were forced to perform nonsensical tasks. . . . They felt debased . . . and preferred even harder work when it produced something useful. . . ." Even Dallin, who has built his whole book on the thesis that the purpose of Russian camps is to provide cheap labor, is forced to admit the inefficiency of camp labor, *op. cit.*, p. 105. —The current theories about the Russian camp system as an economic measure for providing a cheap labor supply would stand clearly refuted if recent reports on mass amnesties and the abolition of concentration camps should prove to be true. For if the camps had served an important economic purpose, the regime certainly could not have afforded their rapid liquidation without grave consequences for the whole economic system.

enormous, costly extermination factories and transported
millions of people back and forth.[12] In the eyes of a
strictly utilitarian world the obvious contradiction between
these acts and military expediency gave the whole enterprise an air of mad unreality.

This atmosphere of madness and unreality, created by
an apparent lack of purpose, is the real iron curtain which
hides all forms of concentration camps from the eyes of the
world. Seen from outside, they and the things that happen
in them can be described only in images drawn from a life
after death, that is, a life removed from earthly purposes.
Concentration camps can very aptly be divided into three
types corresponding to three basic Western conceptions
of a life after death: Hades, Purgatory, and Hell. To Hades
correspond those relatively mild forms, once popular even
in nontotalitarian countries, for getting undesirable elements of all sorts—refugees, stateless persons, the asocial
and the unemployed—out of the way; as DP camps, which
are nothing other than camps for persons who have become superfluous and bothersome, they have survived the
war. Purgatory is represented by the Soviet Union's labor
camps, where neglect is combined with chaotic forced
labor. Hell in the most literal sense was embodied by
those types of camp perfected by the Nazis, in which the
whole of life was thoroughly and systematically organized
with a view to the greatest possible torment.

All three types have one thing in common: the human
masses sealed off in them are treated as if they no longer
existed, as if what happened to them were no longer of

[12] Apart from the millions of people whom the Nazis transported to the extermination camps, they constantly attempted
new colonization plans—transported Germans from Germany
or the occupied territories to the East for colonization purposes. This was of course a serious handicap for military actions and economic exploitation. For the numerous discussions
on these subjects and the constant conflict between the Nazi
civilian hierarchy in the Eastern occupied territories and the
SS hierarchy see especially Vol. XXIX of *Trial of the Major
War Criminals,* Nuremberg, 1947.

any interest to anybody, as if they were already dead and some evil spirit gone mad were amusing himself by stopping them for a while between life and death before admitting them to eternal peace.

It is not so much the barbed wire as the skillfully manufactured unreality of those whom it fences in that provokes such enormous cruelties and ultimately makes extermination look like a perfectly normal measure. Everything that was done in the camps is known to us from the world of perverse, malignant fantasies. The difficult thing to understand is that, like such fantasies, these gruesome crimes took place in a phantom world, which, however, has materialized, as it were, into a world which is complete with all sensual data of reality but lacks that structure of consequence and responsibility without which reality remains for us a mass of incomprehensible data. The result is that a place has been established where men can be tortured and slaughtered, and yet neither the tormentors nor the tormented, and least of all the outsider, can be aware that what is happening is anything more than a cruel game or an absurd dream.[13]

The films which the Allies circulated in Germany and elsewhere after the war showed clearly that this atmosphere of insanity and unreality is not dispelled by pure reportage. To the unprejudiced observer these pictures are just about as convincing as snapshots of mysterious substances taken at spiritualist séances.[14] Common sense re-

---

[13] Bettelheim, *op. cit.*, notes that the guards in the camps embraced an attitude toward the atmosphere of unreality similar to that of the prisoners themselves.

[14] It is of some importance to realize that all pictures of concentration camps are misleading insofar as they show the camps in their last stages, at the moment the Allied troops marched in. There were no death camps in Germany proper, and at that point all extermination equipment had already been dismantled. On the other hand, what provoked the outrage of the Allies most and what gives the films their special horror —namely, the sight of the human skeletons—was not at all typical for the German concentration camps; extermination was

acted to the horrors of Buchenwald and Auschwitz with the plausible argument: "What crime must these people have committed that such things were done to them!"; or, in Germany and Austria, in the midst of starvation, over-population, and general hatred: "Too bad that they've stopped gassing the Jews"; and everywhere with the skep-tical shrug that greets ineffectual propaganda.

If the propaganda of truth fails to convince the average person because it is too monstrous, it is positively dan-gerous to those who know from their own imaginings what they themselves are capable of doing and who are therefore perfectly willing to believe in the reality of what they have seen. Suddenly it becomes evident that things which for thousands of years the human imagination had banished to a realm beyond human competence can be manufactured right here on earth, that Hell and Purgatory, and even a shadow of their perpetual duration, can be established by the most modern methods of destruction and therapy. To these people (and they are more nu-merous in any large city than we like to admit) the to-talitarian hell proves only that the power of man is greater than they ever dared to think, and that man can realize hellish fantasies without making the sky fall or the earth open.

These analogies, repeated in many reports from the world of the dying,[15] seem to express more than a des-perate attempt at saying what is outside the realm of hu-man speech. Nothing perhaps distinguishes modern masses as radically from those of previous centuries as the loss of faith in a Last Judgment: the worst have lost their fear

---

handled systematically by gas, not by starvation. The condition of the camps was a result of the war events during the final months: Himmler had ordered the evacuation of all extermina-tion camps in the East, the German camps were consequently vastly overcrowded, and he was no longer in a position to assure the food supply in Germany.

[15] That life in a concentration camp was simply a dragged-out process of dying is stressed by Rousset, *op. cit., passim.*

and the best have lost their hope. Unable as yet to live without fear and hope, these masses are attracted by every effort which seems to promise a man-made fabrication of the Paradise they had longed for and of the Hell they had feared. Just as the popularized features of Marx's classless society have a queer resemblance to the Messianic Age, so the reality of concentration camps resembles nothing so much as medieval pictures of Hell.

The one thing that cannot be reproduced is what made the traditional conceptions of Hell tolerable to man: the Last Judgment, the idea of an absolute standard of justice combined with the infinite possibility of grace. For in the human estimation there is no crime and no sin commensurable with the everlasting torments of Hell. Hence the discomfiture of common sense, which asks: What crime must these people have committed in order to suffer so inhumanly? Hence also the absolute innocence of the victims: no man ever deserved this. Hence finally the grotesque haphazardness with which concentration-camp victims were chosen in the perfected terror state: such "punishment" can, with equal justice and injustice, be inflicted on anyone.

In comparison with the insane end-result—concentration-camp society—the process by which men are prepared for this end, and the methods by which individuals are adapted to these conditions, are transparent and logical. The insane mass manufacture of corpses is preceded by the historically and politically intelligible preparation of living corpses. The impetus and what is more important, the silent consent to such unprecedented conditions are the products of those events which in a period of political disintegration suddenly and unexpectedly made hundreds of thousands of human beings homeless, stateless, outlawed and unwanted, while millions of human beings were made economically superfluous and socially burdensome by unemployment. This in turn could only happen because the Rights of Man, which had never been philosophically

established but merely formulated, which had never been
politically secured but merely proclaimed, have, in their
traditional form, lost all validity.

The first essential step on the road to total domination is
to kill the juridical person in man. This was done, on the
one hand, by putting certain categories of people outside
the protection of the law and forcing at the same time,
through the instrument of denationalization, the nontotalitarian world into recognition of lawlessness; it was done,
on the other, by placing the concentration camp outside
the normal penal system, and by selecting its inmates outside the normal judicial procedure in which a definite
crime entails a predictable penalty. Thus criminals, who
for other reasons are an essential element in concentration-
camp society, are ordinarily sent to a camp only on completion of their prison sentence. Under all circumstances
totalitarian domination sees to it that the categories gath-
ered in the camps—Jews, carriers of diseases, representatives of dying classes—have already lost their capacity for
both normal or criminal action. Propagandistically this
means that the "protective custody" is handled as a "preventive police measure,"[16] that is, a measure that deprives
people of the ability to act. Deviations from this rule in
Russia must be attributed to the catastrophic shortage of
prisons and to a desire, so far unrealized, to transform the
whole penal system into a system of concentration
camps.[17]

The inclusion of criminals is necessary in order to make
plausible the propagandistic claim of the movement that
the institution exists for asocial elements.[18] Criminals do

[16] Theodor Maunz, *Gestalt und Recht der Polizei*, Hamburg,
1943, p. 50, insists that criminals should never be sent to the
camps for the time of their regular sentences.

[17] The shortage of prison space in Russia has been such that
in the year 1925–26, only 36 per cent of all court sentences
could be carried out. See Dallin, *op. cit.*, p. 158 ff.

[18] "Gestapo and SS have always attached great importance
to mixing the categories of inmates in the camps. In no camp

not properly belong in the concentration camps, if only because it is harder to kill the juridical person in a man who is guilty of some crime than in a totally innocent person. If they constitute a permanent category among the inmates, it is a concession of the totalitarian state to the prejudices of society, which can in this way most readily be accustomed to the existence of the camps. In order, on the other hand, to keep the camp system itself intact, it is essential as long as there is a penal system in the country that criminals should be sent to the camps only on completion of their sentence, that is when they are actually entitled to their freedom. Under no circumstances must the concentration camp become a calculable punishment for definite offenses.

The amalgamation of criminals with all other categories has moreover the advantage of making it shockingly evident to all other arrivals that they have landed on the lowest level of society. It soon turns out, to be sure, that they have every reason to envy the lowest thief and murderer; but meanwhile the lowest level is a good beginning. Moreover it is an effective means of camouflage: this happens only to criminals and nothing worse is happening than what deservedly happens to criminals.

The criminals everywhere constitute the aristocracy of the camps. (In Germany, during the war, they were replaced in the leadership by the Communists, because not even a minimum of rational work could be performed under the chaotic conditions created by a criminal administration. This was merely a temporary transformation

---

have the inmates belonged exclusively to one category" (Kogon, *op. cit.*, p. 19).

In Russia, it has also been customary from the beginning to mix political prisoners and criminals. During the first ten years of Soviet power, the Left political groups enjoyed certain privileges; only with the full development of the totalitarian character of the regime "after the end of the twenties, the politicals were even officially treated as inferior to the common criminals" (Dallin, *op. cit.*, p. 177 ff.).

of concentration camps into forced-labor camps, a thoroughly atypical phenomenon of limited duration.)[19]
What places the criminals in the leadership is not so much the affinity between supervisory personnel and criminal elements—in the Soviet Union apparently the supervisors are not, like the SS, a special elite trained to commit crimes[20]—as the fact that only criminals have been sent to the camp in connection with some definite activity. They at least know why they are in a concentration camp and therefore have kept a remnant of their juridical person. For the politicals this is only subjectively true; their actions, insofar as they were actions and not mere opinions or someone else's vague suspicions, or accidental membership in a politically disapproved group, are as a rule not covered by the normal legal system of the country and not juridically defined.[21]

To the amalgam of politicals and criminals with which concentration camps in Russia and Germany started out, was added at an early date a third element which was soon to constitute the majority of all concentration-camp inmates. This largest group has consisted ever since of people who had done nothing whatsoever that, either in their own consciousness or the consciousness of their tormentors,

[19] Rousset's book suffers from his overestimation of the influence of the German Communists, who dominated the internal administration of Buchenwald during the war.
[20] See for instance the testimony of Mrs. Buber-Neumann (former wife of the German Communist Heinz Neumann), who survived Soviet and German concentration camps: "The Russians never . . . evinced the sadistic streak of the Nazis. . . . Our Russian guards were decent men and not sadists, but they faithfully fulfilled the requirements of the inhuman system" (*Under Two Dictators*, New York, 1951).
[21] Bruno Bettelheim, "Behavior in Extreme Situations," in *Journal of Abnormal and Social Psychology*, Vol. XXXVIII, No. 4, 1943, describes the self-esteem of the criminals and the political prisoners as compared with those who have not done anything. The latter "were least able to withstand the initial shock," the first to disintegrate. Bettelheim blames this on their middle-class origin.

had any rational connection with their arrest. In Germany, after 1938, this element was represented by masses of Jews, in Russia by any groups which, for any reason having nothing to do with their actions, had incurred the disfavor of the authorities. These groups, innocent in every sense, are the most suitable for thorough experimentation in disfranchisement and destruction of the juridical person, and therefore they are both qualitatively and quantitatively the most essential category of the camp population. This principle was most fully realized in the gas chambers which, if only because of their enormous capacity, could not be intended for individual cases but only for people in general. In this connection, the following dialogue sums up the situation of the individual: "For what purpose, may I ask, do the gas chambers exist?"— "For what purpose were you born?"[22] It is this third group of the totally innocent who in every case fare the worst in the camps. Criminals and politicals are assimilated to this category; thus deprived of the protective distinction that comes of their having done something, they are utterly exposed to the arbitrary. The ultimate goal, partly achieved in the Soviet Union and clearly indicated in the last phases of Nazi terror, is to have the whole camp population composed of this category of innocent people.

Contrasting with the complete haphazardness with which the inmates are selected are the categories, meaningless in themselves but useful from the standpoint of organization, into which they are usually divided on their arrival. In the German camps there were criminals, politicals, asocial elements, religious offenders, and Jews, all distinguished by insignia. When the French set up concentration camps after the Spanish Civil War, they immediately introduced the typical totalitarian amalgam of politicals with criminals and the innocent (in this case the stateless), and despite their inexperience proved remarkably inventive in creating meaningless categories of in-

[22] Rousset, *op. cit.*, p. 71.

mates.[23] Originally devised in order to prevent any growth of solidarity among the inmates, this technique proved particularly valuable because no one could know whether his own category was better or worse than someone else's. In Germany this eternally shifting though pedantically organized edifice was given an appearance of solidity by the fact that under any and all circumstances the Jews were the lowest category. The gruesome and grotesque part of it was that the inmates identified themselves with these categories, as though they represented a last authentic remnant of their juridical person. Even if we disregard all other circumstances, it is no wonder that a Communist of 1933 should have come out of the camps more Communistic than he went in, a Jew more Jewish, and, in France, the wife of a Foreign Legionary more convinced of the value of the Foreign Legion; it would seem as though these categories promised some last shred of predictable treatment, as though they embodied some last and hence most fundamental juridical identity.

While the classification of inmates by categories is only a tactical, organizational measure, the arbitrary selection of victims indicates the essential principle of the institution. If the concentration camps had been dependent on the existence of political adversaries, they would scarcely have survived the first years of the totalitarian regimes. One only has to take a look at the number of inmates at Buchenwald in the years after 1936 in order to understand how absolutely necessary the element of the innocent was for the continued existence of the camps. "The camps would have died out if in making its arrests the Gestapo had considered only the principle of opposition,"[24] and toward the end of 1937 Buchenwald, with less than 1,000 inmates, was close to dying out until the November pogroms brought more than 20,000 new ar-

[23] For conditions in French concentration camps, see Arthur Koestler, *Scum of the Earth*, New York, 1941.

[24] Kogon, *op. cit.*, p. 6.

rivals.[25] In Germany, this element of the innocent was furnished in vast numbers by the Jews after 1938; in Russia, it consisted of random groups of the population which for some reason entirely unconnected with their actions had fallen into disgrace.[26] But if in Germany the really totalitarian type of concentration camp with its enormous majority of completely "innocent" inmates was not established until 1938, in Russia it goes back to the early thirties, since up to 1930 the majority of the concentration-camp population still consisted of criminals, counterrevolutionaries and "politicals" (meaning, in this case, members of deviationist factions). Since then there have been so many innocent people in the camps that it is difficult to classify them—persons who had some sort of contact with a foreign country, Russians of Polish origin (particularly in the years 1936 to 1938), peasants whose villages for some economic reason were liquidated, deported nationalities, demobilized soldiers of the Red Army who happened to belong to regiments that stayed too long abroad as occupation forces or had become prisoners of war in Germany, etc. But the existence of a political opposition is for a concentration-camp system only a pretext, and the purpose of the system is not achieved even when, under the most monstrous terror, the population becomes more or less voluntarily co-ordinated, *i.e.*, relinquishes its political rights. The aim of an arbitrary system is to destroy the civil rights of the whole population, who ultimately become just as outlawed in their own country as the stateless and homeless. The destruction of a man's rights, the killing of the juridical person in him, is a prerequisite for dominating him entirely. And this applies not only to spe-

[25] See *Nazi Conspiracy*, IV, 800 ff.

[26] F. Beck and W. Godin, *Russian Purge and the Extraction of Confession*, New York, 1951, state explicitly that "opponents constituted only a relatively small proportion of the [Russian] prison population" (p. 87), and that there was no connection whatever between "a man's imprisonment and any offense" (p. 95).

cial categories such as criminals, political opponents, Jews, homosexuals, on whom the early experiments were made, but to every inhabitant of a totalitarian state. Free consent is as much an obstacle to total domination as free opposition.[27] The arbitrary arrest which chooses among innocent people destroys the validity of free consent, just as torture—as distinguished from death—destroys the possibility of opposition.

Any, even the most tyrannical, restriction of this arbitrary persecution to certain opinions of a religious or political nature, to certain modes of intellectual or erotic social behavior, to certain freshly invented "crimes," would render the camps superfluous, because in the long run no attitude and no opinion can withstand the threat of so much horror; and above all it would make for a new system of justice, which, given any stability at all, could not fail to produce a new juridical person in man, that would elude the totalitarian domination. The so-called "Volksnutzen" of the Nazis, constantly fluctuating (because what is useful today can be injurious tomorrow) and the eternally shifting party line of the Soviet Union which, being retroactive, almost daily makes new groups of people available for the concentration camps, are the only guaranty for the continued existence of the concentration camps, and hence for the continued total disfranchisement of man.

The next decisive step in the preparation of living

[27] Bruno Bettelheim, "On Dachau and Buchenwald," when discussing the fact that most prisoners "made their peace with the values of the Gestapo," emphasizes that "this was not the result of propaganda . . . the Gestapo insisted that it would prevent them from expressing their feelings anyway" (pp. 834–35).

Himmler explicitly prohibited propaganda of any kind in the camps. "Education consists of discipline, never of any kind of instruction on an ideological basis." "On Organization and Obligation of the SS and the Police," in *National-politischer Lehrgang der Wehrmacht,* 1937. Quoted from *Nazi Conspiracy,* IV, 616 ff.

corpses is the murder of the moral person in man. This is
done in the main by making martyrdom, for the first time in
history, impossible: "How many people here still believe
that a protest has even historic importance? This skepti-
cism is the real masterpiece of the SS. Their great accomplishment. They have corrupted all human solidarity. Here
the night has fallen on the future. When no witnesses are
left, there can be no testimony. To demonstrate when
death can no longer be postponed is an attempt to give
death a meaning, to act beyond one's own death. In order
to be successful, a gesture must have social meaning. There
are hundreds of thousands of us here, all living in absolute
solitude. That is why we are subdued no matter what
happens."[28]

The camps and the murder of political adversaries are
only part of organized oblivion that not only embraces
carriers of public opinion such as the spoken and the
written word, but extends even to the families and friends
of the victim. Grief and remembrance are forbidden. In
the Soviet Union a woman will sue for divorce immediately after her husband's arrest in order to save the lives of
her children; if her husband chances to come back, she will
indignantly turn him out of the house.[29] The Western
world has hitherto, even in its darkest periods, granted the
slain enemy the right to be remembered as a self-evident
acknowledgment of the fact that we are all men (and *only*
men). It is only because even Achilles set out for Hector's
funeral, only because the most despotic governments
honored the slain enemy, only because the Romans allowed
the Christians to write their martyrologies, only because
the Church kept its heretics alive in the memory of men,
that all was not lost and never could be lost. The concentration camps, by making death itself anonymous
(making it impossible to find out whether a prisoner is

[28] Rousset, *op. cit.*, p. 464.
[29] See the report of Sergei Malakhov in Dallin, *op. cit.*,
pp. 20 ff.

dead or alive) robbed death of its meaning as the end of a fulfilled life. In a sense they took away the individual's own death, proving that henceforth nothing belonged to him and he belonged to no one. His death merely set a seal on the fact that he had never really existed.

This attack on the moral person might still have been opposed by man's conscience which tells him that it is better to die a victim than to live as a bureaucrat of murder. Totalitarian terror achieved its most terrible triumph when it succeeded in cutting the moral person off from the individualist escape and in making the decisions of conscience absolutely questionable and equivocal. When a man is faced with the alternative of betraying and thus murdering his friends or of sending his wife and children, for whom he is in every sense responsible, to their death; when even suicide would mean the immediate murder of his own family—how is he to decide? The alternative is no longer between good and evil, but between murder and murder. Who could solve the moral dilemma of the Greek mother, who was allowed by the Nazis to choose which of her three children should be killed?[30]

Through the creation of conditions under which conscience ceases to be adequate and to do good becomes utterly impossible, the consciously organized complicity of all men in the crimes of totalitarian regimes is extended to the victims and thus made really total. The SS implicated concentration-camp inmates—criminals, politicals, Jews— in their crimes by making them responsible for a large part of the administration, thus confronting them with the hopeless dilemma whether to send their friends to their death, or to help murder other men who happened to be strangers, and forcing them, in any event, to behave like murderers.[31] The point is not only that hatred is diverted from those who are guilty (the *capos* were more hated than

[30] See Albert Camus in *Twice A Year*, 1947.
[31] Rousset's book, *op. cit.*, consists largely of discussions of this dilemma by prisoners.

the SS), but that the distinguishing line between perse-
cutor and persecuted, between the murderer and his
victim, is constantly blurred.[32]

Once the moral person has been killed, the one thing
that still prevents men from being made into living corpses
is the differentiation of the individual, his unique identity. In a sterile form such individuality can be preserved
through a persistent stoicism, and it is certain that many
men under totalitarian rule have taken and are each day
still taking refuge in this absolute isolation of a personality without rights or conscience. There is no doubt that this
part of the human person, precisely because it depends so
essentially on nature and on forces that cannot be controlled by the will, is the hardest to destroy (and when
destroyed is most easily repaired).[33]

The methods of dealing with this uniqueness of the
human person are numerous and we shall not attempt to
list them. They begin with the monstrous conditions in the
transports to the camps, when hundreds of human beings
are packed into a cattle-car stark naked, glued to each
other, and shunted back and forth over the countryside for
days on end; they continue upon arrival at the camp, the
well-organized shock of the first hours, the shaving of the
head, the grotesque camp clothing; and they end in
the utterly unimaginable tortures so gauged as not to kill
the body, at any event not quickly. The aim of all these
methods, in any case, is to manipulate the human body—
with its infinite possibilities of suffering—in such a way as

[32] Bettelheim, *op. cit.*, describes the process by which the
guards as well as the prisoners became "conditioned" to the
life in the camp and were afraid of returning to the outer
world.

Rousset, therefore, is right when he insists that the truth is
that "victim and executioner are alike ignoble; the lesson of
the camps is the brotherhood of abjection" (p. 588).

[33] Bettelheim, *op. cit.*, describes how "the main concern of
the new prisoners seemed to be to remain intact as a personality" while the problem of the old prisoners was "how to live
as well as possible within the camp."

to make it destroy the human person as inexorably as do certain mental diseases of organic origin.

It is here that the utter lunacy of the entire process becomes most apparent. Torture, to be sure, is an essential feature of the whole totalitarian police and judiciary apparatus; it is used every day to make people talk. This type of torture, since it pursues a definite, rational aim, has certain limitations: either the prisoner talks within a certain time, or he is killed. To this rationally conducted torture another, irrational, sadistic type was added in the first Nazi concentration camps and in the cellars of the Gestapo. Carried on for the most part by the SA, it pursued no aims and was not systematic, but depended on the initiative of largely abnormal elements. The mortality was so high that only a few concentration-camp inmates of 1933 survived these first years. This type of torture seemed to be not so much a calculated political institution as a concession of the regime to its criminal and abnormal elements, who were thus rewarded for services rendered. Behind the blind bestiality of the SA, there often lay a deep hatred and resentment against all those who were socially, intellectually, or physically better off than themselves, and who now, as if in fulfillment of their wildest dreams, were in their power. This resentment, which never died out entirely in the camps, strikes us as a last remnant of humanly understandable feeling.[34]

The real horror began, however, when the SS took over the administration of the camps. The old spontaneous bestiality gave way to an absolutely cold and systematic destruction of human bodies, calculated to destroy human dignity; death was avoided or postponed indefinitely. The camps were no longer amusement parks for beasts in human form, that is, for men who really belonged in

[34] Rousset, *op. cit.*, p. 390, reports an SS-man haranguing a professor as follows: "You used to be a professor. Well, you're no professor now. You're no big shot any more. You're nothing but a little runt now. Just as little as you can be. I'm the big fellow now."

mental institutions and prisons; the reverse became true: they were turned into "drill grounds," on which perfectly normal men were trained to be full-fledged members of the SS.[35]

[35] Kogon, *op. cit.*, p. 6, speaks of the possibility that the camps will be maintained as training and experimental grounds for the SS. He also gives a good report on the difference between the early camps administered by the SA and the later ones under the SS. "None of these first camps had more than a thousand inmates. . . . Life in them beggared all description. The accounts of the few old prisoners who survived those years agree that there was scarcely any form of sadistic perversion that was not practiced by the SA men. But they were all acts of individual bestiality, there was still no fully organized cold system, embracing masses of men. This was the accomplishment of the SS" (p. 7).

This new mechanized system eased the feeling of responsibility as much as was humanly possible. When, for instance, the order came to kill every day several hundred Russian prisoners, the slaughter was performed by shooting through a hole without seeing the victim. (See Ernest Feder, "Essai sur la Psychologie de la Terreur," in *Synthèses*, Brussels, 1946.) On the other hand, perversion was artificially produced in otherwise normal men. Rousset reports the following from a SS guard: "Usually I keep on hitting until I ejaculate. I have a wife and three children in Breslau. I used to be perfectly normal. That's what they've made of me. Now when they give me a pass out of here, I don't go home. I don't dare look my wife in the face" (p. 273).—The documents from the Hitler era contain numerous testimonials for the average normality of those entrusted with carrying out Hitler's program of extermination. A good collection is found in Léon Poliakov's "The Weapon of Antisemitism," published by UNESCO in *The Third Reich*, London, 1955. Most of the men in the units used for these purposes were not volunteers but had been drafted from the ordinary police for these special assignments. But even trained SS-men found this kind of duty worse than frontline fighting. In his report of a mass execution by the SS, an eyewitness gives high praise to this troop which had been so "idealistic" that it was able to bear "the entire extermination without the help of liquor."

That one wanted to eliminate all personal motives and passions during the "exterminations" and hence keep the cruelties to a minimum is revealed by the fact that a group of doctors

The killing of man's individuality, of the uniqueness shaped in equal parts by nature, will, and destiny, which has become so self-evident a premise for all human relations that even identical twins inspire a certain uneasiness, creates a horror that vastly overshadows the outrage of the juridical-political person and the despair of the moral person. It is this horror that gives rise to the nihilistic generalizations which maintain plausibly enough that essentially all men alike are beasts.[36] Actually the experience of the concentration camps does show that human beings can be transformed into specimens of the human animal, and that man's "nature" is only "human" insofar as it opens up to man the possibility of becoming something highly unnatural, that is, a man.

After murder of the moral person and annihilation of the juridical person, the destruction of the individuality is almost always successful. Conceivably some laws of mass psychology may be found to explain why millions of human beings allowed themselves to be marched unresistingly into the gas chambers, although these laws would explain nothing else but the destruction of individuality. It is more significant that those individually condemned to death very seldom attempted to take one of their executioners with them, that there were scarcely any serious revolts, and that even in the moment of liberation there were very few spontaneous massacres of SS men. For to destroy individuality is to destroy spontaneity, man's power to begin something new out of his own resources, something that cannot be explained on the basis of reac-

---

and engineers entrusted with handling the gas installations were making constant improvements that were not only designed to raise the productive capacity of the corpse factories but also to accelerate and ease the agony of death.

[36] This is very prominent in Rousset's work. "The social conditions of life in the camps have transformed the great mass of inmates, both the Germans and the deportees, regardless of their previous social position and education . . . into a degenerate rabble, entirely submissive to the primitive reflexes of the animal instinct" (p. 183).

tions to environment and events.[37] Nothing then remains but ghastly marionettes with human faces, which all
behave like the dog in Pavlov's experiments, which all
react with perfect reliability even when going to their own
death, and which do nothing but react. This is the real
triumph of the system: "The triumph of the SS demands
that the tortured victim allow himself to be led to the
noose without protesting, that he renounce and abandon
himself to the point of ceasing to affirm his identity. And
it is not for nothing. It is not gratuitously, out of sheer
sadism, that the SS men desire his defeat. They know that
the system which succeeds in destroying its victim before
he mounts the scaffold . . . is incomparably the best for
keeping a whole people in slavery. In submission. Nothing
is more terrible than these processions of human beings
going like dummies to their death. The man who sees this
says to himself: 'For them to be thus reduced, what power
must be concealed in the hands of the masters,' and he
turns away, full of bitterness but defeated."[38]

If we take totalitarian aspirations seriously and refuse to
be misled by the common-sense assertion that they are
utopian and unrealizable, it develops that the society of
the dying established in the camps is the only form of
society in which it is possible to dominate man entirely.
Those who aspire to total domination must liquidate all
spontaneity, such as the mere existence of individuality

[37] In this context also belongs the astonishing rarity of
suicides in the camps. Suicide occurred far more often before
arrest and deportation than in the camp itself, which is of
course partly explained by the fact that every attempt was
made to prevent suicides which are, after all, spontaneous
acts. From the statistical material for Buchenwald (*Nazi Conspiracy*, IV, 800 ff.) it is evident that scarcely more than one-
half per cent of the deaths could be traced to suicide, that frequently there were only two suicides per year, although in the
same year the total number of deaths reached 3,516. The reports from Russian camps mention the same phenomenon. Cf.,
for instance, Starlinger, *op. cit.*, p. 57.

[38] Rousset, *op. cit.*, p. 525.

will always engender, and track it down in its most private forms, regardless of how unpolitical and harmless these may seem. Pavlov's dog, the human specimen reduced to the most elementary reactions, the bundle of reactions that can always be liquidated and replaced by other bundles of reactions that behave in exactly the same way, is the model "citizen" of a totalitarian state; and such a citizen can be produced only imperfectly outside of the camps.

The uselessness of the camps, their cynically admitted anti-utility, is only apparent. In reality they are more essential to the preservation of the regime's power than any of its other institutions. Without concentration camps, without the undefined fear they inspire and the very well-defined training they offer in totalitarian domination, which can nowhere else be fully tested with all of its most radical possibilities, a totalitarian state can neither inspire its nuclear troops with fanaticism nor maintain a whole people in complete apathy. The dominating and the dominated would only too quickly sink back into the "old bourgeois routine"; after early "excesses," they would succumb to everyday life with its human laws; in short, they would develop in the direction which all observers counseled by common sense were so prone to predict. The tragic fallacy of all these prophecies, originating in a world that was still safe, was to suppose that there was such a thing as one human nature established for all time, to identify this human nature with history, and thus to declare that the idea of total domination was not only inhuman but also unrealistic. Meanwhile we have learned that the power of man is so great that he really can be what he wishes to be.

It is in the very nature of totalitarian regimes to demand unlimited power. Such power can only be secured if literally all men, without a single exception, are reliably dominated in every aspect of their life. In the realm of foreign affairs new neutral territories must constantly be subjugated, while at home ever-new human groups must be mastered in expanding concentration camps, or, when circumstances require liquidated to make room for others. The question of opposition is unimportant both in foreign and domestic affairs. Any neutrality, indeed any spontaneously given friendship, is from the standpoint of totalitarian domination just as dangerous as open hostility, precisely because spontaneity as such, with its incalculability, is the greatest of all obstacles to total domination over man. The Communists of non-Communist countries, who fled or were called to Moscow, learned by bitter experience that they constituted a menace to the Soviet Union. Convinced Communists are in this sense, which alone has any reality today, just as ridiculous and just as menacing to the regime in Russia, as, for example, the convinced Nazis of the Röhm faction were to the Nazis.

What makes conviction and opinion of any sort so ridiculous and dangerous under totalitarian conditions is that totalitarian regimes take the greatest pride in having no need of them, or of any human help of any kind. Men insofar as they are more than animal reaction and fulfillment of functions are entirely superfluous to totalitarian regimes. Totalitarianism strives not toward despotic rule over men, but toward a system in which men are superfluous. Total power can be achieved and safeguarded only in a world of conditioned reflexes, of marionettes without the slightest trace of spontaneity. Precisely because man's resources are so great, he can be fully dominated only when he becomes a specimen of the animal-species man.

Therefore character is a threat and even the most unjust legal rules are an obstacle; but individuality, anything indeed that distinguishes one man from another, is intolerable. As long as all men have not been made equally superfluous—and this has been accomplished only in concentration camps—the ideal of totalitarian domination has not been achieved. Totalitarian states strive constantly, though never with complete success, to establish the superfluity of man—by the arbitrary selection of various groups for concentration camps, by constant purges of the ruling apparatus, by mass liquidations. Common sense protests desperately that the masses are submissive and that all this gigantic apparatus of terror is therefore superfluous; if they were capable of telling the truth, the totalitarian rulers would reply: The apparatus seems superfluous to you only because it serves to make men superfluous.

The totalitarian attempt to make men superfluous reflects the experience of modern masses of their superfluity on an overcrowded earth. The world of the dying, in which men are taught they are superfluous through a way of life in which punishment is meted out without connection with crime, in which exploitation is practiced without profit, and where work is performed without product, is a place where senselessness is daily produced anew. Yet, within the framework of the totalitarian ideology, nothing could be more sensible and logical; if the inmates are vermin, it is logical that they should be killed by poison gas; if they are degenerate, they should not be allowed to contaminate the population; if they have "slave-like souls" (Himmler), no one should waste his time trying to re-educate them. Seen through the eyes of the ideology, the trouble with the camps is almost that they make too much sense, that the execution of the doctrine is too consistent.

While the totalitarian regimes are thus resolutely and cynically emptying the world of the only thing that makes sense to the utilitarian expectations of common sense, they impose upon it at the same time a kind of supersense which the ideologies actually always meant when they pretended to have found the key to history or the solution to the riddles of the universe. Over and above the senselessness of totalitarian society is enthroned the ridiculous supersense of its ideological superstition. Ideologies are harmless, uncritical, and arbitrary opinions only as long as they are not believed in seriously. Once their claim to total validity is taken literally they become the nuclei of logical systems in which, as in the systems of paranoiacs, everything follows comprehensibly and even compulsorily once the first premise is accepted. The insanity of such systems lies not only in their first premise but in the very logicality with which they are constructed. The curious logicality of all isms, their simple-minded trust in the salvation value of stubborn devotion without regard for specific, varying factors, already harbors the first germs of totalitarian contempt for reality and factuality.

Common sense trained in utilitarian thinking is helpless against this ideological supersense, since totalitarian regimes establish a functioning world of no-sense. The ideological contempt for factuality still contained the proud assumption of human mastery over the world; it is, after all, contempt for reality which makes possible changing the world, the erection of the human artifice. What destroys the element of pride in the totalitarian contempt for reality (and thereby distinguishes it radically from revolutionary theories and attitudes) is the supersense which gives the contempt for reality its cogency, logicality, and consistency. What makes a truly totalitarian device out of the Bolshevik claim that the present Russian system is superior to all others is the fact that the totalitarian ruler draws from this claim the logically impeccable conclusion that without this system people never could have built such a wonderful thing as, let us say, a subway; from this, he again draws the logical conclusion that anyone who knows of the existence of the Paris subway is a suspect because he may cause people to doubt that one can do things only in the Bolshevik way. This leads to the final conclusion that in order to remain a loyal Bolshevik, you have to destroy the Paris subway. Nothing matters but consistency.

With these new structures, built on the strength of supersense and driven by the motor of logicality, we are indeed at the end of the bourgeois era of profits and power, as well as at the end of imperialism and expansion. The aggressiveness of totalitarianism springs not from lust for power, and if it feverishly seeks to expand, it does so neither for expansion's sake nor for profit, but only for ideological reasons: to make the world consistent, to prove that its respective supersense has been right.

It is chiefly for the sake of this supersense, for the sake of complete consistency, that it is necessary for totalitarianism to destroy every trace of what we commonly call human dignity. For respect for human dignity implies the recognition of my fellow-men or our fellow-nations as subjects, as builders of worlds or cobuilders of a common world. No ideology which aims at the explanation of all historical events of the past and at mapping out the course of all events of the future can bear the unpredictability which springs from the fact that men are creative, that they can bring forward something so new that nobody ever foresaw it.

What totalitarian ideologies therefore aim at is not the transformation of the outside world or the revolutionizing transmutation of society, but the transformation of human nature itself. The concentration camps are the laboratories where changes in human nature are tested, and their shamefulness therefore is not just the business of their inmates and those who run them according to strictly "scientific" standards; it is the concern of all men. Suffering, of which there has been always too much on earth, is not the issue, nor is the number of victims. Human nature as such is at stake, and even though it seems that these experiments succeed not in changing man but only in destroying him, by creating a society in which the nihilistic banality of *homo homini lupus* is consistently realized, one should bear in mind the necessary limitations to an experiment which requires global control in order to show conclusive results.

Until now the totalitarian belief that everything is possible seems to have proved only that everything can be destroyed. Yet, in their effort to prove that everything is possible, totalitarian regimes have discovered without knowing it that there are crimes which men can neither punish nor forgive. When the impossible was made possible it became the unpunishable, unforgivable absolute evil which could no longer be understood and explained by the evil motives of self-interest, greed, covetousness, resentment, lust for power, and cowardice; and which therefore anger could not revenge, love could not endure, friendship could not forgive. Just as the victims in the death factories or the holes of oblivion are no longer "human" in the eyes of their executioners, so this newest species of criminals is beyond the pale even of solidarity in human sinfulness.

It is inherent in our entire philosophical tradition that we cannot conceive of a "radical evil," and this is true both for Christian theology, which conceded even to the Devil himself a celestial origin, as well as for Kant, the only philosopher who, in the word he coined for it, at least must have suspected the existence of this evil even though he immediately rationalized it in the concept of a "perverted ill will" that could be explained by comprehensible motives. Therefore, we actually have nothing to fall back on in order to understand a phenomenon that nevertheless confronts us with its overpowering reality and breaks down all standards we know. There is only one thing that seems to be discernible: we may say that radical evil has emerged in connection with a system in which all men have become equally superfluous. The manipulators of this system believe in their own superfluousness as much as in that of all others, and the totalitarian murderers are all the more dangerous because they do not care if they themselves are alive or dead, if they ever lived or never were born. The danger of the corpse factories and holes of oblivion is that today, with populations and homelessness everywhere on the increase, masses of people are continuously rendered superfluous if we continue to think of our world in utilitarian terms. Political, social, and economic events everywhere are in a silent conspiracy with totalitarian instruments devised for making men superfluous. The implied temptation is well understood by the utilitarian common sense of the masses, who in most countries are too desperate to retain much fear of death. The Nazis and the Bolsheviks can be sure that their factories of annihilation which demonstrate the swiftest solution to the problem of overpopulation, of economically superfluous and socially rootless human masses, are as much of an attraction as a warning. Totalitarian solutions may well survive the fall of totalitarian regimes in the form of strong temptations which will come up whenever it seems impossible to alleviate political, social, or economic misery in a manner worthy of man.

XI

Collective Guilt

HANNAH ARENDT

Organized Guilt and Universal Responsibility

The greater the military defeats of the Wehrmacht in the field, the greater becomes that victory of Nazi political warfare which is so often incorrectly described as mere propaganda. It is the central thesis of this Nazi political strategy that there is no difference between Nazis and Germans, that the people stand united behind the government, that all Allied hopes of finding part of the people uninfected ideologically and all appeals to a democratic Germany of the future are pure illusion. The implication of this thesis is, of course, that there is no distinction as to responsibility, that German anti-Fascists will suffer from defeat equally with German Fascists, and that the Allies had made such distinctions at the beginning of the war only for propaganda purposes. A further implication is that Allied provisions for punishment of war criminals will turn out to be empty threats because they will find no one to whom the title of war criminal could not be applied.

That such claims are not mere propaganda but are supported by very real and fearful facts, we have all

From *Jewish Frontier*, Vol. 12 (1945). Reprinted by permission of the author and *Jewish Frontier*.

learned in the past seven years. The terror-organizations
which were at first strictly separated from the mass of the
people, admitting only persons who could show a criminal
past or prove their preparedness to become criminals, have
since been continually expanded. The ban on party membership for members of the army has been dissolved by
the general order which subordinates all soldiers to the
party. Whereas those crimes which have always been a part
of the daily routine of concentration camps since the beginning of the Nazi regime were at first a jealously
guarded monopoly of the SS and Gestapo, today members of the Wehrmacht are assigned at will to duties of
mass murder. These crimes were at first kept secret by
every possible means and any publication of such reports
was made punishable as atrocity propaganda. Later, however, such reports were spread by Nazi-organized whisper-
ing campaigns and today these crimes are openly proclaimed under the title of "measures of liquidation" in
order to force "Volksgenossen" whom difficulties of organization made it impossible to induct into the "Volks-
gemeinschaft" of crime at least to bear the onus of complicity and awareness of what was going on. These tactics
resulted in a victory for the Nazis, as the Allies abandoned
the distinction between Germans and Nazis. In order to
appreciate the decisive change of political conditions in
Germany since the lost battle of Britain, one must note
that until the war and even until the first military defeats
only relatively small groups of active Nazis, among whom
not even the Nazi sympathizers were included, and equally
small numbers of active anti-Fascists really knew what was
going on. All others, whether German or non-German,
had the natural inclination to believe the statements of
an official, universally recognized government rather than
the charges of refugees, which, coming from Jews or So-
cialists, were suspect in any case. Even of those refugees,
only a relatively small proportion knew the full truth and
even a smaller fraction was prepared to bear the odium of
unpopularity involved in telling the truth.

As long as the Nazis expected victory, their terror organizations were strictly isolated from the people and, in time of war, from the army. The army was not used to commit atrocities and SS troops were increasingly recruited from "qualified" circles of whatever nationality. If the planned New Order of Europe should have succeeded, we would have been witnesses of an inter-European organization of terror under German leadership. The terror would have been exercised by members of all European nationalities with the exception of Jews in an organization graded according to the racial classification of the various countries. The German people, of course, would not have been spared by it. Himmler was always of the opinion that authority in Europe should be in the hands of a racial élite, organized in SS troops without national ties.

It was only their defeats which forced the Nazis to abandon this concept and pretend to return to old nationalist slogans. The active identification of the whole German people with the Nazis was part of this trend. National Socialism's chances of organizing an underground movement in the future depend on no-one's being able to know any longer who is a Nazi and who is not, on there being no visible signs of distinction any longer, and above all on the victorious powers' being convinced that there really are no differences between Germans. To bring this about, an intensified terror in Germany, which proposed to leave no person alive whose past or reputation proclaimed him an anti-Fascist, was necessary. In the first years of the war the regime was remarkably "magnanimous" to its opponents, provided they remained peaceful. Of late, however, countless persons have been executed even though, by reason of years without freedom of movement, they could not constitute any immediate danger to the regime. On the other hand, prudently foreseeing that in spite of all precautionary measures the Allies might still find a few hundred persons in each city with an irreproachable anti-Fascist record—testified to by former war prisoners or foreign laborers, and supported by records of imprisonment or concentration camp internment—the Nazis have already provided their own trusted cohorts with similar documentation and testimony, making these criteria worthless. Thus in the case of inmates of concentration camps (whose number nobody knows precisely, but which is estimated at several million), the Nazis can safely either liquidate them or let them escape: in the improbable event of their survival (a massacre of the type which already occurred in Buchenwald is not even punishable under the war crimes provisions)—it will not be possible to identify them unmistakably.

Whether any person in Germany is a Nazi or an anti-Nazi can be determined only by the One who knows the secrets of the human heart, which no human eye can penetrate. Those, at any rate, who actively organize an anti-Nazi underground movement in Germany today—and there are such persons in Germany, of course—would meet a speedy death if they failed to act and talk precisely like Nazis. In a country where a person attracts immediate attention by failing either to murder upon command or to be a ready accomplice of murderers, this is no light task. The most extreme slogan which this war has evoked among the Allies, that the only "good German" is a "dead German," has this much basis in fact: the only way in which we can identify an anti-Nazi is when the Nazis have hanged him. There is no other reliable token.

These are the real political conditions which underlie the charge of the collective guilt of the German people. They are the consequences of a policy which, in the deepest sense, is a- and anti-national; which is entirely determined that there shall be a German people only if it is in the power of its present rulers; and which will rejoice as at its greatest victory if the defeat of the Nazis involves with it the physical destruction of the German people. The totalitarian policy, which has completely destroyed the neutral zone in which the daily life of human beings is ordinarily lived, has achieved the result of making the

existence of each individual in Germany depend either
upon committing crimes or on complicity in crimes. The
success of Nazi propaganda in Allied countries, as expressed in the attitude commonly called Vansittartism, is
a secondary matter in comparison. It is a product of general war propaganda, and something quite apart from the
specific modern political phenomenon described above.
All the documents and pseudo-historical demonstrations
of this tendency sound like relatively innocent plagiarism
of the French literature of the last war—and it makes no
essential difference that a few of those writers who twenty-
five years ago kept the presses rolling with their attacks on
"perfidious Albion" have now placed their experience at
the Allies' disposal.

But even the best-intended discussions between the defenders of the "good Germans" and the accusers of the
"bad" not only miss the essence of the question but plainly
do not even apprehend the magnitude of the catastrophe.
Either they are betrayed into trivial general comments on
good and bad people, and into a fantastic over-estimation
of the power of education, or they simply adopt an inverted
version of Nazi racial theory. There is a certain danger in
all this only because since Churchill's famous statement
on the subject, the Allies have refrained from fighting an
ideological war and have thus unconsciously given an advantage to the Nazis (who, without regard to Churchill,
are organizing their defeat ideologically) and a chance of
survival to all racial theories.

The true problem however is not to prove what is self-
evident, namely that Germans have not been potential
Nazis ever since Tacitus' times, nor what is impossible,
that all Germans harbor Nazi views. It is rather to consider how to conduct ourselves and how to bear the trial
of confronting a people among whom the boundaries divid-
ing criminals from normal persons, the guilty from the
innocent, have been so completely effaced that nobody
will be able to tell in Germany whether in any case he is
dealing with a secret hero or with a former mass murderer.

In this situation we will not be aided either by a definition of those responsible, nor by the punishment of "war criminals." Such definitions by their very nature can apply only to those who not only took responsibility upon themselves, but produced this whole inferno—and yet strangely enough are still not to be found on the lists of war criminals. The number of those who are responsible *and* guilty will be relatively small. There are many who share responsibility without any visible proof of guilt. There are many more who have become guilty without being in the least responsible. Among the responsible in a broader sense must be included all those who continued sympathetic to Hitler as long as it was possible, who aided his rise to power, and who applauded him in Germany and in other European countries. Who would dare to brand all these ladies and gentlemen of high society as war criminals? And as a matter of fact they really do not deserve such a title. Unquestionably they have proved their inability to judge modern political groupings, some of them because they regarded all principles as moralistic nonsense in politics, others because they were affected by a romantic predilection for gangsters whom they confused with "pirates" of an older time. Yet these people, who were co-responsible for Hitler's crimes in a broader sense, did not incur any guilt in a stricter sense. They, who were the Nazis' first accomplices and their best aides, truly did not know what they were doing nor with whom they were dealing.

The extreme horror with which particularly persons of good will react whenever the case of Germany is discussed is not evoked by those irresponsible co-responsibles, nor even by the particular crimes of the Nazis themselves. It is rather the product of that vast machine of administrative mass murder, in whose service not only thousands of persons, nor even scores of thousands of selected murderers, but a whole people could be and was employed: In that organization which Himmler has prepared against the defeat, everyone is either an executioner, a victim, or an automaton, marching onward over the corpses of his comrades—chosen at first out of the various storm troop formations and later from any army unit or other mass organization. That everyone, whether or not he is directly active in a murder camp, is forced to take part in one way or another in the workings of this machine of mass murder—that is the horrible thing. For systematic mass murder—the true consequence of all race theories and other modern ideologies which preach that might is right—strains not only the imagination of human beings, but also the framework and categories of our political thought and action. Whatever the future of Germany, it will not be determined by anything more than the inevitable consequences of a lost war—consequences which in the nature of the case are temporary. There is no political method for dealing with German mass crimes, and the destruction of seventy or eighty million Germans, or even their gradual death through starvation (of which, of course, nobody except a few psychotic fanatics dream), would simply mean that the ideology of the Nazis had won, even if power and the rights of might had fallen to other peoples.

Just as there is no political solution within human capacity for the crime of administrative mass murder, so the human need for justice can find no satisfactory reply to the total mobilization of a people for that purpose. Where all are guilty, nobody in the last analysis can be judged.* For that guilt is not accompanied by even the mere appearance, the mere pretense of responsibility. So long as punishment is the right of the criminal—and

* That German refugees, who had the good fortune either to be Jews or to have been persecuted by the Gestapo early enough, have been saved from this guilt is of course not their merit. Because they know this and because their horror at what might have been still haunts them, they often introduce into discussions of this kind that insufferable tone of self-righteousness which frequently and particularly among Jews, can turn into the vulgar obverse of Nazi doctrines; and in fact already has.

this paradigm has for more than two thousand years been the basis of the sense of justice and right of Occidental man—guilt implies the consciousness of guilt, and punishment evidence that the criminal is a responsible person. How it is in this matter has been well described by an American correspondent, in a story whose dialogue material is worthy of the imagination and creative power of a great poet.

Q. Did you kill people in the camp? A. Yes.

Q. Did you poison them with gas? A. Yes.

Q. Did you bury them alive? A. It sometimes happened.

Q. Were the victims picked from all over Europe? A. I suppose so.

Q. Did you personally help kill people? A. Absolutely not. I was only paymaster in the camp.

Q. What did you think of what was going on? A. It was bad at first but we got used to it.

Q. Do you know the Russians will hang you? A. (Bursting into tears) Why should they? *What have I done?* (Italics mine. PM, Sunday, Nov. 12, 1944.)

Really he had done nothing. He had only carried out orders and since when has it been a crime to carry out orders? Since when has it been a virtue to rebel? Since when could one only be decent by welcoming death? What then had he done?

In his play, "Last Days of Mankind" about the last war, Karl Kraus rang down the curtain after Wilhelm II had cried, "I did not want this." And the horribly comic part of it was that this was the fact. When the curtain falls this time, we will have to listen to a whole chorus calling out, "We did not do this." And even though we shall no longer be able to appreciate the comic element, the horrible part of it will still be that this is the fact.

In trying to understand what were the real motives which caused people to act as cogs in the mass murder machine, we shall not be aided by speculations about German history and the so-called German national character, of whose potentialities those who knew Germany most intimately had not the slightest idea fifteen years ago. There is more to be learned from the characteristic personality of the man who can boast that he was the organizing spirit of the murder. Heinrich Himmler is not one of those intellectuals stemming from the dim No-Man's Land between the Bohemian and the Pimp, whose significance in the composition of the Nazi élite has been repeatedly stressed of late. He is neither a Bohemian like Goebbels, nor a sex criminal like Streicher, nor a perverted fanatic like Hitler, nor an adventurer like Goering. He is a "bourgeois" with all the outer aspect of respectability, all the habits of a good *paterfamilias* who does not betray his wife and anxiously seeks to secure a decent future for his children; and he has consciously built up his newest terror organization, covering the whole country, on the assumption that most people are not bohemians nor fanatics, nor adventurers, nor sex maniacs, nor sadists, but, first and foremost job-holders, and good familymen.

It was Péguy, I believe, who called the family man the "grand aventurier du 20e siecle." He died too soon to learn that he was also the great criminal of the century. We had been so accustomed to admire or gently ridicule the family man's kind concern and earnest concentration on the welfare of his family, his solemn determination to make life easy for his wife and children, that we hardly noticed how the devoted *paterfamilias*, worried about nothing so much as his security, was transformed under the pressure of the chaotic economic conditions of our time into an involuntary adventurer, who for all his industry and care could never be certain what the next day would bring. The docility of this type was already manifest in the very early period of Nazi "gleichschaltung." It became clear that for the sake of his pension, his life insurance, the security of his wife and children, such a man was ready to sacrifice his beliefs, his honor, and his human dignity. It needed only the Satanic genius of Himmler to discover that after such degradation he was entirely prepared to do literally anything when the ante was raised and the bare existence of his family was threatened. The only condition he put was that he should be fully exempted from responsibility for his acts. Thus that very person, the average German, whom the Nazis notwithstanding years of the most furious propaganda could not induce to kill a Jew on his own account (not even when they made it quite clear that such a murder would go unpunished) now serves the machine of destruction without opposition. In contrast to the earlier units of the SS men and Gestapo, Himmler's over-all organization, relies not on fanatics, nor on congenital murderers, nor on sadists; it relies entirely upon the normality of jobholders and family-men.

We need not specially mention the sorry reports about Latvians, Lithuanians, or even Jews who have participated in Himmler's murder organization in order to show that it requires no particular national character in order to supply this new type of functionary. They are not even all natural murderers or traitors out of perversity. It is not even certain that they would do the work if it were only their own lives and future that were at stake. They felt (after they no longer needed to fear God, their conscience cleared through the bureaucratic organization of their acts) only the responsibility toward their own families. The transformation of the family man from a responsible member of society, interested in all public affairs, to a "bourgeois" concerned only with his private existence and knowing no civic virtue, is an international modern phenomenon. The exigencies of our time— "bedenkt den Hunger und die grosse Kaelte in diesem Tale, das von Jammerschallt" (Brecht)—can at any moment transform him into the mob-man and make him the instrument of whatsoever madness and horror. Each time society, through unemployment, frustrates the small man in his normal functioning and normal self-respect, it trains him for that last stage in which he will willingly undertake any function, even that of hangman. A Jew released from Buchenwald once discovered among the SS men who gave him the certificates of release a former schoolmate, whom he did not address but yet stared at. Spontaneously the man stared at remarked: You must understand, I have five years of unemployment behind me. They can do anything they want with me.

It is true that the development of this modern type of man who is the exact opposite of the "citoyen" and whom for lack of a better name we have called the "bourgeois," enjoyed particularly favorable conditions in Germany. Hardly another country of Occidental culture was so little imbued with the classic virtues of civic behavior. In no other country did private life and private calculations play so great a role. This is a fact which the Germans in time of national emergency disguised with great success, but never altered. Behind the facade of proclaimed and propagandized national virtues, such as "love of the Fatherland," "German courage," "German loyalty," etc., there lurked corresponding real national vices. There is hardly another country where on the average there is so little patriotism as Germany; and behind the chauvinistic claims of loyalty and courage, a fatal tendency to disloyalty and betrayal for opportunistic reasons is hidden.

The mob man, however, the end-result of the "bourgeois," is an international phenomenon; and we would do well not to submit him to too many temptations in the blind faith that only the German mob man is capable of such frightful deeds. What we have called the "bourgeois" is the modern man of the masses, not in his exalted moments of collective excitement, but in the security (today one should rather say the insecurity) of his own private domain. He has driven the dichotomy of private and public functions, of family and occupation, so far that he can no longer find in his own person any connection between the two. When his occupation forces him to murder people he does not regard himself as a murderer because he has not done it out of inclination but in his professional capacity. Out of sheer passion he would never do harm to a fly.

If we tell a member of this new occupational class which our time has produced that he is being held to account for what he did, he will feel nothing except that he has been betrayed. But if in the shock of the catastrophe he really becomes conscious that in fact he was not only a functionary but a murderer, then his way out will not be that of rebellion, but suicide—just as so many have already chosen the way of suicide in Germany, where it is plain that there has been one wave of self-destruction after another. And that too would be of little use to us.

It is many years now that we meet Germans who declare that they are ashamed of being Germans. I have often felt tempted to answer that I am ashamed of being human. This elemental shame, which many people of the most various nationalities share with one another today, is what finally is left of our sense of international solidarity, and it has not yet found an adequate political expression. Our fathers' enchantment with humanity was of a sort which not only light-mindedly ignored the national question; what is far worse, it did not even conceive of the terror of the idea of humanity and of the Judeo-Christian faith in the unitary origin of the human race. It was not very pleasant even when we had to bury our false illusions about "the noble savage," having discovered that men were capable of being cannibals. Since then peoples have learned to know one another better and learned more and more about the evil potentialities in men. The result has been that they have recoiled more and more from the idea of humanity and become more susceptible to the doctrine of race which denies the very possibility of a common humanity. They instinctively felt that the idea of humanity, whether it appears in a religious or humanistic form, implies the obligation of a general responsibility which they do not wish to assume. For the idea of humanity, when purged of all sentimentality, has the very serious consequence that in one form or another men must assume responsibility for all crimes committed by men and that all nations share the onus of evil committed by all others. Shame at being a human being is the purely individual and still non-political expression of this insight.

In political terms, the idea of humanity, excluding no people and assigning a monopoly of guilt to no-one, is the only guarantee that one "superior race" after another may not feel obligated to follow the "natural law" of the right of the powerful, and exterminate "inferior races unworthy of survival"; so that at the end of an "imperialistic age" we should find ourselves in a stage which would make the Nazis look like crude precursors of future political methods. To follow a non-imperialistic policy and maintain a non-racist faith becomes daily more difficult because it becomes daily clearer how great a burden mankind is for man.

Perhaps those Jews, to whose forefathers we owe the first conception of the idea of humanity, knew something about that burden when each year they used to say "Our Father and King, we have sinned before you," taking not only the sins of their own community but all human offenses upon themselves. Those who today are ready to follow this road in a modern version do not content themselves with the hypocritical confession, "God be thanked, I am not like that," in horror at the undreamed of potentialities of the German national character. Rather, in fear and trembling, have they finally realized of what man is capable— and this is indeed the precondition of any modern political thinking. Such persons will not serve very well as functionaries of vengeance. This, however, is certain: upon them and only upon them, who are filled with a genuine fear of the inescapable guilt of the human race, can there be any reliance when it comes to fighting fearlessly, uncompromisingly, everywhere against the incalculable evil that men are capable of bringing about.

XII

The Stains of War

J. GLENN GRAY

The Ache of Guilt

The man I interrogated and took to Army proved to be a spy.
. . . I went to Army two days later, after he had been "broken"
by endless interrogation and considerable beating. . . . It recalled the memory of Scarpelini in Italy, whom I also appre-
hended and turned over. . . . One thing contents me, that
these were not innocent soldiers. They knew what they were
facing. The German had been an idealistic Nazi for fifteen
years. . . . Am I responsible for their deaths? Both might well
have escaped had it not been for me. . . . Certainly they had
blood on their hands, and desired to have more. Is their blood
on mine? But I am more fortunate than many soldiers who
must kill more innocent men. Perhaps the hardest thing of all
is that I feel no guilt. (War journal, November 4, 1944)

Nothing revolts the sensitive spirit so much as the bloody
and unjust deeds of warfare that leave no trace of guilt in
the doers and are from every human perspective un-
avenged. If we were not accustomed to evasions of responsibility in ourselves, such behavior would force us
into cynicism of the most nihilistic sort or, at the best, to
complete bewilderment about human nature. Yet a voice

From *The Warriors: Reflections on Men in Battle* (New York:
Harper & Row, 1967). Copyright 1959 by J. Glenn Gray. Reprinted by permission of the author.

within each of us echoes the sentiments of Hamlet: "Use every man after his desert, and who should 'scape whipping?"

The fighting man is disinclined to repent his deeds of violence. Men who in private life are scrupulous about conventional justice and right are able to destroy the lives and happiness of others in war without compunction. At least to other eyes they seem to have no regrets. It is understandable, of course, why soldiers in combat would not suffer pangs of conscience when they battle for their lives against others who are trying to kill them. And if the enemy is regarded as a beast or a devil, guilt feelings are not likely to arise if he is slain by your hand. But modern wars are notorious for the destruction of nonparticipants and the razing of properties in lands that are accidentally in the path of combat armies and air forces. In World War II the number of civilians who lost their lives exceeded the number of soldiers killed in combat. At all events, the possibilities of the individual involving himself in guilt are immeasurably wider than specific deeds that he might commit against the armed foe. In the thousand chances of warfare, nearly every combat soldier has failed to support his comrades at a critical moment; through sins of omission or commission, he has been responsible for the death of those he did not intend to kill. Through folly or fear, nearly every officer has exposed his own men to needless destruction at one time or another. Add to this the unnumbered acts of injustice so omnipresent in war, which may not result in death but inevitably bring pain and grief, and the impartial observer may wonder how the participants in such deeds could ever smile again and be free of care.

The sober fact appears to be that the great majority of veterans, not to speak of those who helped to put the weapons and ammunitions in their hands, are able to free themselves of responsibility with ease after the event, and frequently while they are performing it. Many a pilot or artilleryman who has destroyed untold numbers of terrified noncombatants has never felt any need for repentance or regret. Many a general who has won his laurels at a terrible cost in human life and suffering among friend and foe can endure the review of his career with great inner satisfaction. So are we made, we human creatures! Frequently, we are shocked to discover how little our former enemies regret their deeds and repent their errors. Americans in Germany after World War II, for instance, feel aggrieved that the German populace does not feel more responsibility for having visited Hitler upon the world. The Germans, for their part, resent the fact that few Americans appear to regret the bombing of German cities into rubble and the burning and crushing of helpless women and children. It appears to be symptomatic of a certain modern mentality to marvel at the absence of guilt consciousness in others while accepting its own innocence as a matter of course.

No doubt there are compelling historical reasons why soldiers in earlier times have felt comparatively little regret for their deeds and why modern soldiers in particular are able to evade responsibility so easily. It is wise to assume, I believe, that the soldiers who fight twentieth-century wars are morally little better or worse than their grandfathers or great-grandfathers in previous wars. Nevertheless, there are some novel factors in our time that, taken together with the traditional ways of escape, make it easier for the majority of soldiers to carry the guilt for the destruction of the innocent in contemporary conflicts. These novel factors lie both in our contemporary interpretation of guilt and in the nature of recent combat.

Our age seems peculiarly confused about the meaning of guilt, as well as its value. With the rise of modern psychology and the predominance of naturalistic philosophers, guilt has come to be understood exclusively in a moral sense. Its older religious and metaphysical dimensions have been increasingly forgotten. Moreover, these naturalistic psychologists have tended to view guilt feelings as a hindrance to the free development of personality

and the achievement of a life-affirming outlook. They like
to trace guilt to the darker, subconscious levels of the soul
and emphasize its backward-looking character as opposed to
the future-directed impulses of the natural man. Hence
guilt, when reduced to moral terms, has more and more
been branded as immoral. To some, it is associated with
a species of illness, which must be cured by psychiatric
treatment. Though these modern doctors of the soul
realize that the uninhibited man is not an attainable ideal,
they still strive for the goal of acceptance of oneself and
one's nature for what they are. The individual is released
as far as possible from regret for past deeds and from the
hard duty to improve his character.

Even if these doctrines get modified in actual practice
and are seldom read in their deeper meanings, the basic
ideas filter into the broadest strata of our population and
help to form the dominant mood of our day. Even the
simplest soldier suspects that it is unpopular today to be
burdened with guilt. Everyone from his pastor to his doctor is likely, if he brings up feelings that oppress him, to
urge him to "forget it." Precisely this is what he often
longs to hear, and, so, forgetting becomes such a disquiet-
ing phenomenon of the modern mind.

In war itself, the most potent quieters of conscience are
evidently the presence of others who are doing the same
things and the consciousness of acting under the orders of
people "higher up" who will answer for one's deeds. So
long as the soldier thinks of himself as one among many
and identifies himself with his unit, army, and nation, his
conscience is unlikely to waken and feel the need to respond. All awareness of guilt presupposes the capacity to
respond as an individual to the call of conscience. I am
using the term "respond" in its original meaning of answer
to a question or a demand made on the self. We respond
to conscience only when we can separate ourselves from
others and become conscious, often painfully so, of our
differentness. Though the call of conscience may seem to
be an impersonal voice outside of one, the response is

peculiarly within the individual self. Why did *you* do this? Why did *you* not do that? If we hear at all and if we attempt to answer, the response must begin with the first person singular pronoun. I must begin with myself as I was:

My conscience seems to become little by little sooted. . . . If I can soon get out of this war and back on the soil where the clean earth will wash away these stains! I have also other things on my conscience. . . . [A man named H., accused of being the local Gestapo agent in one small town] was an old man of seventy. His wife and he looked frightened and old and miserable. . . . I was quite harsh to him and remember threatening him with an investigation when I put him under house arrest. . . . Day before yesterday word came that he and his wife had committed suicide by taking poison. Fain and I went back and found them dead in their beds, he lying on his back and reminding me, gruesomely enough, of my father, she twisted over on her side with her face concealed. At the bedside was a card on which he had scrawled: "Wir mussten elend zu Grunde gehen. Der Herr Gott verzeihe uns. Wir haben niemandem leid getan." . . . [We must perish miserably. God forgive us. We have done no one any harm.] The incident affected me strongly and still does. I was directly or indirectly the cause of their death. . . . I hope it will not rest too hard on my conscience, and yet if it does not I shall be disturbed also.

Since conscience normally awakens in guilt in the sense that a troubled conscience is usually our first indication of its existence, it is clear that an important function of guiltiness is to make us aware of our selves. Whatever his response, the person who hears the call of conscience is aware of freedom in the form of a choice. He could have performed differently than he did; an act of his might have been different. The whole realm of the potential in human action is opened to him and with it the fateful recognition that he is in charge of his own course. Conscience is thus in the first instance a form of self-consciousness. It is that form that gives to us an unmistakable sense of free individuality and separates for us the domains of the actual and the ideal. Therewith the life of reflection begins, and the inner history of the individual no longer corresponds to his outer fate.

But the individual need not waken, and, indeed, everything in warfare conspires against such response to the call of freedom. Enemy and ally enclose his little life, and there is little privacy or escape from their presence. Loyalty to his unit is instilled by conscious and unconscious means; the enemy is seeking to destroy that unity and must be prevented from doing so at all costs. He is one with the others in a fraternity of exposure and danger. His consciousness of the others may be vague but is an omnipresent reality; it has much similarity to dream awareness. Directly, he is aware of his pals, the half-dozen or more men he knows relatively well, with a few dozen more who are on the periphery of his consciousness. Beyond them there are thousands who encircle him, whose presence he senses. There is a vast assemblage of unknown "friends" confronting an equally vast mass of unknown "enemies," and he is in the midst of all of them. Their presence makes his situation endurable, for they help to conquer the loneliness that oppresses him in the face of death, actual or possible. Something within him responds powerfully to the appeal of the communal. The orders that he receives from those in charge of his fate hold him where he is in the midst of disorder. He is compelled and controlled as though by invisible threads through the unseen presence of the others, friend and foe.

In an exposed position on the battlefield during action, his consciousness of being a part of an organism is likely to plunge him into contradictory feelings of power and impotence which succeed one another rapidly. "If I don't hit that guy out there or man this machine gun to the last, my buddies will be killed and I'll be the cause of their death. Everything depends on me." A few minutes later he is likely to ask himself what one rifle or machine gun on one tiny portion of the field can possibly matter to the final outcome. His place in the whole complex is lost to sight, and he is in danger of feeling how absolute is his dependence. All the time, he acts as he feels he must, swept by moods of exultation, despair, loyalty, hate, and many others. Much of the time he is out of himself, acting simply as a representative of the others, as part of a super-personal entity, on orders from elsewhere. He kills or fails to kill, fights courageously or runs away in the service of this unit and unity. Afterward, he hears no voice calling him to account for his actions, or, if he does hear a voice, feels no need to respond.

In less sophisticated natures, this presence of the others is projected also into the weapons and instruments of war. They become personalized, and the soldier becomes attached to them as an extension of himself. They afford him a vast comfort in difficult positions as a protection and a shield, a second skin. On the one hand, these weapons help to prevent the soldier from feeling responsible for the lives he takes. "I did not kill, my gun or grenade did it" is the subconscious suggestion. On the other hand, guns help to fill the intermediate spaces between him and the others. They help to cement the wall of comradeship that encloses him and ties him to his own side while at the same time preventing the enemy from becoming too real. Unless he is caught up in murderous ecstasy, destroying is easier when done at a little remove. With every foot of distance there is a corresponding decrease in reality. Imagination flags and fails altogether when distances become too great. So it is that much of the mindless cruelty of recent wars has been perpetrated by warriors at a distance, who could not guess what havoc their powerful weapons were occasioning.

Where weapons and comrades are insufficient to dampen self-awareness and personal responsibility, the soldier can often draw aid and comfort from the earth itself. His relation to nature is likely to be quite different from that elemental sense of belonging, which can also arouse in the perceptive person the most poetic and blissful feelings. The combat soldier hugs earth and trees as protection, as "cover" in the expressive military phrase. He does not now think of nature as the source of his life, but as his possible means of preserving it against those who would isolate and destroy him. Nature is part of his situation; it, too, is a presence in the special way that his weapons and his buddies are. If earth becomes dear, for example, the walls of his foxhole, trees, breastworks, clouds, and sun, it is not as part of nature that these things are dear. They are dear as instruments that shield him from the enemy. Everything is there for him, as it were, and yet he is there only for the others. He makes everything into an instrument, himself included. He is a trigger finger, a tank driver, a bombardier, a scout, and he can take delight in being an instrument. So everything conspires to prevent his coming to himself, and, as often as not, the soldier is a semiconscious accomplice in it as well. Why should he undergo the pain of reflection, the dangerous isolation acute self-awareness can bring with it?

In highly mechanized armies, many a soldier gains a certain fulfillment in serving the machine with which he is entrusted. The automatism of military life has been immeasurably increased by the perfection and intricacy of instruments and weapons, and it is certain that the human beings who serve them are actually influenced by their automatic character. Combat soldiers must adjust themselves to the laws of these mechanisms, and their habits become of necessity more and more mechanized. Individuality is inevitably suppressed when a group of soldiers have to co-ordinate their movements and all their daily activities in the proper functioning of an instrument of war. But the significant thing is that so many take pleasure in it. There is, I suppose, a perverse kind of freedom here, the freedom from reacting in novel and unpredictable ways. Whatever the source, love for the machine—and the more complicated and exacting, often the greater the love—is an important element in modern combat. The hardened German tanker cited earlier who broke down and cried at the loss of his tank is far from an isolated instance. Those thinkers who believe that a new type of man is bound to emerge as a product of our technological development might well study in detail over the last century the varying relation of men to their weapons of war.

In totalitarian countries, this willingness to become a functionary is much further developed because it is consciously pursued by the dictator at the summit. Self-awareness is fought as an enemy of communal enthusiasms. In 1944 and 1945 I had to listen to Fascist and Nazi police and party functionaries exclaim with nauseating regularity when they were captured: "My conscience is clear!" It made no difference how heinous the deeds were in which they had taken part, always the refrain was the same: "I have done nothing wrong. My conscience is clear." Despite early suspicions that these protestations masked real guilt feelings, I became convinced in the end that most of these men knew no genuine regrets for what they had done. As functionaries, guilt was for them, in any case, an empty word. If their consciences had ever awakened, the lack of response had long since silenced the call. The inhumanity that so appalled me about them was more often than not a kind of absence of feeling rather than sadistic perversion. Machines cannot respond; they can only perform, being at the service of something or someone else.

It was peculiarly abhorrent to me that these people expected the same treatment at my hands that they had meted out to their victims. One particularly repulsive officer of the Security Service, nicknamed "Genickschuss" from his reputation for shooting Polish underground fighters and hapless Jews in the back of the neck, hastily wrote a farewell note to his wife and children after I had interrogated him and consigned him to a jail cell. The jailer brought me his letter within the hour, asking me what to do with it. When I had read it, I was puzzled by the references to his imminent death.

"Does he mean to commit suicide?" I asked the German jailer.

He looked incredulous and answered simply, "Not a chance. He expects you to treat him as he treated his prisoners."

In a kind of baffled rage at the thought of his fearful crimes, I cried out, "And if I did what was right, that is just exactly what I should do."

I shall never forget the jailer's quiet reply. "Sir, it is necessary," he said.

For many soldiers, however, a much more conscious escape from responding to conscience is the fact that they are acting "under orders." Their superiors who issue the orders must take the blame and bear the consequences. When one asked, as I did, which superiors would bear responsibility, the answer was usually vague. Pressed far enough, it usually turned out to be the commander in chief who was to carry all the weight of guilt for deeds that, if committed in peacetime, would have brought heavy penalties.

I was amazed how many American civilian soldiers appeared to put great weight on taking the oath of the soldier. Frequently, I heard the remark: "When I raised my right hand and took that oath, I freed myself of the consequences for what I do. I'll do what they tell me and nobody can blame me." Of course, in a legal sense it is and has been customary in military organizations to hold the highest ranking officer responsible for deeds of his men committed under orders. But Anglo-Saxon lands have long since learned to distinguish between legal and moral responsibility, at least in peacetime. It was clear, however, that most of the soldiers who cited the oath felt that the moral responsibility was being shifted as well. The satisfaction in thus sloughing off responsibility was often plainly visible. Becoming a soldier was like escaping from one's own shadow. To commit deeds of violence without the usual consequences that society visits upon the violent seemed at first a bit unnatural but for many not unpleasant. All too quickly it could become a habit.

In a more legalistic nation like Germany, where the distinction between law and right or between state justice and private morality has never been sharply drawn, the abrogation of personal responsibility for one's deeds is even less complicated. It is hard for civilian America to comprehend the mental and moral conversion involved for a professional German soldier to oppose in full consciousness a military command. To most of us, it sounded like an easy excuse when Hitler's officers protested at Nuremberg and elsewhere that they were "carrying out orders" when they committed atrocities. To most of them, however, this was a sufficient explanation and excuse for their deeds. I suspect that the majority of Germans remain unconvinced that any soldier should be legally punished for "doing his duty," regardless of its inhumane character. I hardly need to add that many Americans, both professional military men and others, are also unpersuaded.

To be sure, since the Nuremberg trials, Western nations have officially denied the soldier's right to obey orders that involve him in crimes. He must distinguish between illegitimate orders and those that are in line with his duty as a soldier. Presumably, the distinction is always clear according to official pronouncements, but in reality under the conditions of total war few things are more difficult to distinguish. Our age is caught in a painful contradiction for which there is no resolution other than the renunciation of wars or at least of the way we have been waging them in this generation. On the other hand, we have come to believe in total victory over the foe, with the use of every means thinkable to effect this goal. Since the opponent's residual strength rests in his industrial potential and civilian labor force, we have found it necessary to disregard the age-old distinction between combatant and noncombatant. In these wars moral considerations become, as a consequence, increasingly irrelevant while the war is in progress. The longer they last the more nearly do the opposing sides approach that boundary where everything is allowed.

However, once the question of victory is decided, we are shocked beyond measure at such moral license and require stern punishment of the vanquished for violations of the rules of war. When reason gains some ascendancy over passion at the end of a war, nearly everyone can see that to turn over individual rights to desperate men, intent on victory at whatever cost, is to invite moral chaos. It seems that the more we transgress in recent wars upon everything essential to individual dignity, the more convinced we become afterward of the necessity of maintaining individual rights inviolate. Small wonder, however, that the majority of soldiers, dimly conscious of this contradiction, refuse to involve themselves in issues so confused and troubling.

Not at all certain whether they will later be considered by their own people as heroes or as scoundrels, great numbers find it simpler to ignore the moral problems by thinking of them as little as possible. Better to let the conscience sleep, to do as the others are doing and as one is told to do, and the future will bring what it will. Who knows whether there will be a future anyway? Most soldiers in wartime feel caught in the present so completely that they surrender their wills to their superiors and exist in the comforting anonymity of the crowd.

Though the above may be a correct, external description of the response or lack of response on the part of most soldiers to individual guilt in waging war, it nevertheless misses all the subtle ways in which guilt is incurred in conflict and made present to the conscience of the minority. There are degrees and kinds of guilt, and not merely a formal declaration of simple guilt or innocence by the inner tribunal. Those soldiers who do respond to the call of conscience find themselves involved in the most baffling situations, in which any action they could take is inappropriate. They learn soon that nearly any of the individual's relations to the world about him can involve him in guilt of some kind, particularly in warfare. It is as pervasive in life and reflection as is human freedom itself. Awakened to his personal responsibility in one aspect of combat action, the soldier is not necessarily awakened to finer nuances of guilt. Yet it sometimes happens that the awakening is thorough and absolute in character, demanding of the subject an entirely different set of relations to friend and enemy.

It is a crucial moment in a soldier's life when he is ordered to perform a deed that he finds completely at variance with his own notions of right and good. Probably for the first time, he discovers that an act someone else thinks to be necessary is for him criminal. His whole being rouses itself in protest, and he may well be forced to choose in this moment of awareness of his freedom an act involving his own life or death. He feels himself caught in a situation that he is powerless to change yet cannot himself be part of. The past cannot be undone and the present is inescapable. His only choice is to alter himself, since all external features are unchangeable.

What this means in the midst of battle can only inadequately be imagined by those who have not experienced it themselves. It means to set oneself against others and with one stroke lose their comforting presence. It means to cut oneself free of doing what one's superiors approve, free of being an integral part of the military organism with the expansion of the ego that such belonging brings. Suddenly the soldier feels himself abandoned and cast off from all security. Conscience has isolated him, and its voice is a warning. If you do this, you will not be at peace with me in the future. You can do it, but you ought not. You must act as a man and not as an instrument of another's will.

I shall always remember the face of a German soldier when he described such a drastic awakening as this. At the time we picked him up for investigation in the Vosges in 1944, he was fighting with the French Maquis against his own people. To my question concerning his motives for deserting to the French Resistance, he responded by describing his earlier involvement in German reprisal raids against the French. On one such raid, his unit was ordered to burn a village and to allow none of the villagers to escape. (Possibly the village was Oradour and the soldier was one of the participants in that grisly atrocity; at that time we knew little of what was happening elsewhere and I did not ask him for names.) As he told how women and children were shot as they fled screaming from the flames of their burning homes, the soldier's face was contorted in painful fashion and he was nearly unable to breathe. It was quite clear that this extreme experience had shocked him into full awareness of his own guilt, a guilt he feared he would never atone. At the moment of that awakening he did not have the courage or resolution to hinder the massacre, but his desertion to the Resistance soon after was evidence of a radically new course. Terrible as was his self-reproach at what now could not be undone, he had won himself through this experience and would never again be available as a functionary.

In the Netherlands, the Dutch tell of a German soldier who was a member of an execution squad ordered to shoot innocent hostages. Suddenly he stepped out of rank and refused to participate in the execution. On the spot he was charged with treason by the officer in charge and was placed with the hostages, where he was promptly executed by his comrades. In such an act the soldier has abandoned once and for all the security of the group and exposed himself to the ultimate demands of freedom. He responded in the crucial moment to the voice of conscience and was no longer driven by external commands. In this case we can only guess what must have been the influence of his deed on slayers and slain. At all events, it was surely not slight, and his example on those who hear of the episode cannot fail to be inspiriting. Were it not for the revelation of nobility in mankind, which again and again appears in time of war, we could scarcely endure reading the literature of combat.

These are, of course, extreme examples and not to be taken as typical. Normally, the awakening of guilt is much more gradual, and the achievement of clarity about duty to one's country and duty to oneself a matter of anguished doubt, sometimes lasting for months or years. But the primary realization is the same in all cases: there is a line that a man dare not cross, deeds he dare not commit, regardless of orders and the hopelessness of the situation, for such deeds would destroy something in him that he values more than life itself. He may decide that his commander, his army, or his people may justly demand his life but may not command him to do what is in violation of his deepest self. However clear he may be about this momentous conclusion in moments of quiet and repose, the soldier is not thereby steeled against anxiety and fear of death. In the melee of conflict he may at times feel as do his unawakened comrades, that life is all he has, after all. Personal resolution is constantly attacked by the strain and disorder of combat life. His body, he discovers, is not always subject to his will. Impulses and emotions sweep him away, causing him to act again and again contrary to his sense of right. Against his innermost desire, he involves himself in guilt. Conscience within him is a voice long before it is a power; he desires to respond long before he has the required resolution. Though the voice is insistent, more clamorous impulses are able to dominate him in moments of violent action.

Nevertheless, his conscience has established an image of the ideal, a man who will acquit himself in whatever situation with independence and dignity. His inner history henceforth in combat will be the struggle to live up to this ideal. It may be that the soldier is contending against fear that he will involuntarily desert his comrades in a critical moment and be responsible for their death. It may be that he has qualms against killing enemy soldiers. Or he may be utterly persuaded of the justice of his country's

cause and of the necessity of destroying lives to realize
that cause, yet strongly opposed to this or that means his
side is employing. He may be struggling to acquit himself
well in a tangle of personal relationships common to military organizations in times of tension and peril. The occasions and situations are manifold in which the soldier who
can no longer pass responsibility for his acts to others
must struggle to gain full possession of himself. The voice
of conscience is forever convicting him of inadequacy and
insufficiency, urging him to better efforts. The ideal of
acquitting himself like a man comes to appear utopian
when he is confronted with certain situations.

Guilt is likely to come upon him in many other ways
than as a consequence of natural fear of pain or death.
Modern wars are full of border situations where a soldier
is forced to choose between evils and where every choice is
like leaping into the dark because its consequences are un-
foreseeable. Rarely will he find a situation as clearly wrong
as the shooting of hostages or the strafing of fleeing
civilians. On the contrary, he will often have to choose
between helping a wounded comrade to safety or remain-
ing at his post to protect others whom he does not know.
Sometimes he will have to choose the welfare of his unit
at the expense of other units or the civilian populace.
Hunger and cold and animal needs are everywhere in war
in the midst of superfluity of food and warmth and deli-
cacies. When he gives up his food or warm room in favor
of some pitiful urchin or haggard mother, such charity can
hardly comfort him because it is so transient. In the face
of the need, his efforts will seem inconsequential to the
point of futility. Even though the soldier may become a
relatively selfless man in the service of the civil populace
and his weaker comrades, he will seldom be at ease with
himself. In some degree he will feel guilty of omitting to
do what he ought, or doing what he ought not. This is inevitable, of course, for he is an individual who thinks of
himself and others as ends in themselves in a situation
where human beings are means for superpersonal goals.

Men are materials to be expended for national interests, real or imagined. All the awakened soldier can hope to do in such a society is to meliorate the lot of the less fortunate, to act in an inhumane environment as humanely as possible. Opportunities to be humane are ordinarily plentiful enough in combat zones, but his freedom is constricted on all sides. It is like moving on a rack.

Such a soldier is likely to suffer most of all from the commands of military superiors when they are close to the border zone of the forbidden, that is, when they transgress the line that he cannot cross if he is to live with his conscience. The satisfaction that the unawakened conscience takes in making itself an instrument of higher wills is for the awakened conscience a leading source of its misery. To be required to carry out orders in which he does not believe, given by men who are frequently far removed from the realities with which the orders deal and often motivated by abstract hatred—this is the familiar lot of the combat soldier. The man of conscience can survive morally only by following the letter of such orders and disobeying their intention.

It is a great boon of front-line positions that this disobedience is frequently possible, since supervision is not very exact where danger of death is present. Many a conscientious soldier has discovered he could reinterpret military orders in his own spirit before obeying them. The fortunate ones have escaped difficulties with their commanders; the unfortunate have often ended in disciplinary barracks or even a death cell. At all events, the tension in such a soldier between the voice of conscience and the demands made upon him as a means and instrument of higher authority will rarely relax. The alternatives to this tension are for him either the surrender of his conscience to superiors or open defiance of their orders with fateful consequences to his life and freedom. Both alternatives he will seek to avoid as long as possible.

Here is a personal example. For several months in World War II, I was attached to an infantry division whose divisional intelligence officer, a colonel, was an insensitive military tyrant. He was pleased to have our detachment of six men under his control and at the same time was deeply resentful of our superior educational backgrounds and independence of mind. He liked to meddle with our somewhat specialized job of interrogating the civilian populace in the search for spies and saboteurs the retreating Germans might have left behind or sent over the front. Increasingly, I found myself resenting and resisting his often harsh orders for civilian restrictions and prohibitions. As linguists, we were his only means of communication with the civilian populace, who were regarded by him as an infernal nuisance to be tolerated only because they could not be conveniently expelled from combat areas.

When our division entered the first towns of Alsace, we encountered numerous young Alsatians in civilian clothes who had deserted from the German armies when on furlough and hidden out at the risk of their lives while awaiting our advance. The Alsatians had helped to hide these youths from the ruthless clutches of the Gestapo. Some of them had previously served with the French against the Germans, but when Alsace and Lorraine were incorporated in Germany with the defeat of France in 1940, they had been conscripted into Hitler's armies, only to desert at the first opportunity. There was, of course, much rejoicing now that they could at last leave their hiding places and greet old friends and neighbors publicly once more. Many of them came to us and offered their help in intelligence work. Hard pressed as we were for help (only two in our detachment knew German well enough to be effective), we found much for them to do.

But the colonel had noticed the appearance of young men on the streets here in contrast to France, where male youth had been conspicuously absent. He called our detachment commander by telephone and demanded an explanation. With our briefing, the captain gave him the facts of the situation. The colonel's response was immediate: "Do they have discharge papers from the German

Army?" It was explained to him that deserters were never supplied with discharge papers, that being contrary to the usage of the German Army. His conclusion was breath-taking. In that case, these men were prisoners of war, and we were to round them up and ship them in prisoner trucks through regular channels to the huge camps in France. The colonel insisted on quick action. Our captain, who was sympathetic with us but afraid of the colonel, begged us to arrest the deserters the next day as ordered.

I was fortunate in having as a German-speaking colleague a strong-minded and intelligent young man of Boston Irish descent. He was profane, not overly scrupulous on moral issues, but fair-minded. He and I determined not to obey the order. To obey it would be the one way to alienate completely this friendly and much-mistreated Alsatian people. For parents to see their sons, who had risked their lives escaping from the German Army, loaded on the same trucks with hated German soldiers and transported to prison camps would be to embitter relations with their "liberators" from the beginning. Moreover, the orders were manifestly unjust to these young men, who felt themselves to be allies and wanted in every way to aid our cause. The two of us hoped to avoid the issue by simply ignoring the order and continuing our other work, of which we had more than enough. But the colonel called again and was this time insulting and insistent. Still we ignored him, though our captain begged us to act. The third day, the colonel was threatening us with court-martial and worse for disobeying a direct order.

What were we to do? The two of us talked it over and decided to continue to refuse. It was not so much courage on my part as physical weariness and moral disgust at the injustices of warfare. In the most obscene language, my associate declared that the Army could court-martial him a hundred times and he would not obey such a stupid, senseless command. His mood was one of weary, sullen resistance to the vast stupidity of higher headquarters. He had been much longer in the war than I, having served with distinction in Africa and Sicily as well as in Italy and France. If his concern with the injustice of the order was not as great as mine, his resoluteness was greater, and fortified me. I had visions of the forbidding disciplinary barracks we had glimpsed in North Africa, of a dishonorable discharge and the disgrace it would bring on my aged father, who would not be able to understand why I had to disobey. Still, I knew that if I did not draw the line here I would be unable to draw it anywhere. If I did not refuse to become a party to the arrest of innocent, wronged men, I could not refuse to do anything that this or any other colonel ordered. I felt myself to be at the end of a tether. This was to be a showdown, and I had little doubt as to the winner. The loneliness and isolation of spirit that swept over me served to teach me how much I had hitherto been sustained by the silent approval of "the others." Even my partner in disobedience could not lift from me the heavy spiritual burden, for he was bitter and cynical about the whole affair.

Fortunately, things turned out in very different fashion from the expected. The colonel decided to call up army headquarters and report our insubordination before taking further action. He chanced to reach an intelligent officer who knew us both slightly, and this officer wanted to know why we persisted in disobeying orders. This the colonel had never stopped to determine, but when he did communicate the cause, Army Intelligence found our reasons good and within a day or two sent through an order that all Alsatian deserters were to be left with their families and in no case to be transported anywhere with German prisoners of war.

We had unexpectedly won the day and drew comfort afterward from the report that where our division had gone through Alsace the population was distinctly more pro-American than in other parts of Alsace-Lorraine. In areas where the deserters had been arrested, they had been forced to undergo manifold hardships and humiliations in prisoner-of-war camps, ironically enough because they were not in uniform, and were treated by our troops as cowardly and unworthy the respect accorded regular prisoners.

This was only an incident of war, not objectively important except as it influenced sectors of a population for or against the Allied cause. But subjectively it was for me a kind of turning point. As a result of it, I gained no great confidence in my ability to withstand extreme pressures from official authority, yet I had determined that a line could be drawn between personal rights and military demands. Though I knew that sheer good fortune had prevented the normal consequences of disobedience from falling upon me, I felt, nevertheless, immensely strengthened for a possible second refusal. More important, the incident cleared my mind on the vexed question of the relation of the individual to his state. Hard as they were to assert, I now felt convinced that the individual had his absolute rights even in the desperate struggle for survival that is modern war. And survival without integrity of conscience is worse than perishing outright, or so it seemed to me. Nothing had furthered my self-knowledge so much since my encounter with the old man of the mountain in Italy the year before.

I have no doubt that many others have found themselves in much more crucial difficulties in warfare than this example illustrates. Yet, curiously enough, most contemporary war novels deal with nearly every agony of combat except this one. Where matters of conscience are taken up, as in the immensely popular *Caine Mutiny*, there is frequently an ambivalence in the attitude of the author toward the rights of conscience against military organization. In Wouk's novel, for instance, the reader is left in doubt about the moral justification for "the mutiny," despite the fact that the captain of the *Caine* is portrayed in the worst possible light. He is cowardly, completely neurotic, a pathological liar, and incapable of giving orders that will save his ship from destruction. Yet, the

author reminds us, he is a commander in the United States
Navy, of long service, and as such an early fighter against
the evil enemies of his country. Perhaps he should be
obeyed despite his incapacity, since the principles of
obedience and discipline count for more in a war of survival than individual conscience and private morality. This
is typical of the modern confusion about the spheres of
individual right and state authority in the era of total war.

However, the man of awakened conscience actually
caught in this dilemma, as contrasted with the author
writing a book about it, will usually be clear that duty to
himself prohibits him from acting contrary to his voice,
regardless of his fears and the personal consequences.
He may obey such orders, but at the cost of his moral
integrity. The safe observer has no right to blame him,
for the sternest self-discipline is demanded. Few men in
any age have had the moral stamina of a Socrates, who
many centuries ago decided for himself that it was a right
and duty to disobey his state and people when he felt they
were wrong, but not his right to flee from their punishment for that disobedience. If few young men can be
expected to attain the resolution of a mature Socrates, the
reflective soldier is nearly certain to share the Socratic trust
in the reliability of his conscience when it is in conflict with
the group will.

This is particularly true of the conscience that is supported by faith in its divine origin. A secure religious faith
has enabled many a soldier to act in defiance of unjust
commands or to overcome the temptation to save himself
at the cost of others. As I have pointed out elsewhere, the
testimony of those condemned officers and soldiers who
struck against Hitler in 1944 is eloquent and instructive
evidence of this fact. Judging from their last letters to
friends and family members, not all of them had religious
support for their consciences. Those who had no religious
faith or hope for life after death acted as courageously as
the others and faced the end with confidence in the justice
of their cause. Nevertheless, their sadness stands in sharp

contrast with the tranquillity and even exaltation of those who were believers. Both groups seemed immensely relieved to be freed from the pressure of conformity to a system and a party they had learned to despise. The difference between them was that those of religious faith took leave of their lives as though the physical end was the beginning of something mysterious yet marvelous.

There is a kind of guilt that transcends the personal responsibility of the sensitive conscience and burdens that soldier particularly who retains faith in the cause and the country for which he is fighting. It is the guilt the individual shares as a member of a military unit, a national fighting force, a people at war. We may call it social or political or collective guilt; it is not essentially different for the civilian than for the soldier, and it is inescapable. No matter how self-contained and isolated in spirit the man of conscience may feel, he cannot avoid the realization that he is a participant in a system and an enterprise whose very essence is violence and whose spirit is to win at whatever cost. For the soldier, it is his squad or company or division that performs deeds abhorrent to him. No matter how strongly he abjures personal responsibility for this or that deed, he cannot escape social responsibility. So long as he wears the same uniform as his fellows, he will be regarded by outsiders as one of them. His fellows, too, treat him as a member of the fraternity of men at arms. The conscience within him may be more and more appalled by the heedlessness of group behavior and the mechanical ruthlessness of an organization whose dedication to violence gives it an unholy character. I was appalled and yet I could not escape it. I wrote in my journal one day at the height of the war:

Yesterday we caught two spies, making our recent total five. We are getting a reputation as a crack detachment. One had to be severely beaten before he confessed. It was pretty horrible, and I kept away from the room where it was done . . . though I could not escape his cries of pain. . . . I lay

awake until three o'clock this morning. . . . I thought of the
Hamlet line as most appropriate, "Tis bitter cold and I am sick
at heart."

A soldier with an awakened conscience who is a member of such a community, coarse, vulgar, heedless, violent,
realizes with overpowering clarity the possibility of being
alienated from his own kind. This uniformed, machine-like
monster, the combat unit, drives him back into himself and
repels him utterly. Toward individuals who make it up, he
can gain many relationships, but the collectivity itself
chokes him without mercy.

Toward his nation as a nation he may well come to
experience in his innermost self the same lack of relationship. A state at war reveals itself to the penetrating eye
in its clearest light and the spectacle is not beautiful.
Nietzsche's likeness of it to a cold snake is, from one perspective, not greatly exaggerated. The awakened conscience will recognize a part of this spirit of the nation in
the hate-filled speeches of politician-patriots, in the antipathy toward dissenting opinions about the utter virtue
of its cause, in the ruthlessness with which the individual
is sacrificed for real or alleged national advantages. It will
despise the fanaticism with which this state makes morally
dubious and historically relative ends into absolutes, its
perversity in maintaining pride at whatever price in human
misery.

At the same time, justice will force this soldier to admit that these are his people, driven by fear and hatred,
who are directing this vast mechanism. If he is honest
with himself he will admit that he, too, is a violent man
on occasion and capable of enjoying the fruits of violence.
Legally, and more than legally, he belongs to the community of soldiers and to the state. At some level of his
being he can understand why they perform as they do and
can find it in his heart to feel sorry for some of the politicians and higher officers. In their place he wonders if he
would do any better than they. He is bound to reflect

that his nation has given him refuge and sustenance, provided him whatever education and property he calls his own. He belongs and will always belong to it in some sense, no matter where he goes or how hard he seeks to alter his inheritance. The crimes, therefore, that his nation or one of its units commits cannot be indifferent to him. He shares the guilt as he shares the satisfaction in the generous deeds and worthy products of nation or army. Even if he did not consciously will them and was unable to prevent them, he cannot wholly escape responsibility for collective deeds.

He belongs and yet he does not belong. "I did not ask to be born," he is likely to tell himself while struggling with his responsibility for collective deeds, "and I did not choose my nation. Had I been given a choice of places to grow up at various stages in my education I might have chosen other than the nation in which I was accidentally born. I am, of course, a citizen of this nation and am willing to expose my life in its defense. But in my inner being I belong only to the community that I have freely chosen, my friends, my club, my church, my profession. All other associations of mine are external and accidental, however little I may have realized it earlier. This does not free me from the guilt that this nation is heaping upon itself, so long as I participate in its defense. I shall always be guilty as long as I belong to a nation at all. Yet there is no good life apart from some nation or other."

It is clear to him that his political guilt is of a different sort from the personal, since the latter stems from his freedom in a direct way, the former only in part. The nation was in being long before him and will presumably continue in being after his death. Hence his capacity to change its course is immeasurably limited by its history as well as by his own powers. For the politically conscious soldier, this does not mean, however, that it is negligible. Insofar as his political guilt is in direct relation to his freedom, he will become conscious of what he has done or failed to do to promote or hinder the humanizing of mili-

tary or political means and objectives. He will be certain
at all events that he has not done enough. On this or that
occasion he has been silent when he should have spoken
out. In his own smaller or larger circle of influence he has
not made his whole weight felt. Had he brought forth the
civil courage to protest in time, some particular act of injustice might have been avoided. Whatever the level of
influence the soldier commands, from the squad or pla-
toon to the command of armies, in some manner he is
able to affect the course of group action.

When the nation for which he is fighting has enjoyed
a free government and been previously responsive to its
citizens' wishes, he will be conscious of greater responsibility than will the soldier whose government is authoritarian or totalitarian. The greater the possibility of
free action in the communal sphere, the greater the degree of guilt for evil deeds done in the name of everyone.
Still, the degrees of guilt are impossible to assess for anyone else, and hardly any two people share an equal burden
of communal guilt. The soldier may have been too young
as a civilian to have exerted much influence on events or
he may have been too poorly informed or confused to
know where his political duty lay. As a soldier, he may be
in too isolated or insignificant a location to make effective
use of his freedom. No citizen of a free land can justly
accuse his neighbor, I believe, of political guilt, of not having done as much as he should to prevent the state of
war or the commission of this or that state crime. But
each can—and the man of conscience will—accuse himself
in proportion to the freedom he had to alter the course of
events.

The peculiar agony of the combat soldier's situation is
that, even more than in his struggle with his own ideal
self, he is aware of the puniness of his individual powers
to effect a change. War not only narrows the limits of personal freedom, but it likewise constricts the individual's
communal liberty, his capacity to make his power felt
in significant ways. The sense of impotence will weigh

upon him day after day. Though the man of awakened conscience will hardly believe that the war is a natural catastrophe, he will not know how any individual can alter its seemingly inexorable course. Personal guilt can be in some measure atoned and the struggle to improve can be taken up every morning anew. But communal guilt comes upon him in ever increasing measure in any war, and he is likely to feel utterly inadequate either to atone for it or prevent its accumulation.

For instance, when the news of the atomic bombing of Hiroshima and Nagasaki came, many an American soldier felt shocked and ashamed. The combat soldier knew better than did Americans at home what those bombs meant in suffering and injustice. The man of conscience wherever he was realized intuitively that the vast majority of the Japanese in both cities were no more, if no less, guilty of the war than were his own parents, sisters, or brothers. In his shame, he may have said to himself, as some of us did: "The next atomic bomb, dropped in anger, will probably fall on my own country and we will have deserved it." Such a conviction will hardly relieve him of the heavy sense of wrong that his nation committed and the responsibility for which he must now in some measure share. All the arguments used in justification—the shortening of the war by many months and the thousands of American lives presumably saved—cannot alter the fact that his government was the first to use on undefended cities, without any warning, a monstrous new weapon of annihilation.

Worst of all about such deeds is that millions accepted and felt relief. Hearing this near-exultation in the enemy's annihilation, one can only conclude that political guilt has another source than the freedom of the individual to affect group action. It lies in the degree of his identification with the goals and the means of realizing them that his nation adopts. The person who inwardly approves an immoral action of his government or military unit testifies to his own probable decision had he possessed the freedom and opportunity of the actors. Freedom is possible, therefore, not only in the power to do or prevent, but also in inner assent and consent to action by others. With a relative criterion like this it is, of course, impossible to be exact in estimating even one's own guilt. Yet the jubilation in evil deeds allows little room for doubt that inner consent is often forthcoming. So do thousands of people increase their political guilt in wartime beyond the range of their direct action.

To some extent after World War I and explicitly after World War II, doctrines of collective guilt have become common. The German nation, for example, and particularly the German Army is often said to be guilty for having fought for Hitler in his aggressive wars of conquest and rapine. However innocent the individual soldier may have been of any personal misconduct, the fact that he was a member of a criminal conspiracy to deprive other peoples of their independence by violent means made him guilty. What justice is there in such a claim? To what extent is a German soldier in the last war guilty who kept himself free of personal crimes but was forced to experience, more or less directly, atrocities committed by his fellow soldiers and who was not blind to Hitler's mad ambitions? Is he not in an utterly different position from the soldier of a nation like ours who fought the war defensively to repel aggression?

In terms of what I have previously said, the answer can only be that no outsider has a moral right to make such an accusation about either the soldiery or the people as a whole. For an anti-Nazi soldier to have interfered with some act of injustice carried out by his fellow countrymen would have resulted in his prompt execution, as enough recorded instances prove. Apart from the demands of courage and determination that such an act requires, the question that tormented some soldiers in this situation was: What political purpose will my sacrifice serve? Many a conscientious German soldier might have screwed up his courage to open interference had he seen clearly in what

way his death would have helped prevent further crimes.
Fortunate soldiers found the right moment and the right
deed with which to strike against the system they despised,
and their chance to witness made them content to die.
Others fought to the end of the war without such opportunities or without the necessary courage. Only those who
sacrificed themselves in similar situations have the right
to accuse them, and probably few of them would care
to do so, if they were alive and able. For my own deeds
I am responsible and can be held accountable, even if I
act under the orders of another. For the deeds of my fellow
men, specifically my fellow countrymen, my responsibility
cannot be a public or legal one, for it is too dependent
on my estimate of my ability to hinder criminal acts and
of my inner consent to their commission.

Yet if accusations of collective guilt are unjustified, the
sensitive German soldier could hardly escape the consciousness of his own political guilt. A burning sense of
shame at the deeds of his government and the acts of horror committed by German soldiers and police was the
mark of a conscientious German at the close of the war.
"I am ashamed to be a German" was a not infrequent remark when friend was speaking to friend as the revelations
of what the Third Reich had done became generally
known. To be sure, those without conscience considered
that they had atoned sufficiently for their political "mis-
takes" by their suffering during and after the war, and
rejected with indignation any imputation of collective
guilt. They wanted to hear nothing of their vicarious part
in the crimes of their fellow citizens.

The reflective man knows in his heart what rarely
crosses his lips, that the sins of his fellows are not so remote from him as he would like. If he is a soldier, he, too,
has yielded at times to the temptations of power and the
license that violence evokes in all of us. However free he
may have kept himself from external participation in evil
deeds and however foreign cruelty may be to his better
nature, he will be aware that there is in nearly all men the

capacity for criminal deeds and the obscure yearning for license to act without consequences, hence his recognition of the chains of communal responsibility and his knowledge that atonement in this sphere is largely chimerical. No human power could atone for the injustice, suffering, and degradation of spirit of a single day of warfare. All of us shared the guilt, as I wrote in my journal on two occasions.

I talked yesterday to a young Viennese deserter . . . he had had nothing to eat but potato soup. . . . The picture he gave of the prison was grim enough. . . . One man, suspected of being a spy, was given nothing to eat for six days and was now past hunger. If he talked he would be shot as a spy, if he didn't he would starve—a difficult choice. The youth was strong, courteous. . . . He finally asked me in German, "Do I have to go back to Epinal?" And his whole soul was in the question and in his eyes. I said no, that was all past for him, and his face was suddenly illumined. I felt in a moment the whole stark tragedy of this war. What bitter cruelty all of us exercise! We are guilty and deserve the extreme penalty. Nothing that happens to me in future will I ever feel unjust and unmerited.

This morning was spent in attempting to control the mass of refugees streaming around here, some 2000 in a town whose population hardly exceeds 5000. This fate is pathetic, and more and more this problem of displaced persons becomes tremendous. Germany was really a slave state on a gigantic scale. Almost all of these foreign workers are on the roads, a few hours after their liberation, going they know not where, but away from the front and toward home, they hope, though thousands must know that they have no longer a home. But this afternoon Seitz and I saw something ten times worse. There was a concentration camp not far from here, and last Saturday the German guards loaded the inmates onto freight trains and tried to haul them away. When they discovered that the trains could not proceed, they left them near a town named Osterburken. We found them there this afternoon, some 880, half-dead, horribly starved people, among them 300 French Maquis, political prisoners. . . . To see these living deaths in their striped suits in rags, dragging their feet, was a sight that I would have done without. To add to its gruesomeness, there was a dead German soldier deserter, who had been hanged and whose body was lying by the road under a tree. Someone had cut him down but the rope was still around his neck and his feet were tied. He had been an attractive youngster, and one could pretty well guess his story. The SS who had hanged him will one day have to pay, and those who were responsible for the unimaginable suffering of these concentration-camp inmates will pay also.

The realization of political guilt is poignantly expressed in a poem by Albrecht Haushofer, one of the determined and long-standing opponents of Hitler, who was imprisoned and finally executed near the end of the war. His little book of poems entitled *Moabiter Sonette*, written in a Berlin prison while his hands were shackled, testifies to political guilt of a man who had already atoned more than is required of most of us. In the sonnet entitled *Schuld* (Guilt), he begins by noting how easy it is for him to carry the guilt that his Nazi court trial wanted to load upon him. To them he was a traitor to his people in the plot against Hitler. Then he concludes in the German version, to which I have added a literal translation:

> *Doch schuldig bin ich anders als ihr denkt,*
> *ich müsste früher meine Pflicht erkennen*
> *ich müsste schärfer Unheil Unheil nennen—*
> *mein Urteil hab ich viel zu lang gelenkt . . .*
>
> *Ich klage mich in meinem Herzen an:*
> *Ich habe mein Gewissen lang betrogen*
> *Ich hab mich selbst und andere belogen—*
>
> *ich kannte früh des Jammers ganze Bahn—*
> *ich hab gewarnt—nicht hart genug und klar!*
> *Und heute weiss ich, was ich schuldig war . . .*

> Yet I am guilty otherwise than you think.
> I should have known my duty earlier
> And called evil by its name more sharply—
> My judgment I kept flexible too long . . .

In my heart I accuse myself of this:
I deceived my conscience long
I lied to myself and others—

Early I knew the whole course of this misery—
I warned—but not hard enough or clearly!
Today I know of what I am guilty . . .

Thus the conscientious German soldier may well feel greater political guilt than a conscientious Allied soldier, depending on the measure of assent he had given to the National Socialist regime and the freedom of action he possessed. But the quality of his political guilt will hardly be different, for the warfare was not carried on by angels against devils, but by soldiers in a relatively just cause fighting soldiers in a relatively unjust cause. If the character of Hitler and his paladins gave to the Allied side a moral justification unusual in warfare, the Western nations have no reason to forget their share of responsibility for Hitler's coming to power or their dubious common cause with the Russian dictator. The reflective soldier on both sides of the conflict will see no escape from political guilt as long as he remains a member of a state. If, in his disillusionment, he is tempted to renounce his nation and pledge his allegiance to the human race alone, this, too, will prove illusory, for mankind collectively is doubtless as predisposed to injustice as nations are.

It is precisely this realization that may lead the soldier to a recognition that personal and political guilt are hardly resolvable on their own levels. They involve a guilt that can only be called metaphysical, because it concerns man's very being and its relations to the rest of the cosmos. The root of the guilt problem lies in human nature itself, in our failure as human beings to live in accordance with our potentialities and our vision of the good. Because we do fail, our spirits are isolated and closed to each other. None of us can be to another as we really desire to be, for we strike against something strange and alien in him. The sympathies of even the most reflective and sensitive do not extend far enough to overcome entirely the antipathy toward his fellows that is in nearly all of us. In some facet of our being we are closed and indifferent, not open to others or concerned with their fate. Though most of us are capable of feeling compassion for the suffering of men, and recognize our common kinship in isolation and loneliness, this recognition is rarely strong enough to influence our action decisively. We cannot love enough either our fellow men or our common mother, the nature from which we originate and to which we return. As human beings, we are in a perpetual state of disequilibrium with the rest of creation, neither humble enough to recognize our dependence nor bold enough to actualize our powers.

If this is capable of oppressing many of us in time of peace, it is easy to imagine with how much greater force it strikes a reflective soldier in combat. Everywhere he experiences himself and his comrades as violators of the earth. The ruthlessness with which organized warriors deal with the order of nature in order to defend their miserable lives will appall him, all the more so in modern times, when the scorched-earth policy has been succeeded by atomic destruction. The crimes against horses and other animals that men press into the service of their insane passions, the recklessness in destroying human habitations and works of art, full of the dignity and genius of human labor, will rob him forever of any exaggerated hope for the species. When his martial passions are kindled, this pygmy of creation is capable of defying the creative source of all life and flinging away all that he has formerly cherished. Like the ancient Titans of fable, he seems intent on storming the ramparts of heaven and calling down upon himself a novel kind of punishment.

Faced with this presumptuousness of the human creature, his closedness and dearth of love, the awakened soldier will be driven to say in his heart: "I, too, belong to this species. I am ashamed not only of my own deeds, not only of my nation's deeds, but of human deeds as well. I am ashamed to be a man." This is the culmination of a passionate logic which begins in warfare with the questioning of some act the soldier has been ordered to perform contrary to his conscience. Consciousness of failure to act in response to conscience can lead to the greatest revulsion, not only for oneself, but for the human species. How many soldiers have experienced in battle a profound distaste for the human creature! I wrote of my own despair:

It is eleven o'clock at night, and raining. The town is quiet, a fresh breeze, rain-laden, is blowing. I sit alone in my room and ponder my own limitations, wondering why the whole mystery of the universe must be closed, why I must plod on in the path of so many others, subject to the same temptations and weaknesses. Such nights as these have for years beaten in upon me my failures, my blindness, and the impenetrable nature of the world.

The combat soldier who experiences this guilt of the human creature deeply is likely to be caught in a serious inner crisis. On the one hand, he perceives the degraded and degrading level of human life, as battle experiences can so well teach it. And this degradation does not seem to be a consequence of war conditions so much as war conditions are a consequence of it. His whole being rebels against this condition; his conscience warns him that it ought not to be. Neither he nor the others deserve to be spared. All are such caricatures of what they should be that death appears to be the only fitting resolution. On the other hand, he is plunged into doubt about the possibility of attaining to any other state. Perhaps men are what they are by virtue of some hidden necessity in the nature of things. Is it wise to expect anything else than the spectacle now offered? The despairing soldier seeks for a reason why men are the creatures they show themselves to be in combat, and the reason that has appealed over many generations is the idea of necessity. Freedom may be after all an illusion, and the conscience within me, always protesting, be fatally wrong.

This classic struggle between freedom and necessity often tears the heart of one who has advanced a little in the consciousness of guilt. Perhaps the feeling of necessity is the final refuge of that spirit in us which resists all attempts at self-reproach, that uncivilizable ego which stops at nothing to justify the self in its lowest, most aggressive manifestations. Or it may be simply the hopelessness of the effort to rid oneself of metaphysical guilt that makes belief in necessity so attractive. At any rate, for the soldier in battle, the arguments for necessity look very strong indeed. The voice of conscience can be so easily explained away in terms of childhood indoctrination and religious superstition. It is tempting to attack the validity of the feeling of freedom through its questionable origin.

Some survive this crisis of faith only by yielding up their belief in the individual's responsibility for his actions. The moral cynics, which modern wars generate in great numbers, testify to a lost hope in mankind. Where cynicism is not mere shallowness and show, it is the cry of men who have not been able to endure the tension between their inner ideal and outer reality. They resolve not to take the world or themselves seriously any longer and give themselves over to enjoyment. But everyone notices that there is a pathos about their gaiety, and their frivolity is hardly contagious.

The soldier who does not succumb to the seductions of a theory of necessity, but attempts, instead, to resolve the conflict through reason finds himself long exposed to indecisive inner doubts. Gradually he may come to realize that neither freedom nor determinism can be established satisfactorily except in an emotional sense. In practice, it is not difficult to convince himself that he is free to change. On reflection, however, the clarity that practice generates searches the past and finds necessity, the other looks to action in present and future and asserts freedom. In serene moments the soldier may be very clear that he is partly free, in projecting himself into the future and striving for an ideal; partly determined, in being limited by what he has done and been. Yet whether his own freedom is not a tiny aspect of some larger necessity will escape his best efforts at analysis. At times he becomes convinced that the two are not opposed at all, but in a mysterious way two sides of the same coin.

The logic of most soldiers with a deep sense of guilt is a logic of passion, and all the subtleties of the problem will normally be lost on them. If at times such a soldier is too tired out or occupied with other cares to feel distressed in any way, the conflict is likely to be driven deeper into his unconscious mind, there to weigh on his spirit and foster melancholy. What he longs for essentially is a simple piety, an attitude of gratefulness and acceptance for the created. He loses whatever satisfaction he formerly took in the destructive ways of war. Man as *Homo furens* appears now to be a monster to him, for this soldier has learned to cherish solely the human function as preserver and conserver of created things.

Many a soldier in this predicament has found a blessed release in the certainty that there is a higher order of reality where the irresolvable is resolved. It can be—indeed, often is—a rather primitive trust in the ultimate justice and mercy of a heavenly father, in whom justice and mercy are not at odds. In a sense, the surrender here is similar to the satisfaction in believing that necessity is ruler of all. But the difference is apparent in the richness of meaning that religious trust evidently brings. All previous struggles are seen to have been necessary preparation and purification for present assurance. In God all that appears endlessly difficult for human reason is mysteriously purposeful and clear. Apart from the validity of the religious resolution of guilt (and for the nonbeliever it appears to be little more than an escape mechanism), the efficacy of this path is beyond any other that mortal man has found.

If the soldier possesses a primary religious nature, he

can derive absolution and exaltation from his capacity for
repentance and surrender to the will of the divine. He
loses any need for death and sometimes, too, the fear of
death as well, for he has gained the great virtue of hope,
which is perhaps the strongest hold in life and is that
virtue which is peculiar to religion. If it does not free him
from the usual troubles of the flesh, religious hope does
assure him that there is a realm on the other side of human weakness and guilt. His one desire is to act in accord
with his hope in this supreme reality, and, if he is a Christian, the prayer that will be most often on his lips is: Not
my will but Thine be done. Personal and political guilt,
which may have weighed upon him unendurably before,
are now resolved in this childlike trust in a single interpretation and interpreter.

For the more philosophical temperament, however, there
is no immediate solution or resolution to metaphysical
guilt. If such a soldier is strong enough, the insight gained
through his recognition of this most comprehensive form
of guilt may help him gradually win a new relationship
to his fellows and to the cosmos. Guilt can teach him, as
few things else are able to, how utterly a man can be
alienated from the very sources of his being. But the recognition may point the way to a reunion and a reconciliation
with the varied forms of the created. In short, he may pass
beyond his rejection of the human species and gain a new
grasp of his world. Such a soldier will discover his future
mission in life to be as far removed as possible from the
destructive work of war. He will be absorbed in the reconstructive, the simple, and the truly humane arts. Atonement will become for him not an act of faith or a deed,
but a life, a life devoted to strengthening the bonds between men and between man and nature. He will not
be in any obvious way a reformer or a social worker or a
preacher. But among his friends he will be known as
extraordinarily gentle, sane, and wise.

These are some of the outcomes of a metaphysical conviction of guilt. Some it can drive mad; some to the barely

covert wish for death. Others are overwhelmed by the belief that all is necessary, and conclude very often that nothing really matters except pleasures of the senses. Still others triumph through religious faith or through a philosophical reconciliation with man and nature, thus using guilt as a means to a firmer and more enduring hold on life. Metaphysical guilt may well be as prevalent in peace as in war, since all men incur it to greater or lesser extent. Frequently, however, it necessitates an excess of moral and political guilt to force our acceptance of this reality. In this sphere, too, some men require the utter exposure and extreme experiences of combat to come to their true selves.

I find it hard to believe that in the wars of our day any great number of soldiers attain the possibilities that lie in the acceptance of guilt. As I indicated earlier, the reasons appear to lie in a dominant mood of our times and in the different nature of warfare. Yet it is hard to be sure, for few people care to admit the guilt they sometimes feel. Possibly the profound aversion to war that is widespread at the mid-century is not entirely due to the political and economic fruitlessness of recent wars and their unprecedented fury. Many who reveal no outward evidence may be aware at some level of their being that the moral issues of war are hardly resolvable on present capital. They may realize that since wars cannot teach nations repentance and humility, they must be abandoned if we are not to lose our inherited humanistic culture. Cut loose from traditional ties, *Homo furens* is seen to be too exclusively devoted to the devastation of the natural and human soil on which he has hitherto been nourished.

If guilt is not experienced deeply enough to cut into us, our future may well be lost. Possibly more people realize this than I suspect; and veterans who did not show any traces of it as warriors may now be feeling it keenly. At all events, there are some who have made that secret journey within the conscience and are building their lives on principles very different from those they knew as un-awakened ones.

Last night I lay awake and thought of all the inhumanity of it, the beastliness of the war. . . . I remembered all the brutal things I had seen since I came overseas, all the people rotting in jail, some of whom I had helped to put there. . . . I thought of Plato's phrase about the wise man caught in an evil time who refuses to participate in the crimes of his fellow citizens, but hides behind a wall until the storm is past. And this morning when I rose, tired and distraught from bed, I knew that in order to survive this time I must love more. There is no other way. . . . (War journal, December 8, 1944)

The Literature of Guilt

A BIBLIOGRAPHY

The bibliography includes works from a number of disciplines and represents various approaches to the problem of guilt.

ADKINS, ARTHUR W. H. *Merit and Responsibility: A Study in Greek Values* (Clarendon Press: Oxford, 1960).

AESCHYLUS. *The Oresteian Trilogy,* trans. Philip Vellacott (Baltimore: Penguin, 1965).

ANDERS, GUNTHER. "Reflections on the H Bomb," *Dissent* (1956) III: 146–55.

ARENDT, HANNAH. *Eichmann in Jerusalem: A Report on the Banality of Evil,* rev. and enl. ed. (New York: Viking Press, 1964).

AUSUBEL, DAVID P. "Relationships Between Shame and Guilt in the Socializing Process," *Psychological Review* (1955) 62: 378–90.

BENEDICT, RUTH. *The Chrysanthemum and the Sword: Patterns of Japanese Culture* (Boston: Houghton Mifflin, 1946).

BRETT, PETER. *An Inquiry into Criminal Guilt* (London: Sweet and Maxwell, 1963).

BURKE, KENNETH. *The Rhetoric of Religion: Studies in Logology* (Boston: Beacon Press, 1961).

CAHN, EDMOND. *The Predicament of Democratic Man* (New York: Dell, 1962).

CAMUS, ALBERT. *The Fall,* trans. Justin O'Brien (New York: Vintage Books, 1956).

CLARK, WALTER VAN TILBURG. *The Ox-Bow Incident* (New York: Vintage Books, 1957).

DAUBE, DAVID. "Two Notes on Communal Responsibility," *Sociological Review* (1944) XXXVI: 24–42.

DEVLIN, LORD. "The Sense of Guilt as an Instrument of Law and Order," *The Listener* (1965) LXXIII: 438–39, 480–81.

DOSTOEVSKY, FYODOR. *The Brothers Karamazov,* trans. Constance Garnett (New York: Modern Library, 1950).

    Crime and Punishment, trans. Constance Garnett (New York: Modern Library, 1950).

    The Possessed, trans. Constance Garnett (New York: Modern Library, 1930).

DOUGLAS, MARY. *Purity and Danger: An Analysis of Concepts of Pollution and Taboo* (New York: Praeger, 1966).

DURKHEIM, ÉMILE. *The Division of Labor in Society,* trans. George Simpson (New York: Free Press, 1964).

DÜRRENMATT, FRIEDRICH. *The Visit,* trans. Patrick Bowles, (New York: Grove, 1962).

EBERHARD, WOLFRAM. *Guilt and Sin in Traditional China* (Berkeley: University of California Press, 1967).

ELLIOTT, WARD. "Guilt and Overguilt: Some Reflections on Moral Stimulus and Paralysis," *Ethics* (1968) 78: 247–54.

ERIKSON, ERIK H. *Childhood and Society,* 2d ed. (New York: Norton, 1963) Ch. 7.

ERIKSON, KAI T. *Wayward Puritans: A Study in the Sociology of Deviance* (New York: Wiley, 1966).

FAULKNER, WILLIAM. *Requiem for a Nun* (New York: Random House, 1951).

FINGARETTE, HERBERT. *On Responsibility* (New York: Basic Books, 1967).

FRANKEL, CHARLES. "The Rediscovery of Sin," in *The Case for Modern Man* (Boston: Beacon Press, 1959) Ch. VI.

FRAZER, JAMES G. "The Scapegoat," in *The Golden Bough,* 3d ed. (New York: St. Martin's Press, 1966) 9.

FREUD, SIGMUND. *Civilization and Its Discontents,* trans. James Strachey (New York: Norton, 1962).

    Moses and Monotheism, trans. Katherine Jones (New York: Vintage Books, n.d.).

    Totem and Taboo, trans. James Strachey (New York: Norton, 1962).

FROMM, ERICH. "Conscience, Man's Recall to Himself," in *Man for Himself* (Greenwich, Conn.: Fawcett, 1965) 145–75.

GENET, JEAN. *The Blacks: A Clown Show,* trans. Bernard Frechtman (New York: Grove Press, 1960).

GIDE, ANDRÉ. *Lafcadio's Adventures,* trans. Dorothy Bussy (New York: Vintage Books, 1953).

GOLDING, WILLIAM. *Lord of the Flies* (New York: Capricorn Books, 1959).

GREEVES, FREDERICK. *The Meaning of Sin* (London: Epworth Press, 1956).

HAIGH, GERALD. "Existential Guilt: Neurotic and Real," *Review of Existential Psychology and Psychiatry* (1961) I: 120–30.

HALBERSTAM, MICHAEL. "Are *You* Guilty of Murdering Martin Luther King?" *The New York Times Magazine* (June 9, 1968).

HALLE, LOUIS J. "Collective Guilt?" *Encounter* (1965) XXIV: 61–62.

HAMMER, RICHARD. *One Morning in the War* (New York: Coward-McCann, 1970).

HAWTHORNE, NATHANIEL. *The Scarlet Letter* (New York: Norton, 1962).

HEIDEGGER, MARTIN. *Being and Time*, trans. John Macquarrie and Edward Robinson (New York: Harper & Row, 1962).

HERSH, SEYMOUR. *My Lai 4* (New York: Random House, 1970).

HOCHHUTH, ROLF. *The Deputy* (New York: Grove Press, 1964).

HORNEY, KAREN. *The Neurotic Personality of Our Time* (New York: Norton, 1937).

INTERNATIONAL CONGRESS ON MENTAL HEALTH. *Proceedings of the International Conference on Medical Psychotherapy* (London: Lewis, 1948) III.

JASPERS, KARL. *The Question of German Guilt*, trans. by E. B. Ashton (New York: Capricorn Books, 1961).

—— and AUGSTEIN, RUDOLF. "The Criminal State and German Responsibility: A Dialogue," *Commentary* (1966) 41: 33–39.

JONES, ERNEST. *Hamlet and Oedipus* (New York: Norton, 1949).

JUNG, C. G. "After the Catastrophe," in *The Collected Works of C. G. Jung*, ed. Herbert Read, Michael Fordham, and Gerhard Adler (New York: Pantheon, 1953–) 10: 194–217.

"A Psychological View of Conscience," *Collected Works* 10: 437–55.

KAFKA, FRANZ. *The Trial*, trans. Willa and Edwin Muir (New York: Modern Library, 1937).

KEEN, ERNEST. "Scheler's View of Repentance and Rebirth and Its Relevance to Psychotherapy," *Review of Existential Psychology and Psychiatry* (1966) VI: 84–87.

KIERKEGAARD, SØREN. *Fear and Trembling* and *The Sickness Unto Death,* trans. Walter Lowrie (Garden City, N.Y.: Doubleday Anchor, 1954).

KNIGHT, JAMES A. *Conscience and Guilt* (New York: Appleton-Century-Crofts, 1969).

KOESTLER, ARTHUR. *Darkness at Noon* (New York: Modern Library, n.d.).

LANG, DANIEL. *Casualties of War* (New York: McGraw-Hill, 1969).

LECKY, ROBERT S. and WRIGHT, H. ELLIOTT, ed. *Black Manifesto: Religion, Racism, and Reparations* (New York: Sheed and Ward, 1969).

LIFTON, ROBERT JAY. " 'Thought Reform' of Western Civilians in Chinese Communist Prisons," *Psychiatry* (1956) 19: 173–95.

LOCKE, JOHN. *The Second Treatise of Government* and *A Letter Concerning Toleration,* ed. J. W. Gough (New York: Barnes & Noble, 1966).

LYND, HELEN MERRELL. *On Shame and the Search for Identity* (New York: Science Editions, 1961).

MACDONALD, DWIGHT. "The Responsibility of Peoples," *Politics* (1945) 2: 82–93.

MALINOWSKI, BRONISLAW. *Crime and Custom in Savage Society* (Paterson, N.J.: Littlefield, Adams, 1962).

MATTHEWS, HONOR. *The Primal Curse; The Myth of Cain and Abel in the Theatre* (New York: Schocken, 1967).

MAY, ROLLO. *The Meaning of Anxiety* (New York: Ronald Press, 1950).

—— et al. *Existence: A New Dimension of Psychiatry and Psychology* (New York: Basic Books, 1958).

MELVILLE, HERMAN. *Billy Budd, Foretopman,* in Jay Leyda, ed., *The Portable Melville* (New York: Viking Press, 1952).

MENNINGER, KARL. *The Crime of Punishment* (New York: Viking Press, 1968).

MOWRER, O. HOBART. *The Crisis in Psychiatry and Religion* (New York: Van Nostrand, 1961).

NIEBUHR, REINHOLD. *Moral Man and Immoral Society* (New York: Scribner's, 1932).

NIETZSCHE, FRIEDRICH. *The Genealogy of Morals,* in *The Birth of Tragedy* and *The Genealogy of Morals,* trans. Francis Golffing (Garden City, N.Y.: Doubleday Anchor, 1956). "Homer's Contest," in Oscar Levy, ed., *The Complete Works of Friedrich Nietzsche* (London: Allen & Unwin, 1911) 2: 49–62.

NOVICK, PETER. *The Resistance Versus Vichy: The Purge of Collaborators in Liberated France* (New York: Columbia University Press, 1968).

PIAGET, JEAN. *The Moral Judgment of the Child,* trans. Marjorie Gabain (New York: Free Press, 1965).

PIERS, GERHART and SINGER, MILTON B. *Shame and Guilt: A Psychoanalytic and a Cultural Study* (Springfield, Ill.: Thomas, 1953).

RAMSEY, PAUL. "God's Grace and Man's Guilt," *Journal of Religion* (1951) XXXI: 21–37.

RANULF, SVEND. *Moral Indignation and Middle Class Psychology* (New York: Schocken, 1964).

REIK, THEODOR. *Myth and Guilt: The Crime and Punishment of Mankind* (New York: Braziller, 1957).

RICOEUR, PAUL. *The Symbolism of Evil,* trans. Emerson Buchanan (Boston: Beacon Press, 1969).

ROGOW, ARNOLD A. and LASSWELL, HAROLD D. *Power, Corruption, and Rectitude* (Englewood Cliffs, N.J.: Prentice-Hall, 1963).

SARTRE, JEAN-PAUL. *The Condemned of Altona,* trans. Sylvia and George Leeson (New York: Vintage Books, 1963). *The Respectful Prostitute,* in *No Exit and Three Other Plays,* trans. Stuart Gilbert and Lionel Abel (New York: Vintage Books, n.d.).

SENECA. "On Clemency," in *The Stoic Philosophy of Seneca,* trans. Moses Hadas (Garden City, N.Y.: Doubleday Anchor, 1958) 137–65.

SMITH, ROGER W. "Notes on the Sociology of Punishment," *Theoria* (1968) 31: 45–49.

SOPHOCLES. *The Theban Plays,* trans. E. F. Watling (Baltimore: Penguin, 1947).

STEINER, FRANZ. *Taboo* (Baltimore: Penguin, 1967).

TILLICH, PAUL. *The Courage to Be* (New Haven: Yale University Press, 1952).

TOURNIER, PAUL. *Guilt and Grace: A Psychological Study*, trans. A. W. Heathcote (Harper & Row, 1962).

TRESTON, H. J. *Poine: A Study in Ancient Greek Blood-Vengeance* (London: Longmans, Green, 1923).

WHITING, JOHN W. M. "Sorcery, Sin, and Superego," in M. R. Jones, ed., *Nebraska Symposium on Motivation, 1959* (Lincoln: University of Nebraska Press, 1959) 174-95.

WOODWARD, C. VANN. *The Burden of Southern History* (New York: Vintage Books, 1961).